Chaucer's Afterlife

Chaucer's Afterlife

Adaptations in Recent Popular Culture

KATHLEEN FORNI

McFarland & Company, Inc., Publishers
Jefferson, North Carolina, and London

LIBRARY OF CONGRESS CATALOGUING-IN-PUBLICATION DATA

Forni, Kathleen.
  Chaucer's afterlife : adaptations in recent popular culture / Kathleen Forni.
      p.   cm.
  Includes bibliographical references and index.

  ISBN 978-0-7864-7344-1
  softcover : acid free paper ∞

  1. Chaucer, Geoffrey, d. 1400—Adaptations—History and criticism. 2. Chaucer, Geoffrey, d. 1400—Influence. I. Title.
  PR1872.F67 2013
  821'.1—dc23   2013001064

BRITISH LIBRARY CATALOGUING DATA ARE AVAILABLE

© 2013 Kathleen Forni. All rights reserved

No part of this book may be reproduced or transmitted in any form or by any means, electronic or mechanical, including photocopying or recording, or by any information storage and retrieval system, without permission in writing from the publisher.

Front cover: drawing of Geoffrey Chaucer (Photos.com/Thinkstock); Heath Ledger as William Thatcher and Paul Bettany as Geoffrey Chaucer, in *A Knight's Tale,* 2001 (Sony Pictures/Photofest); ornamentals (Photos.com/Thinkstock)

Manufactured in the United States of America

McFarland & Company, Inc., Publishers
  Box 611, Jefferson, North Carolina 28640
  www.mcfarlandpub.com

For Wes, Jack, and Jesse

Acknowledgments

The book would not have been possible without the generous financial support provided by Loyola University in Maryland, the intellectual and social support of my colleagues in the English Department, and the emotional support of friends and family. All allowed me the time away from my usual institutional and familial obligations to write this book. My Chaucer students at Loyola proved to have a sharp eye for contemporary Chauceriana and graciously directed my attention to many of the primary sources included here. I am especially grateful for the insights, warm encouragement, and corrections of those who have read sections of the manuscript in its various drafts and incarnations. For their time and patience, a great debt is also owed to the librarians at Loyola University in Maryland, the Eisenhower Library at Johns Hopkins University, and the Faculty of Letters at Katholieke Universiteit Leuven. Many thanks to *Parergon* for their kind permission to reprint previously published material on the BBC's *Canterbury Tales* (25 [2008]: 171–89).

Table of Contents

Acknowledgments	vi
Preface	1
Introduction: The Popular and the Professional	7
1. Modes of Intertextual Engagement	21
2. Chaucer the Detective	61
3. Chaucer on the TV Screen: The BBC's *Canterbury Tales* and Jonathan Myerson's *Canterbury Tales*	84
4. The Canterbury Pilgrimage and African Diaspora	106
5. The Chaucer Brand	122
Chapter Notes	133
Bibliography	151
Index	165

Preface

The project began with the simple question of who values Chaucer, and why. Perhaps it's an odd question for a mid-career Chaucerian. But with the specter of relevance increasingly raised in the allocation of resources to the humanities, and some sense of crisis, or at least concern, on the part of medievalists regarding the perceived institutional marginality of the discipline, it's neither an unreasonable nor a disinterested query. Given the sustained high profile of medievalism in popular culture and the prominence of cultural studies in the humanities, there is a growing consensus that medievalists might more productively engage with the popular, especially in their teaching. This study seeks to demonstrate that Chaucer's contemporary popular afterlives, that is, his reception and reproduction by nonprofessional readers, have both educational and critical value. Approached as adaptations and appropriations, pedagogical engagement with popular Chaucer requires not only a familiarity with the Chaucerian text and critical tradition but also some knowledge of popular genre conventions and the politics of popular culture. More compellingly, critical engagement with Chaucer's popular reception can provide the professional with some insight into his functioning canonicity, a cultural valuation that is not confined to academic discourse. Indeed, from a popular culture perspective it is Chaucer's very presence in popular discourse that attests to his continuing relevance, to the amenability of his text and persona to the construction of value and the creation of pleasure.

Exploring the intersection between literary canonicity and popular culture, this study contributes to work on Chaucer's post-medieval reception that examines the various historical constructions of Chaucer (as laureate, moralist, philosopher, courtier, monarchist, iconoclast, proto-Protestant, love poet, liberal humanist, feminist) by a variety of successive readers (imitators, modernizers, antiquarians, belletristic critics, and early editors).[1] Part of that reception history, although sometimes considered tangential to an evolutionary narrative of critical understanding and appreciation, is Chaucerian medievalism — popularizations embodied in eighteenth- and nineteenth-century political broadsides, modernizations for a common readership, proverb collections, periodicals, stage adaptations, and children's literature.[2] The conceptual difference between historical constructions (often by eminent readers) and popular valuations might have once been distinguished by the degree of the reader's perceived ideological, emotive, or commercial interest. But the distinction between popularizations in which, to follow the evolutionary metaphor, Chaucer is adapted to or made fit for a variety of cultural and social environments and the history of nascent philological and critical investigation, has gradually blurred, as reflected in recent discussions about the difficulty in making clear methodological distinctions between medieval studies and medievalism.[3] Although within contemporary Chaucerian discourse there is some collapsing of the distinction between medieval studies and medievalism, the distinction between professional and nonprofessional responses to Chaucer would seem more apparent. But while the professional and nonprofessional represent different kinds of critical discrimination, they nonetheless contribute to a continuum of Chaucerian cultural production and consumption. That is, if Chaucer's historical canonization is a product of his reception history (a reception history that by modern standards of bibliographical, textual, and critical scholarship is necessarily a history of Chaucerian medievalism), it would seem inarguable that his contemporary canonicity is in part based on the continued circulation of his name in the larger cultural economy.

This study continues the developing narrative of Chaucer's modern popular reception initiated by Steve Ellis's *Chaucer at Large: The Poet in the Modern Imagination* and Candace Barrington's *American Chaucers*.[4] Mainly focusing on the twentieth century, both Ellis and Barrington show how Chaucer has been adapted to meet changing social and cultural interests and ideologies. Ellis's broad overview, concentrated largely on Britain, finds Chaucer's popular reproduction to be both diffuse and variable; common refrains, however, associate the Chaucerian with a nostalgia for preindustrial community and nativist constructions of Englishness. And in a series of compelling case studies, Barrington focuses on Chaucer's adaptability to key features of American ideology: "the undergirding religious purpose, the conglomeration of various voices and genres, the rowdiness and bawdiness coupled with profound piety, the easy communion between the high, middling and low elements of society" (3). The most conspicuous feature of the American Chaucer, however, is his paradoxical and ideologically flexible association with both populist and hegemonic values, that is, the malleability of his poetry to articulate "lower-class concerns while simultaneously inculcating values that benefit the upper class" (15).

The focus here is predominantly on the ample supply of contemporary manifestations of Chaucer's popular afterlife that have appeared in the past two decades or so, clustered around the millennium, material that has received relatively little critical attention.[5] Concentrating on examples in the public domain that are available for examination and further analysis, the following chapters provide both some sense of the generic and intertextual diversity of this fecund field and more detailed analyses into some modern genres and trends. Chaucer's frequent appearance in popular culture is a product of both his continued presence in secondary and higher educational curricula and the sustained popularity of recreational medievalisms. And modern media technologies have also made many of the primary sources, once by nature ephemeral or archival, more permanently available to a far wider audience. Chaucer's contemporary afterlife embodies a highly diverse range of texts and the theoretical approach here, although emphasizing the socio-cultural critique integral to popular culture theory, is necessarily catholic, drawing on interpretive approaches informed by several different but related fields: intertextuality, adaptation theory, and genre study. The assumption throughout is that this cultural recycling attests to the continued symbolic and commercial value of Chaucer's name and texts across a range of cultural fields.

The introduction, "The Popular and the Professional," explores more fully the contention that Chaucer's popular reproduction contributes to the vitality of his contemporary canonicity. Popular and professional Chaucerian production and consumption would appear to be separate spheres of discourse, demarcated chiefly by the expertise of their producers and consumers. One might assume that Chaucer's high cultural status (as attested to by his inclusion in secondary and higher educational curricula) would be maintained by professional critical discourse. But from a cultural studies approach, both professional and popular discrimination of Chaucer's poetry reflect the ideological and cultural usefulness and relevance of his texts and thus constitute part of a spectrum of Chaucerian cultural production. Since the popular is, however, by definition in tension with high or dominant discourses, Chaucer's popular reception also represents both a challenge and critique of academic valuations. As such, a consideration of the popular provides fuller understanding of Chaucer's functioning canonicity, providing some insight into why Chaucer's texts continue to make meaning in the larger cultural economy in ways in which John Lydgate's and John Gower's, for instance, seemingly do not. In short, within the context of popular culture theory, the fact that Chaucer has a popular afterlife attests to his continued cultural vitality.

Chaucer's contemporary popular reception covers a broad range of genres representing different degrees of interpretive engagement — ranging from formal adaptations to allusions—with Chaucer's texts. The long first chapter, "Modes of Intertextual Engagement," provides a survey of these contemporary primary sources with the intention of teasing out some patterns of popular meaning making. While extant theories of intertextuality address the range of signification found within individual texts, they often fail to address the range of signification involving an individual work across a broad array of texts. In an effort to make some sense of the levels of interpretation with Chaucer's texts found in the popular corpus, this chapter offers a provisional model for classifying the various modes of intertextuality found in a group of texts with little else in common besides their engagement with Chaucer and their exclusion from professional discourse. In the case of allusion, Chaucer often simply functions as an iconic literary figurehead whose cultural status lends canonical imprimatur to the popular text. But across a range of genres one finds a number of recurring motifs that might be described as both populist and pluralist. The Chaucerian is, for instance, consistently associated with social satire targeting snobbery of any kind. And one finds the pilgrimage and tale-telling structure most often recreated as a literary space providing the opportunity for confessional chat that fosters communal camaraderie.

Subsequent chapters explore in detail the more compelling instances of adaptation and appropriation, focusing on some generic trends in Chaucer's contemporary popular reception. "Chaucer the Detective" explores how *The Canterbury Tales* and Chaucerian biography are reproduced within the genre of mystery fiction, the most common manifestation of Chaucer's popular afterlife. Although embodying loosely Chaucerian themes like a suspicion of institutional religion and a derision for social pretension, Chaucerian mystery fiction reflects the social and ideological concerns common to detective and crime genres, particularly middle-class aspirations and anxieties. But while Chaucerian mystery fiction reflects genre conventions in maintaining that social stability is predicated on the perpetuation of the status quo, a frequent subtext suggesting that social inequality is a factor for criminal behavior nonetheless infiltrates the largely conservative ethos found in the genre. Chaucer, who commonly transcends social categories and is immune to what is imagined as a rigid social hierarchy, functions as an aspirational figure with whom the reader can imaginatively identify. The reader, with Chaucer, is made aware of the gross social injustice that often precipitates criminal behavior, but the suggested response is a fundamental passive conservatism in the guise of optimistic fatalism.

"Chaucer on the TV Screen" utilizes adaptation theory to explore how genre expectations and industrial constraints affect the interpretive approaches in the two most recent television adaptations of *The Canterbury Tales*. The BBC's *Canterbury Tales* adapts several of Chaucer's tales to prime-time television melodramas set in modern Britain. Although reflecting melodramatic conventions, particularly the representation of romantic love as the source of transcendent meaning, the episodes also channel social criticism, exploring how female agency and male identity are affected by both sociocultural changes (immigration, urbanization) and institutionalized socioeconomic inequities. The animated *Canterbury Tales* takes advantage of the abstraction and fabrication afforded by the medium to package some of Chaucer's mature themes (rape, murder) for a juvenile audience. Most conspicuously, the inherent fluidity of the visual image serves to emphasize the themes of transformation and metamorphosis in Chaucer's tales, especially the illusiveness of human identity. Although the generic retrofitting produces radically different interpretations of Chaucer's text, both the melodramatic and animated versions are marked by an anti-elitist spirit common to the popular aesthetic and by a markedly pessimistic assessment of human nature.

"The Canterbury Pilgrimage and African Diaspora" examines how African and African American creative academic writers have appropriated Chaucerian pilgrimage as a structural template for exploring the complex legacies of colonialism and African diaspora. Marilyn Nelson (*The Cachoeira Tales*), Karen King-Aribisala (*Kicking Tongues*), and Gloria Naylor (*Bailey's Café*) seize on the conceptual connection between pilgrimage and diaspora and reconfigure *The Canterbury Tales* as a vehicle for exploring both contemporary categories of difference and the cultural plurality of contemporary black identities. Each undertakes a tropological revision, inspiring Chaucer's pilgrims with the voices of the alienated and dispossessed, and jettisoning the competitive aspect of Chaucer's frame in favor of bonding, communal testimonials. While representing very different kinds of modern pilgrimage — spiritual, political, and psychological — each embodies the sense of exile and the desire for understanding and self-transformation inherent in medieval Christian pilgrimage. But more important perhaps is the plurality of narrative voices afforded by Chaucer's frame, reconfigured by these writers as a social dialogue essential to the formation of collective identity. Indeed, the assimilation of Chaucer as canonical representative represents aesthetically the cultural and social synthesis and accommodation that the authors model in their texts.

The final chapter, "The Chaucer Brand," turns from literary production to material consumption. While no doubt catering to niche markets, Chaucer's name continues to serve as a viable commodity, providing a meaningful symbolic resource for addressing social aspirations and anxieties. In contrast to those who use Chaucer as a creative resource, "Chaucer" as a brand has a number of prestige associations — organic craftsmanship, British cultural heritage, authenticity — appealing to the upscale consumer with a sense of nostalgic conservatism. But Chaucer's primary commercial function is as a cultural icon representing intellectual distinction. The attendant social distinction presumably embodied in the acquisition of Chaucerian literacy is, however, consistently disavowed. The curious dialectic of avowal and abnegation of status found in Chaucerian niche commodities perhaps reflects consumer anxiety about both the durability and desirability of the cultural capital provided by the humanities. But it also reflects a fundamental paradox of Chaucer's popular function, revealing a tension between the high cultural status of the canonical author and the modest, self-effacing fictional persona whose imaginative pilgrimage embodies a vision of social comity.

Like the history of Chaucerian medievalism, Chaucer's contemporary extra-academic reception resists a neat metanarrative. But a strain of aesthetic and cultural populism is certainly discernible. This is in part the inevitable product of his appropriation into the rhetoric of popular culture genres, reflecting both an engagement with and resistance to the dominant Chaucerian discourses of the academy. A metonymic stimulus-response test, however, would most often associate "Chaucer," not surprisingly, first with "pilgrimage," with "satire" a close second." The highly durable Chaucerian brand of pilgrimage is repeatedly appropriated and reproduced as a narrative structure useful for exploring and satirizing the roots of social divisiveness and exclusion. Providing a platform for competing discourses and modeling democratic inclusiveness, the construct mirrors Tobin Siebers's notion of postmodern utopia, "where community is based on the inclusion of differences, where different forms of talk are allowed to exist simultaneously, and where heterogeneity does not inspire conflict."[6] As for the man himself, the popular corpus most often constructs Chaucer as both social aspirant and anti-elitist, a people's poet, purveyor of the pithy proverb, valued for the very lack of "high seriousness" that Matthew Arnold found wanting in his poetry.

Introduction: The Popular and the Professional

The concept of popular Chaucer might still seem like an oxymoron to some. He lacks the kind of cult following Jane Austen enjoys, or the mythic and affective celebrity of Charles Dickens or Mark Twain, and his presence on the cultural radar certainly pales in comparison to the global phenomenon of "Shakespop."[1] But in just the past decade Chaucer has been adapted to film, television, stage, ballet, and opera, translated into hip-hop, and resurrected as a sleuth in historical detective fiction. The pilgrimage structure has been appropriated within the genres of science fiction, travelogue, postcolonial critique, romance, scientific debate, and zombie thriller. Chaucer's name is used to sell products ranging from dessert wines to teddy bears. And he has a blog. The impulse might be to view some manifestations of Chauceriana as ephemera, if not disposable and debased representations, then certainly pale reflections of Chaucer's literary and cultural value. But if Chaucer's popular reproduction is considered within the context of reception history, one might appeal to the notion that canonicity is based on successive acts of valuation, or that accumulated dialogues institutionalize a work's reputation, or that old texts are refracted, reconstituted, and revivified through the prism of new texts.[2]

And from the perspective of cultural studies, Chaucer's circulation in popular culture would attest to the continuing value of his texts as a meaningful resource in the construction of social identities and the articulation of social interests. Chaucer's relatively fulsome afterlife arguably reflects the vitality of his contemporary canonicity, a cultural viability that is not solely created by or confined to academic discourse. An examination of his popular reception can therefore offer some insight into the mechanisms of Chaucer's cultural renown, that is, why Chaucer continues to make meaning and give pleasure to a wide range of taste cultures. Indeed, those under a pop culturalist persuasion would argue not only that Chaucer's popular reproduction indicates his continuing cultural relevance, but also that to dismiss the legitimacy of such meanings and pleasures has less to do with critical or aesthetic discrimination than the assertion of cultural distinction and the defense of social privilege.

Designating Chaucer's extra-academic reception as "popular" follows established precedent.[3] But the subject would appear to be misnomered since the texts examined here represent a range of cultural production including both conventionally-designated high and low genres, from poetry, metafiction, and dark comedy to animation and pulp fiction. Moreover, many of the texts examined here as "popular" will probably be unfamiliar to most readers. Therefore, a clarification of nomenclature is probably warranted. The quality of statistical popularity might be "the *sine qua non* of popular culture," but "popularity" itself is notoriously difficult to quantify.[4] Popular culture encompasses a number of definitions, connoting texts, products, or practices that are well liked by many, judged inferior or in contrast to a high culture, created for primarily commercial purposes, and widely accessible.[5] Depending upon the conceptual approach, popular culture has also been associated with products that are mass produced, widely disseminated, and consumed as a form of entertainment or leisure. But with the exception of commercial visual media such as Brian Helgeland's *A Knight's Tale*, or the genre of mystery fiction, few of the texts examined in this study would seem to qualify.[6] Given the semantic ambiguity of the term, however, John Storey maintains that popular culture is both an "*empty* conceptual category" and a "residual category," dependent upon context and always defined in contrast to what is considered a high or dominant culture.[7]

Within the circumscribed context of contemporary Chaucerian cultural production, high culture is certainly academic discourse, or what Derek Brewer calls "the Chaucer industry," that is, "the professional criticism of Chaucer by salaried academics."[8] Carolyn Collette suggests that by the end of the nineteenth century, "Chaucer the man … disappeared into the academy to become the subject of professional study"; and by the 1930s any effort to extract and survey the industry's voluminous scholarly output would be, Brewer contends, "rash, if not suicidal."[9] The split between institutionalized hermeneutic discourse and interpretive commentary accessible to common readers is often traced to the formation of departments of English literature in the late nineteenth and early twentieth centuries. A number of factors contributed to the gradual transformation of literary study as part of a belletristic public culture to professional criticism, including the expansion of the university system, increasing specialization, the collapse of the literary periodical, and the influence of conceptual paradigms of expertise from the hard sciences.[10] The study of English literature, and medieval studies in particular, was from its inception characterized by a bifurcated theoretical approach, partly created by the perceived need for professional credibility. On the one hand, the approach to the study of English was influenced by a Romantic, humanistic tradition with an emphasis on the cultural, ethical, and spiritual value of the study of literary aesthetics. On the other, the adoption of a German disciplinary model with a focus on the scientific rigors of philology, empirical analysis, and the production of knowledge helped to place the professional study of literature on par with the natural sciences and classics. Lee Patterson suggests that early Chaucerians such as George Lyman Kittredge embodied this conceptual split in their work, producing both philological analyses of Chaucer's language and descriptive literary interpretation accessible and of interest to a wider reading audience.[11]

Despite their emphasis on the intuitive accessibility of Chaucer's poetry, however, Kittredge's lectures (collected in *Chaucer and His Poetry*) were hardly pitched at a wide audience in the same manner as, for instance, Percy MacKaye's contemporaneous popular adaptations of *The Canterbury Tales* for stage, pageant, and comic opera.[12] Indeed, popularizations and popular appropriations, or what Barrington characterizes as "secondary transmissions" for the "uninformed" and "illiterate," are not represented in Brewer's extracts of Chaucer's pre-professional critical heritage.[13] While popularizations are briefly documented in Caroline Spurgeon's collection of criticism and allusions, the narrative of Chaucer's early reception has been dominated largely by the learned medievalism of tutored eminents.[14] And a century of the professionalization and specialization of scholarly labor has resulted in a relatively clear demarcation between critical commentary intended for scholars and their students and Chaucer's imaginative reproduction and reception outside of an educational context. Thus, modern manifestations of Chaucer's extra-academic afterlife are called "popular" to make a distinction between his academic or professional reception — that is, work on Chaucer that is largely produced by and for specialists and educators, circulating within an interpretive community of largely professional scholars and teachers — and creative works produced primarily (although not exclusively) by and for nonprofessionals. Because Chaucer's quantitative popularity is certainly provisional, "Chaucer's afterlife" (a notion that connotes some wrangling over a celebrity's legacy) or Chaucerian "intertextuality" (some forms of intertextuality explore the conjunction between literary influence and socio-political power) will also serve as descriptors for his non-academic reception. But preference has been given to the concept of the "popular" which carries the primary theoretical baggage — the metanarrative of opposition to the cultural elitism of an authoritative discourse — that attends the study of popular culture and that permeates Chaucer's popular reception.

Those professionals who produce high Chaucerian discourse have taken an increasing interest in how Chaucer is reproduced in popular culture. The critical attention to Chaucer's contemporary afterlives (or what David Wallace has called "new Chaucer topographies") is in part a product of the pervasive popularity of medievalism, both as a professional field of inquiry and in its recreational manifestations, and the legitimation of the study of popular culture as an interpretive methodology in literary studies.[15] But the growing consideration of popular culture on the part of medievalists, particularly as part of a pedagogical strategy, also reflects larger institutional concerns about the viability of the discipline within the larger cultural economy, manifested in the perceived marginalization of medieval studies and the real dwindling supply of medieval literature tenure track lines.[16] David Marshall, for instance, suggests that for scholars of the Middle Ages who feel that they "must explain their usefulness," the study of medievalism in popular culture "opens avenues for medievalists to further engage in the social debates that occupy other areas of academic inquiry."[17] In her study of the successes of nineteenth-century popularizers, Charlotte Morse provides a bleak appraisal of the current discipline:

> Chaucer's fame, together with the popularity of medievalized romance in book and film, may keep medieval English literature in circulation. If Chaucer loses currency in the twenty-first-century university, the rest of English medieval literature, and perhaps all medieval literature except Dante's *Commedia,* may almost cease to circulate.[18]

Morse concludes that in order to attract customers, "Chaucerians should be more willing than they have been to engage with popular culture" (117). And although acknowledging "a time of few jobs and much pessimism about our discipline," Richard K. Emmerson perceives a healthier industry in his review of the state of medieval studies at the beginning of the new millennium (based on Medieval Academy memberships, conference attendance, and a vigorous output of scholarship).[19] He nonetheless also contends that "For medieval studies to flourish in the future," medievalists should engage with "popular representations of things 'medieval' and make use of them to direct the interest of students and the general public" (26–7).

All suggest appropriating the popular as a way to promote our own academic product. But in *Chaucer at Large,* the pioneering analysis of Chaucer's place in the modern imagination, Ellis often finds dubious value in popular estimations of the poet's work. With some notable exceptions, Ellis concludes that "Chaucer's present popular status is firmly down-market."[20] He finds a consistent "reductive appreciation" of Chaucer's poetry, in which the poet is constructed, among other things, as a nostalgic icon representing "the easy, inebriated amity of a static Merrie England" or as an embodiment of "uncomplicated bawdy affability" (162–64). Among the reasons for this "relative obscuring" of Chaucer in the culture at large is the difficulty of Middle English, Chaucer's association with patriarchal tradition and, most importantly, his appropriation by academics. That is, because primary intellectual and aesthetic work done on Chaucer only addresses others within the academy rather than the general public, "the persistence of reductive ideas about Chaucer is hardly to be dissociated from the difficulty of access to the means of enlightenment" (165). What Ellis hopes for is better communication between the academy and the reading public, and he looks forward to a new generation of teachers who will bear a "more modern outlook" and exploit more popular responses to Chaucer (e.g., translations) as an adjunct to academic commentary in the classroom.

This study suggests a somewhat different approach to the relationship between the estimation of Chaucer's cultural value and his representation in popular culture, positing a continuum rather than a chasm between the professional and popular modes of cultural production. Ellis suggests that there are two Chaucers (the one in the culture at large and the one owned by the academy) and wants better communication between Chaucerians and the reading public in order to correct what professional readers not unreasonably might see as the trivialization and infantilization of Chaucer in the modern imagination. An examination of Chaucer's popular reception should, in short, serve as a wake-up call for those responsible for communicating Chaucer's aesthetic distinction to the general reader. Similarly, Barrington concedes in her seminal study of Chaucer's remarkable adaptability to key features of American ideology that readers might be wont to dismiss Chaucer's popular progeny as "bastard children begotten by ignorant lowbrows."[21] From the perspective of cultural studies, however, all forms of Chaucerian cultural production contribute to his cultural valuation. All cultural production — high and low, professional and popular — is a social practice that reflects the mediation of social relations and the articulation of social identities. An important aspect of the mediation of social power and privilege is in the very distinction itself between high and low cultural forms. Thus, the hierarchical distinction between professional and popular valuations of Chaucer is problematic, having less to do with aesthetic evaluation than with an assertion and defense of institutional privilege. In short, Chaucer's circulation in the cultural imagination, that is, his functioning canonicity, is predicated on his continued meaning making in both professional and popular culture.

Ellis's distinction between the two Chaucers is not perverse and does reflect efforts to make conceptual distinctions between elite and popular cultures. Academic discourse and popular culture would appear to represent two separate spheres of Chaucerian reception, distinguished by the motives for their production and consumption. The difference between the Chaucer of professional and popular culture—between a monograph, such as David Carlson's revisionary biography, *Chaucer's Jobs*, and something like Helgeland's *A Knight's Tale*—would seem obvious.[22] The two might be easily differentiated on the basis of production, distribution, and consumption, or by the nature of their creators, suppliers, and users, the basic categories often used to distinguish between high and low cultural products.[23] Most distinctions between elite and popular culture emphasize the commercial motives of the producers and suppliers, the accessibility and distribution of the product to a wide audience, and, more ambiguously, the motives or disposition of the reader or consumer. Academic writing is created primarily by and intended for what Gans calls "*professional* taste cultures," which ostensibly enjoy at least a relative degree of commercial autonomy.[24] The monograph is seemingly not solely produced for profit either by the author or the publisher (although the former will hope for some form of compensation in the form of salary increase, promotion, or professional prestige, and the latter will obviously hope for a financial return on its investment).[25] Distribution is quite limited (print runs are often several hundred copies) and access is restricted either by the prohibitive price of the monograph ($95 for Carlson's hardcover; $30 for paper) or by the relative inaccessibility (geographical, financial) of university library holdings. John Street suggests that high culture is "less accessible both practically and socially," but in this case, since the audience for high Chaucerian culture is restricted and exclusive, requiring a highly specialized Chaucerian cultural literacy, accessibility is primarily limited by education.[26] The product will likely be consumed as a form of scholarly labor, providing information or aesthetic insight, rather than as a form of leisure. In Carlson's case, the monograph radically rewrites some traditional perceptions of Chaucer as a congenial humanist fostering individualism and social aspiration.

Looking at a popular culture product such as *A Knight's Tale* from the perspective of production, distribution, and consumption appears to yield very different results. First, and perhaps most importantly, the film is produced by "an industry organized for profit."[27] Because the product costs tens of millions of dollars to create, profit is based on consumption, consumption is predicated on wide distribution, and wide distribution is dependent upon accessibility. Accessibility presumably demands the comfort of ritual: stereotypes, formulae, homogeneity, and standardization. Using a demographic model, Gans distinguishes between high and popular culture primarily by the nature of the audience (the education, income, and opportunity of the product's users, with education being the most important) and how the cultural product is consumed: "The popular arts are, on the whole, *user-oriented* and exist to satisfy audience values and wishes."[28] In this case the film peddles the mythical American dream of upward mobility, specifically the Nike-esque fantasy of material success made possible by athletic prowess. The character of Chaucer, who facilitates the rise of the commoner and fosters the dream that he can change his stars (i.e., social class) resembles the ideologically accommodating figure that Carlson seeks to dismantle. Similarly, John Fiske suggests that in contrast to aesthetic discrimination, "popular discrimination" prizes social relevance and functionality, that is, how the text can be related to everyday life.[29] Conventional genres allow a plurality of meanings, and the popular text is read selectively, treated as a "resource bank" from which meanings are extracted as they are serviceable. In the case of *A Knight's Tale*, notwithstanding the ostensible invocation of the Chaucerian text, very little is found relevant from the original with the exception of a heterosexual love interest and the spectacle of male chivalric combat. Chaucer's Boethian romance is transformed into a rags-to-riches romance, but it is the film's generic superficiality itself that, rather than closing down the play of meaning, provides any number of readings. Pleasure might be had in the demonstration of the powerful efficacy of male camaraderie and mentoring in overcoming social barriers. Or perhaps pleasure is derived from the violence committed against the cheating aristocrat, a representative of the dominant class who is exposed rigging the system to maintain his social domination.

Louise Fradenburg suggests that the "*pietas*" of academic expertise is often defined in contrast to the enjoyment associated with popular manifestations of medievalism: "But the differences between academic and popular medievalism are of course *made*, and sometimes are made to occlude similarities."[30] One could easily problematize the apparent stark difference between these two cultural products, emphasizing continuum rather than antithesis. *A Knight's Tale*, for instance, both reflects Chaucerian critical tradition and has itself become an object of professional scrutiny. Helgeland's apparently idiosyncratic construction of Chaucer's character as a silver-tongued ne'er-do-well is not created ab ovo, unanchored from academic discourse. Helgeland represents Chaucer as outside, or above, a rigid class hierarchy, occupying a curiously ambiguous social position, equally at home penning sentiments of *fin amors* or participating in a farting contest. In short, he is a master of self-fashioning. This image of the poet has a long critical pedigree, dating back at least to the Renaissance when Chaucer appears to have been valued for his knowledge of courtesy, courtly love, and proper courtiership because of the attendant promise of social advantage that such knowledge might bring.[31] Chaucer's run-in with "Peter" the Pardoner and "Simon" the Summoner who threaten to take their Shakespearean pound of flesh for his gambling debts reflects the erstwhile critical assumption that the pilgrims are based on historical individuals (c.f., John Manly's *Some New*

Light on Chaucer [1926]).[32] And the belief that Chaucer's biting ecclesiastical satire emanates from personal animosity might be traced to Thomas Speght (1598) who first floated the engaging anecdote of Chaucer's "beating a Franciscane fryar in Fleetstreete."[33] The film has also excited a surprising amount of academic attention. Considered by several professional readers to be an important contribution to medievalism and to the reception history of Chaucer's *Knight's Tale*, the film has been variously read through the lens of masculinity, heteronormativity, capitalist ideology, historiography, and American myth.[34] And the film itself enjoys a fulsome afterlife in fandom as slash, speculative fiction that develops the homoerotic subtexts and romantic possibilities left unexplored in the film (the slash "/" takes the place of the ampersand "&" conventionally used to denote lovers).[35] In the spirit of early continuations of *The Canterbury Tales* such as John Lydgate's *Siege of Thebes* or the anonymous *Tale of Beryn*, online contributors interpret, criticize, and rewrite Helgeland's narrative, developing, for instance the implications of the kiss between Chaucer and Wat, or casting Laura the smithy as a more proper and appealing romantic partner for William or Chaucer (or both, at the same time).

Notwithstanding the subversive pleasures of slash, as evaluative responses to Chaucer's poetry one would like to insist on a distinction between expertise and entertainment. But as cultural valuations of Chaucer, the distinction becomes more difficult. Gans concedes that high culture requires "formal training" and is more "comprehensive"; but he maintains that while various taste cultures are "aesthetically different," they are nonetheless of "equal worth."[36] And for Fiske, the privileging of aesthetic over popular discrimination is simply part of a "disciplinary system" intended to reinforce social differences: "Aesthetics is naked cultural hegemony."[37] Neither denies that conceptual or descriptive differences between elite and popular culture can be made. But both argue that such differences often carry implicit evaluative judgments that are based less on defensible qualitative criteria than on an interest in asserting social dominance. From the perspective of cultural studies, the hierarchical distinction itself between Chaucer's cultural value as determined by his professional readers and his reception in the culture at large reproduces a privileged form of intellectual/aesthetic discrimination.[38]

Indeed, British cultural studies posits that all cultural production (and therefore cultural distinctions) reflects a negotiation of social relations involving the distribution of social power.[39] Lawrence Grossberg suggests that cultural studies "tends to look at culture itself as the site of the production and struggle over power, where power is understood, not necessarily in the form of domination, but always as an unequal relation of forces in the interests of particular fractions of the population."[40] Cultural production, and the distinction among cultural products, is a medium through which a normative establishment (groups with economic, educational, or social power) seeks to exert and legitimate social privilege.[41] Thus, one might view the academic as part of an elite intelligentsia, protecting the integrity of Chaucerian discourse against the caricatures produced by the mass media (Chaucer as a byword for farts and booze), or the misapprehension of other academic fields (for instance, the notion that subjectivity was invented in the Renaissance),[42] or what Jonathan Brody Kramnick describes as the defense of "professional norms" against public "anti-intellectualism" and "the national skepticism about academic labor."[43] That is, the notion of the Arnoldian academic engaged in "the disinterested and active use of reading, reflection, and observation, in the endeavor to know the best that can be known" would simply be a mystification of other more clearly ideological or social pursuits.[44]

Both Chaucer's own cultural production and elite cultural status would similarly be attributed to his ideological usefulness in exerting or exercising social difference and reproducing unequal social relations. In other words, regarding the ideological value of cultural products, both the liberal pluralist critique of canon formation and cultural studies share similar assumptions about why texts or products attain cultural prominence. Canonized texts embody the ideological values of dominant groups, endorsing the existing status quo—an equilibrium that is based on exclusion. Carlson's Marxist critique, for instance, asserts that Chaucer's poetry worked to enforce social discipline and sustain ruling-class control. Carlson does not deny that Chaucer was "a good poet."[45] But what made him the father of English poetry was that he was a useful poet—by pretending in *The Canterbury Tales*, for instance, that class divisions and inequities did not exist ("and by pretending contributed something towards making it so"), or suggesting that "questioning established order unleashes anarchy," or concluding *The Canterbury Tales* by advocating obedience to institutional religious authority, or, via his love poetry, peddling and sustaining "an aristocratic culture of vacuity" (57, 61, 74). Chaucer's ideological usefulness presumably would be dependent upon historical context. But his continued circulation in both university and secondary educational institutions might suggest that Chaucer remains useful to dominant interests.[46] Assuming that art fulfills a social function of legitimizing social differences, Chaucer's abiding presence in the educational canon might be attributed to any number of ideological functions intended to reproduce "the structure of social relations, a structure of complex and ramifying inequality."[47] He might serve as founding "father" of a Western literary tradition, a totemic figure useful in promoting both British and Eurocentric nationalism. Perhaps it is the ostensible anomalous social identity embodied in his biography and his narrative persona that obscures continuing socioeconomic divisions.⁴⁸ Or, perhaps it is what Alcuin Blamires calls his strategy of "containment," working to fulfill ideological functions not dissimilar to those Carlson describes:

> Chaucer is committed to the "dominant" social view and categorically does not sympathize with political dissent. "Containment" is the key to his positioning. He seeks to divert and thereby contain the resentment of the economically underprivileged. Such deflection of resentment away from its logical target is the familiar ruse of a threatened power structure: it is the familiar impulse to contain threat by dispersing its energies among scapegoats.⁴⁹

Part of Chaucer's institutional usefulness springs from the fact that his poetry remains highly amenable to contemporary critical trends (e.g., neo-Marxism, feminism, new historicism, cultural materialism). And notwithstanding the liberal pluralist critique eschewing Chaucerian aesthetics in favor of ideology, Chaucer's high cultural status is certainly perpetuated by such high culture academic critique.⁵⁰ But if Chaucer's canonicity is in part a reflection of his ideological and institutional usefulness, his popular afterlife suggests an alternative ideological function, constituting a form of resistance to professional Chaucerian discourse. Culture is a site where dominant groups, those with social entitlement, seek to legitimate that power. One of the ways in which that power is perpetuated or naturalized is by the very distinction itself between high and low culture. Although it is difficult to make categorical, evaluative distinctions between high and low culture, within the broader cultural economy few of the texts that constitute Chaucer's popular afterlife would be considered popular (i.e., commercial, accessible, inferior, widely known). But within the context of Chaucerian cultural production the popular can be defined as both in contrast to and inherently oppositional to the dominant Chaucerian discourse.⁵¹ In a *New Yorker* review of Peter Ackroyd's retelling of *The Canterbury Tales*, for instance, Joan Acocella insists that the "new, dark-minded, always ironical Chaucer" recently favored by "critics" who have "wearied of the sun-kissed Chaucer" is a gross characterization of "the freshest, clearest, and sweetest of the great English poets."⁵² Deriding recent critical trends, Acocella goes on to praise Chaucer not only for his realism and ribaldry ("How he loves fart jokes!") but also for his charity and tenderness: "One of the qualities that make [*sic*] Chaucer so lovable is that he seems to love us." *The New Yorker* is not by any conventional definition a low or popular culture magazine, and this kind of professional rivalry between journalism and the academy has a long history.⁵³ But Acocella's antagonism in the wrangling over a cultural product reflects the semiotic resistance, "the power to construct meanings, pleasures, and social identities," that Fiske sees as a hallmark of the popular: "The challenge it [popular culture] offers lies both in *what* meanings are made and in *who* has the power and the ability to make them."⁵⁴

Thus, popular Chaucerian culture can be produced (and often is) by representatives of the dominant discourse.⁵⁵ One might consider, for instance, Brantley L. Bryant's *Geoffrey Chaucer Hath a Blog*, a "pop culture parody" written by a "Chaucerian persona" whose popularity struck even its professional creator as unlikely.⁵⁶ The blog is a parody of a celebrity blog, a self-promotional media platform that can serve as an online journal, a gossip column, and as a way to connect with fans bypassing the distortions of mainstream celebrity news outlets. Written as a pleasurable break from Bryant's own academic labor, "the blog was meant to offer a Chaucer without canonical fame, to blend specialist medieval scholarship with pop culture, and to throw the medieval and the contemporary together in a way that would inextricably link them."⁵⁷ Chaucer's posts describe his daily life as a customs and court official and middle-class father, the developing plan of the *Tales*, his frequent impecuniousness, and his unabashed enthusiasm for the marvels of popular culture and modern media technologies. He monitors an advice column covering topics from unrequited love to plumbing, and sidebars provide links to electronic educational resources, professional organizations, medievalist blogs, charities, what is "Playing on My iPod," and a "Marketplace for Myn Liverie." Certainly one of the more engaging manifestations of Chaucer in new social media, part of the attraction derives from the participatory pleasure of interactive fiction and the intellectual pleasure of parsing the tissues of intertextualities. Currently closing in on 400,000 hits the blog can be considered a manifestation of fan culture, for Fiske "formed outside and often against official culture," appropriating and reworking "certain values and characteristics of that official culture to which it is opposed."⁵⁸

The blog is neomedievalist in its playful blurring of past and present and its tapestry of incongruous conceptual, linguistic, and temporal allusions.⁵⁹ Modern idioms are put into mock archaic spelling ("Ich am really psychede"; "Hekke yes") and modern vernacular is sprinkled into what Bryant modestly calls his "cod-Middle-English" (Chaucer is "sexiled" one night while "Tommy" Usk entertains the mysterious Margaret). Victimized by modern litigiousness and intellectual property rights, Chaucer is charged with plagiarizing Boccaccio. He describes a familiar fit of anti-French political sentiment preceding the naval battle at Sluys: "And thus we eten of 'Magna Carta fries' and 'Magna Carta breed'" (Sept. 2006). Chaucer writes an elegy on the passing of his good friend Sir Ulrich von Lichtenstein/ William Thatcher (a.k.a. Heath Ledger): "For blessed on earthe are al who had the chaunce/ To walk in the gardyn of his turbulaunce" (Nov. 2008). And his various biographical adventures are packaged in modern popular genres: he is captured by "the drede pyrate Robertson," whose accoutrements include a "pegge leg and a copye of the *De Doctrina Christiana*" (July 2006), and he and Richard II experience fear and loathing on a road trip to Las Vegas. Written for cultural omnivores, decoding the allusive parodies requires the privilege of what Jostein Gripsrud calls "double access" to both specialist knowledge and contemporary popular culture.[60]

The Chaucer persona, which Bryant describes as "defanged" and "a pleasurable disorientation of the canonical Chaucer,"[61] reflects the privileging of authorial presence, the desire for authorial incarnation embodied in the critical tradition and prevalent in his popular corpus as well.[62] Bryant's blogger is "nice," "congenial," and "modest"—but not without his caustic moments and hobby-horses, including an "unmitigated hatred" for John Gower, who, besides being a sycophant and a show-off, is selfish with his cellphone minutes (March 2006).[63] Much of the humor arises from the disjunction between the canonical poet, or what Thomas Prendergast describes as the "disembodied and transcendent" genius,[64] and the gross corporality of the daily indignities he must suffer: catering to Richard II's idiosyncratic whims and moods, having little Lewis prefer Gaunt's gift of an "Exeboxe CCCLX" to his astrolabe, seeing to his wife's demands ("Philippe ys on me aboute payntynge the porche"), or having Kalamazoo reject his paper proposal ("...the whiche ys a thynge of much ridiculousnesse, for the papere was on myn selfe! Thou woldst thynke that ich was somedeel of an expert on that subiecte" [May 2006]). In contrast with the ostensible *pietas* of academic labor, what Pierre Bourdieu might call the "barbarous" pleasure here is in the "continuity between art and life," the privileging of "norms of morality or agreeableness" common to the popular aesthetic.[65]

The indignity of having his paper proposal rejected reflects the sense of intimacy and pattern of identification often found in fan culture. But fandom is also a form of empowerment, with pleasure derived from its opposition to or subversion of the dominant discourse of those who control the means of cultural production. Indubitably, part of the pleasure here is in the violation of professional norms. Pushing back against what Stephanie Trigg calls the suspicion "of both the metaphysics and the politics of authorial presence and readerly identification with that presence,"[66] Chaucer is unashamedly constructed in the image of many of his fans—underpaid cultural omnivores and bibliophiles ("As messier John of Gaunt loueth women, so ich loue bokes: without limit or discriminacioun") whose temporal sensibilities straddle the medieval and the modern. And in parodic contrast to the coy critical toying with Chaucer's queerness or his quarrel with Gower, we have the overt outing of his youthful affair with the *Pearl* poet on "Mont Dorse-Quasse" (March 2006), and his iterative insistence that his fellow poet is a "wanker."[67]

Within fan culture, the construction of posthumous celebrity is a site of contention where competing groups lay claim to the meaning of a celebrity's legacy.[68] As a manifestation of popular culture, the claim on a cultural product, that is, the power of constructing meaning and pleasure, represents a negotiation, albeit symbolic, of social relations and identities. But fandom is also finally an expression of both affection and ownership. As this study will attest, nonprofessionals (and perhaps a popular impulse in professionals) prefer a nice Chaucer, whose optimistic poetic vision embodies inclusivity and social comity, who professes an egalitarian spirit and affirms the promise of social opportunity, whose poetry provides a mirror on historical reality, who was politically engaged in the prominent political events of his age, and who is ready with philosophical platitudes notwithstanding his predilection for scatological humor. As such, Chaucer's popular reception both complements and challenges a professional estimate of his cultural value. But the fact that Chaucer has a popular afterlife attests to his continued relevance as a cultural product over which groups with competing interests lay claim. His broad cultural circulation is indicative of a continued meaning making, of the amenability of his text and persona to the construction of value and the creation of pleasure. Chaucer's canonicity finally resides in a number of cultural functions that represent a mix of competing interests and values, a negotiated mixture of meanings across a range of high and low taste cultures.

1
Modes of Intertextual Engagement

Chaucer's popular afterlife consists of a bewildering variety of imaginative responses, spanning a broad spectrum of genres, and dealing almost exclusively with *The Canterbury Tales*. Indeed, Ellis suggests that it is in part "the extremely diffuse nature of the subject" that accounts for the relative lack of critical attention to Chaucer's reception in the modern imagination.[1] In order to give the reader a sense of the images and motifs found across a range of recent popular responses, this chapter provides an overview of Chaucer's contemporary afterlives categorized according to various modes of intertextual engagement. Chaucer's reproduction in popular culture as manifested in the various kinds of adaptations, appropriations, and allusions examined here yields a wide variety of author functions, a "proliferation of significations" in Michel Foucault's phrase, not without contradictions.[2] Nonetheless, one finds a number of recurring ideological and aesthetic uses in Chaucer's contemporary popular reproduction. The communal pilgrimage is most often reconceived as a vehicle for examining social divisions, and tale telling is consistently reimagined as an exploration of social identity in the form of autobiographical confession. Social divisions arise from categories of difference (religion, age, race, gender, sexuality). But discord is also a product of elitism and social pretension, frequently the targets of popular Chaucerian satire. And while "Chaucer" as an iconic persona is often metonymic shorthand for the cultural capital of canonical authorship and Western literary tradition, he is also consistently associated with an egalitarian ethos, particularly the belief in social mobility.

Intertextuality is admittedly a loose expression, if not, as Graham Allen suggests, "one of the most commonly used and misused terms in contemporary critical vocabulary."[3] The term variously connotes the interrelationships between texts, or the perception that all literary texts are constructed from other texts, or the inexhaustible permutations of meaning afforded by the interaction between text and reader. In an effort to construct a framework to make sense of a wide variety of otherwise unrelated texts, the approach here, however, is concerned less with ontological definition than with practical description. John Frow suggests that "the identification of an intertext is an act of interpretation. The intertext is not a real and causative source but a theoretical construct formed by and serving the purposes of a reading."[4] In this case, the relatively small referential frame constructs Chaucer (as persona, historical figure, metonymic concept) or the Chaucerian text as the primary source of signification. The taxonomies—adaptation, appropriation, invocation, and citation—are meant to be descriptive rather than evaluative, without hidden value judgments regarding the fidelity to or interpretive use of Chaucer's texts. While the categories fall across a continuum and are inevitably overlapping, the modes of engagement are differentiated by the explicitness of the use of the Chaucerian text, the extent to which the interpretation of the source text is sustained, and the aesthetic or symbiotic function of the Chaucerian text in the production of meaning.

The categories draw on concepts from some well-known theoretical approaches to adaptation and intertextuality. Useful, for instance, is Linda Hutcheon's approach to adaptations as evolutionary acts of creative cultural recycling and salvaging.[5] David Cowart appropriates a biological metaphor describing the interactions between organisms and species for his notion of "literary symbiosis" in which a guest text engages in aesthetic or thematic revision and undertakes an "epistemic dialogue" with the original.[6] Drawing on metaphors from musicology, travel, and the paranormal, Julie Sanders offers some useful distinctions based on how explicitly literary adaptations and appropriations are announced.[7] Gérard Genette invokes the image of reused parchment to reinforce the notion that all writing is rewriting and examines various kinds of "transtextuality," offering several well-known analytical categories to describe the ways in which previous texts influence interpretation and reception.[8] And Marko Juvan has generated what he calls a "descriptive poetics" of intertextuality based on the extent to which the referentiality is signposted and on the semantic complexity of the appropriation.[9] These established distinctions are not eschewed out of a willful perversity for novelty nor do the following simple classifications reinvent the intertextual wheel. Extant conceptual models, however, are largely tailored to the range of signification found within an individual text. The categories here address the case in which the reader is interested in the types of intertexual engagement with an individual text or author across a broad array of texts.

There remains the problem of the balance between authorial intention and reader response, and the related issue of the professional reading the popular. There are no simple answers, and the agency of the reader in the production of meaning remains an outstanding issue in both intertextuality and popular culture theory.[10] Neither the production nor the consumption of popular culture is necessarily relevant to the reading strategies posited by intertextual theorists, who, whether prioritizing the author, text, or reader as the agent of meaning, are generally concerned with examples involving highly allusive and self-referential texts being read by highly trained readers.[11] On the other hand, literary critics don't necessarily respond to products of popular culture in the same ways that genre connoisseurs or "participant natives" might.[12] There is no pretense that the following observations reflect how nonprofessional readers might respond to the various degrees of Chaucerian intertextuality found in his popular oeuvre. But the assumption is that the examples below constitute what Juvan calls "citational texts," that is, ones "for which the reader can, in a given context of literary life, justifiably suppose its author intentionally acquired other pre-texts, counting on the public not only to be able to recognize citational connections but to interpret them as an aesthetically and semantically relevant writing strategy."[13] The validity in interpretation is predicated on the competence of the interpreter and the purposive context, which in this case is an effort by a professional to assess the various ways nonprofessional producers engage with Chaucer and his texts. But the interpretive engagement in any given case is necessarily dependent not only on the reader's intertextual literacy (familiarity with both the Chaucerian source and the popular artist or genre) but also on the reader's energy, interest, and ingenuity.

Adaptation

An adaptation is a "deliberate, announced, and extended" revisitation or version of a prior work.[14] The text is overt in its relationship with the original, dependent upon the reputation of that text either for marketing (i.e., as a way to sell itself) or as a primary source of signification. Second, an adaptation is sustained, marked by an extended intertextual engagement with the source text. Adaptation theory recognizes different levels of sustainment — roughly falling into the categories of literal, faithful, and loose — generally distinguished by the degree of substantive and interpretive fidelity to the original. Popular adaptation is here limited to the faithful category, or what Geoffrey Wagner calls a "transposition" across genres "with the minimum of apparent interference."[15] In Chaucer's case, adaptations involve linguistic and generic translation in the effort to carry across the medieval text into Modern English and modern artistic genres. But even in the case of an intentionally close rendering, adaptation is never simply imitation but necessarily requires an interpretation of the prior work in order to make the text relevant, comprehensible, and appealing to new audiences.

Screen adaptations of *The Canterbury Tales* that manage to retain some defining characteristics — the pilgrimage frame, the association of tale with teller, the authorial narrator, and the narrative substance of the tales—are relatively rare. The artistic challenges are not insubstantial: the poem is capacious, episodic, and unfinished, a loosely-related series of self-contained versified short stories in a sparsely sketched and unfinished framework. There is no plot in an Aristotelian sense (beginning, middle, end), no three-act structure, no central conflict, and no quest (except for Jerusalem celestial, hardly a teaser). The *General Prologue* is heavily diegetic, featuring a long series of static descriptive portraits. One might add that while many of Chaucer's thematic concerns are broadly transhistorical (the miseries of marriage, clerical corruption, civil and cosmic justice), they are articulated through the prism of the culturally topical (glossing, pardons, chivalry). While substantial, none of these obstacles is insurmountable given cinema's temporal and spatial fluidity and its facility in translating verbal description into visual images. What is insurmountable, however, is the primary institutional contingency of film: the need to turn a profit. Film is the most expensive art form and production costs for *A Knight's Tale*, for instance, ran to some 40 million dollars. Since film adaptations of literary texts are ubiquitous, often seen as "safe bets with a ready audience," one would assume that Chaucer might be attractive as a pre-sold commodity, *The Canterbury Tales* carrying name recognition thanks to its being well ensconced in the educational canon.[16] But notwithstanding Chaucer's cultural prominence, perhaps the crucial difference is that unlike in the case of visual adaptations of popular novels, Chaucer's primary readership is largely compulsory rather than discretionary.

It is not surprising then that most screen adaptations of *The Canterbury Tales* have been made for British public television, partly shielded from purely market-driven considerations and produced at a far lower cost than film productions. Pier Paolo Pasolini's *I racconti di Canterbury* (1972)—still the only cinematic adaptation of the poem — is the exception here.[17] Although the X-rated adaptation immediately inspired a number of knock-offs and now enjoys a cult following, no one has repeated his ambitious and cautionary experiment.[18] The two most recent adaptations—an animated *Canterbury Tales* (1998–2000) with a script by Jonathan Myerson, and the BBC's modernized *Canterbury Tales* (2003)—reflect what Sarah Cardwell sees as a recent trend in British television adaptations, namely, meeting an expectation for both fidelity and artistic innovation.[19] The two shows, examined in more detail in Chapter Three, represent radically different ways of adapting the poem to visual media, with the interpretation of Chaucer's text dictated in large part by the genre to which it is adapted. The three-part animated *Canterbury Tales*, initially intended for holiday family viewing but also enjoying a durable afterlife in the educational market, might be considered a faithful adaptation (albeit translated, highly excised, and paraphrased).[20] Covering ten tales (kicking off with "The Nun's Priest's Tale," ignoring conventional tale order, and saving the fabliaux hits for last) and completing the pilgrimage, the shows use a wide variety of sophisticated animation styles to communicate Chaucer's various narrative modes and philosophical moods. The ostensible historical realism of the frame is distinguished from the fictional tales by the use of three-dimensional (3D) animation, and the focus is on a handful of plasticine pilgrims whose exaggerated features have the effect of the comic grotesque. The leitmotif in the first episode is the miseries of marriage but subsequent links have a trenchant strain of anti-elitism and class antagonism. The ten tales are represented in a variety of aesthetically distinct two-dimensional (2D) styles, tailored to the subject matter and reflecting the animator's interpretive approach to Chaucer's material. What Paul Wells calls the "vocabulary" of animation — including condensation, abstraction, and fluidity — is especially good at expressing psychological and emotional states as well as physical metamorphosis.[21] It is not surprising that what gets highlighted in this version of *The Canterbury Tales* are those themes not only afforded by the inherent artistic features of animation but also those that might appeal to the youthful target demographic: the transient and illusory nature of not only the body, but also self-identity and human relationships.

Pitched to more mature audiences, the BBC's *Canterbury Tales*, a series of six independent episodes, packages Chaucer's narrative plots into primetime social melodramas representing "the identity of Britain today."[22] Although there is no effort to dramatize the pilgrimage frame, an aerial background of Kent in the opening credits provides geographical continuity, signposting the individual episodes on locations along the motorway from London to Canterbury. As with the animated version, the emphasis is on Chaucer's generic diversity, with the individual tales updated to more familiar televisual forms like the romance, ghost story, and tele-noir. But the predominant mood is melodramatic, with a focus on working class characters and domestic themes that address contemporary social and cultural concerns.[23] Reflecting the target audience, the episodes feature strong female leads whose integrity is tested within the context of contemporary social problems: socioeconomic inequality, immigration, racism, and crime. Imagining social conditions that would make Chaucer's plots feasible, the writers also transpose his thematic concerns into a modern idiom. The Wife of Bath (here, an aging actress), for instance, is concerned with a sexual ladder of perfection which equates physical beauty and sexual attractiveness with youth. While loose in terms of fidelity to the Chaucerian text, the BBC series does, for those familiar with the original, encourage Cowart's notion of symbiotic dialogue in the form of a recognition of "the historical and diachronic difference between the voice of one literary age and that of another."[24]

Chaucer has proven far more adaptable to stage than screen.[25] Although obviously also operating for commercial profit, theater can not only target a niche audience but is also far cheaper to produce. One might add that film is characterized by textual economy, dependent upon a visual vocabulary to convey meaning. *The Canterbury Tales*, a text marked by orality (after all, it's about communal storytelling), might lend itself better to the more verbal medium of dramatic form. Mike Poulton's *The Canterbury Tales*, a two-part, six-hour production, and the first serious rival to the often revived *Canterbury Tales — The Musical* (1969), is the most ambitious, recent commercial adaptation of Chaucer's poem.[26] Poulton uses several techniques (some novel, some borrowed) to dramatize the *Tales* for the stage: weaving the *General Prologue* piecemeal throughout the production; expanding the links between tales; using music to punctuate the dialogue; having the characters in the individual tales speak their parts and provide frequent editorial comments; and bringing the characters to Canterbury. Poulton also amplifies what could be called the metafictional rhetorical techniques of Chaucer's poem. He consistently plays with narrative conventions and expectations, particularly in the interaction of Chaucer with his pilgrims and in Chaucer's running commentary on the poor quality of his own poetry. While the two plays have a carnivalesque tenor throughout, there is an effort to balance the courtly, the Christian, and the crude. But the prevailing theme, an echo, perhaps, of John Gardner's elevation of "intentionally bad" art as a hallmark of Chaucerian aesthetics, is that the chief source of comedy in *The Canterbury Tales* arises from the ineptitude of the storytelling.[27]

Since Chaucer's grammar, vocabulary, and pronunciation are the greatest deterrents to modern readers, Chaucer's language has been "updated" rather than "modernized" (the distinction is unclear to me). Although the first play begins in Middle English (to the "astonishment" of at least one audience, according to Steve Orme, who "wondered what they'd let themselves in for"),[28] the actors soon ease into modern vernacular pentameter couplets:

> CHAUCER.
>   A warning, friends. I fear the tale he'll tell
>   Will show us harlotry — bare flesh as well.
>   A shame, I say! That things begun i'th'height
>   *Nods to the* KNIGHT
>   Should sink so low so soon — just to delight
>   The smutty-minded — those of simple wit.
>   I say, good folk, let's stand no more of it:
>   Those who are for high morals and good taste
>   Should now be gone. Depart. Away. Make haste [35].

As this excerpt attests, Chaucer's text is subjected to the radical condensation and substitution that one has come to expect in popular visual or dramatic adaptations of literary sources. The portraits are highly truncated and most of the topical allusions are omitted (i.e., anything that merits an "Explanatory Note" in *The Riverside Chaucer*). And what gets cut from the tales are those parts that retard the narrative pace, viz., Palamon and Arcite's Boethian musings, and the descriptions of the two opposing armies and the three temples in the *Knight's Tale*; the Petrarchan allegorization at the end of the *Clerk's Tale*; the frequent editorial moralizing digressions in the *Man of Law's Tale*; and the *Pardoner's Prologue*. Nonetheless, Poulton (among whose previous credentials include distilling over 40 York mystery plays into the three-and-a-half-hour *York Millennium Mystery Plays*) gives the audience an idea of the scope of Chaucer's work, omitting only *Melibee*, the *Summoner's Tale* (alluded to) and the *Second Nun's Tale* (the *Monk's Tale* is ostensibly told during intermission and briefly summarized by Chaucer).

Given the number of actors on stage, Poulton relies on iteration and stereotyping for coherence, and this accounts for most of his additions to Chaucer's text. The Prioress's role, in addition to her canophilia (her lapdog is, somewhat oddly, eventually trampled by the Squire's horse), is to play the prude. The Wife of Bath embodies a predictable licentious sensibility; Alison is given, for instance, the Host's lines praising the Monk's virility, and she casts a likerous eye on Chaucer. The Knight is the representative of aristocratic decorum, but consistently impatient (a curious character trait also found in Myerson's animated version), the Monk continuously tries to get his "tragical" tale told, and the Pardoner, described as "a eunuch or a queer," is given to stereotypical homosexual feints (60, 134). As for his presentation of Chaucer, who gets drunk within the first ten minutes, Poulton draws on the kinds of popular images, particularly an "easy, inebriated amity," that Ellis finds prevalent in the modern imagination.[29] In keeping with the play's tendency to exaggerate single character traits, however, Chaucer is most conspicuous for his self-effacing anonymity, and Poulton emphasizes the modesty topos throughout: "I'm hopeless, dull, a dunce ... I couldn't tell a tale to save my life" (65); "I don't do tales! Hopeless at it!" (112).

While the emphasis is on ribald bonhomie as one often finds in stage versions of the poem, there is nonetheless some effort to establish a thematic opposition between Chaucer's courtly and religious sensibilities. At the beginning of each play, for instance, an erotic lyric invoking the flower and the leaf (sung by the "drunks" in Part One and the Squire in Part Two) is contrasted with "a morning hymn in honour of St. Thomas" (12, 110). However, one's impression is that Chaucer's forte is primarily bawdy since Poulton highlights this aspect, piling it on, so that the *Reeve's Tale*'s Aleyn, for instance, unnecessarily tells us that he's "stiff as any pole" (54). Several sexually euphemistic songs are added, such as Nicholas's "I have a gentil cock" ("His head is red as coral/ His tail black as jet" [38]) and a knight's song in the *Man of Law's Tale* ("I have a jelly tall and grand/ It has no feet but it can stand/ And it can stab but hath no hand/ You guess what it may be?" [71]). In fact, in Play One, apart from the *Knight's Tale*, every tale has some sexual innuendo, including, however unlikely, the *Prioress's Tale*:

> And through this street of Jews a man might wend
> Access was free — open at either end.
> *Suppressed laughter from* CHAUCER [91].

Although part of the Wife of Bath's role is to foster a libertine tenor, her character also represents a strain of soft-core feminism found in the plays. She frequently provides editorial comments, interrupting the Shipman, for instance, to insist that men should pay for women's finery, or suggesting that had women been in control in the *Physician's Tale*, matters might have turned out differently: "Leave judgement to men? See the mess they make!" (133). Ineptitude, however, is the most conspicuous feature of Chaucer's aesthetics as envisioned by Poulton. For instance, Chaucer describes the innocuous first lines of the *Reeve's Tale* ("At Trumpyngtown, not far from Cantabridge/ There runs a brook, and over it a bridge") as "bad ... very bad" (47), and the opening of the *Cook's Tale* as "dreadful" (58). The *Monk's Tale*, ostensibly told during intermission, has a soporific effect on the pilgrims ("Some ... are asleep, others yawning, all bored stiff" [63]), and the *Squire's Tale*, told by a jejune, nervous, and scatterbrained narrator, is one of the comic highlights of Play Two:

> SQUIRE.
> This Cambyuscan of which I have you told
> Against the sword of winter, keen and cold.
> *Pause.*
> In royal vestments sat upon a dais
> With diadem, full high in his palace...
> I'm sorry I've forgotten it — just the next bit
> A knight comes into the hall ... in his palace
> And gives him three presents:
> A horse made of brass that can fly,
> A mirror in which he can see the truth in men's souls,
> And a ring, which he gives to his daughter ... er...
> CHAUCER.
> Canacee?
> SQUIRE.
> Yes, Canacee — and with the ring she can understand
> The language of birds. That's the best bit.
>   She sees a falcon on a tree, wounding herself because she's in love —
> PRIORESS.
> Canacee or the falcon?

SQUIRE.
What?
PARDONER.
Is it Canacee or the falcon that's in love?
SQUIRE.
The falcon. She's been deserted by her tercelet.
SUMMONER.
Her what?
SQUIRE.
Tercelet — you know, a kind of hawk.
It really is quite good, if I can remember it — Ah wait —
First I will tell you of Cambyuscan [186].

The exchange brilliantly encapsulates the critical tradition of reading the *Squire's Tale* through the lens of dramatic irony and as parody, that is, as the humorous product of the Squire's inadequacies as a story teller. (And as a form of playful self-reflexivity, Chaucer's pejorative critical glosses might also suggest Poulton's poking fun at his own poetic efforts.)[30]

The success of the adaptation as a commercial stage play can be gauged initially by the appraisal of professional reviewers. The Royal Shakespeare Company's production did please critics, who, in addition to being taken with Chaucer's persona of boozy bourgeois benignity, generally praised the diversity of genres, timeless characters, and egalitarian spirit.[31] Joseph Garaventa recommends the experience as "a brilliant way of becoming a Chaucer expert in two evenings."[32] But there can be a bit more depth here, especially for the so-called "Chaucer expert" or what Hutcheon calls the "knowing" reader, not acknowledged by the initial reviews. Those conversant with the primary source might catch such things as an updating of the Physician's portrait ("He keeps his patients waiting hours and hours" [127]); the explicit outing of Boccaccio in a list of Chaucer's sources (65); and the sensible restoration of portions of the *Shipman's Tale*, which should be spoken by a woman, to the Wife of Bath. For nonprofessionals, the plays do provide a hint of the thematic scope and generic variety of Chaucer's poem but perhaps nonetheless reinforce some ingrained stereotypes— particularly the farting and debauchery leavened with a bit of democratic conviviality — that both dog (from an academic's point of view) and perpetuate Chaucer's popular image. But it's clearly the ribald erotics that sell. Poulton's adaptation has itself been adapted (and edited down from six hours) by the Northern Broadsides (March 2010) with a cast drawn from popular British television and with a heavier emphasis on Chaucer's double entendres. Indeed, the spotlight on "swyving" leads one reviewer to conclude that "the germination of English poetry contained the seed of the *Carry On* films."[33]

In an effort to update Chaucer for younger audiences, Baba Brinkman's *Rap Canterbury Tales*, provides vibrant hip-hop versions of four tales

(*Knight's Tale, Miller's Tale, Pardoner's Tale,* and *Wife of Bath's Tale*).[34] In his own General Prologue to the print edition Brinkman explains at length his educational and creative pilgrimage to adapting Chaucer into hip-hop vernacular. Decrying the degeneration of poetry from "its roots in popular entertainment and communal play into something elitist and inaccessible, virtually irrelevant to most people's lives" (35), Brinkman sees Chaucer as a transitional figure who maintained a symbiotic connection between performer and audience before the printing press severed this vital creative link. "An underground legend," Chaucer was also presumably uncompensated for his poetic efforts, thus escaping the taint of mainstream recognition and success. Brinkman constructs Chaucer as the Father of Hip Hop by virtue of his use of structured, formal poetic devices, polysyllabic rhyme, and his "dramatizing live performance and competition explicitly" (22). The storytelling contest in *The Canterbury Tales* is reconceived as a "freestyle battle" ("a freestyle is a rap that is unwritten and unrehearsed, composed by the rapper in the moment of performance, with rhymes that are improvised on beat and, when required, on topic" [13]), with the requisite "quiting," MC (Master of Ceremonies), and most importantly, the central role of audience feedback:

> Chaucer laid out a blueprint in *The Canterbury Tales* for an evolving ideal of poetry's role in society, based on live competitive events controlled by audience feedback, with rhymed narrative verse as its highest expression, empowering the voices of people from all levels of society, a populist poetic meritocracy. Hip hop could hardly be a more perfect fulfillment of Chaucer's vision [51].

Jettisoning Chaucer's iambic pentameter couplets for assonance, alliteration, and slant rhyme, Brinkman emphasizes that while he follows the "spirit" of Chaucer's poetry, remaining "as true to the original story as possible" (49), his versions of the four tales are necessarily interpretations.[35] As he himself documents, he is able to reduce the *Knight's Tale* by 80 percent, mostly by omitting "detailed descriptions," "long speeches," and "many other elements" (49). In other words, what gets cut, in addition to the obvious (the descriptions of the temples, the opposing tournament teams, and the tournament itself) is the whole Boethian subtext raising fundamental questions about human and divine justice, the nature of happiness, and the fragility of friendship. Brinkman reads the *Knight's Tale* as an exposé of dark male aggression with the Knight either complicit in or oblivious to the violence and hypocrisy that courtly language masks, a well-established critical approach to the tale. Drawing a contemporary political analogy whose rhetoric no doubt resonates with American audiences, Theseus destroys Thebes in a "shock and awe campaign" and subjects Creon to "regime change" (64). In terms of the love story, the tale is stripped of the nostalgia and mystification afforded by the language of chivalry and the emphasis throughout is on the knights' simple desire to deflower Emily. Arcite prays to Mars "to be the first to see/ His Emelye no virgin be" (149); and finally given her hand in the end, Palamon can "barely wait/ To take away her cherry state" (185).

Although Brinkman only formally translates the *Wife of Bath's Tale*, he suggests that the *Prologue* can be read as an analogue to the dialogue about wealth and sexuality found in rap music, with Alison providing "the basis of Lil' Kim and Foxy Brown's 'pussy is power' rap personas" (296). Brinkman interprets the *Wife of Bath's Tale* as a piece of "protofeminist propaganda," advocating not social equality but power within the "domestic sphere" to compensate for women's "social disadvantage" (297–8). Like many popularizations of her tale, the pillow sermon on class, age, poverty, and beauty ("You're low-class, wrinkled, and nasty") is a rhetorical casualty, along with the Ovidian Midas anecdote and the myriad protracted answers the knight finds to his query about female desires ("They said: confidence, compliments, comfort, class,/ Compassion, fashion, or for their passion to come back" [309]). Brinkman emphasizes instead the sexual drive; the old woman's "eyes kept climbing his [the knight's] thighs in a slimy way" (319), and the knight is himself invigorated by his wife's transformation: "And his wife saw him standing as stiff as a wooden lance" (333). In other words, the tale is less concerned with transcending gender role restrictions, or the nature of "gentilesse," or exposing patriarchal discourse and authority, than with illustrating the popular romance dictum that sexual attraction is the basis for a happy relationship.

In a similar effort to make Chaucer appealing to youth culture, and manifesting a postmodern blurring of high and low, and adult and juvenile cultural forms, the iconic graphic designer and illustrator Seymour Chwast has adapted *The Canterbury Tales* into a graphic novel that manages, in the epitomy of textual and visual economy, to provide a sequential synopsis of the entire poem in 143 pages.[36] Chwast is known for his unconventional, experimental, and bold designs and for invoking a range of graphic styles whose incongruities often produce a sense of wit and playfulness. Here he deliberately eschews representational realism, employing a naïve, minimalist style distinctive in its lack of visual clutter. The drawings are done in pen and ink outline, without color. Scott McCloud suggests that abstraction in comics both fosters identification and serves to emphasize the textual: "In black and white, the ideas *behind* the art are communicated more *directly*. Meaning transcends form. Art approaches language."[37] Chwast achieves a remarkable narrative economy and clarity both textually, by focusing on action plot points and concrete language, and visually, by omitting distracting detail (background, costuming, physiognomy), by compressing rhetoric into single-image illustrations, and by using diagrams and charts for plot summary. The

Parson's Prologue and Tale, for instance, are managed in two vertical panels; on the top a simple archway marks the "Entrance" to Canterbury next to which the Host declares that they are at the end of their journey and calls on the Parson to "Give us the benefit of your virtuous knowledge." In the lower panel, a gowned clerical figure holds a scroll with two columns, one listing the "Deadly Sin" and the other the "Cure" (142). A similar narrative economy is achieved in the "Doctor's Tale" (*Physician's Tale*) by use of a large panel showing Virginia surrounded by captions describing her virtuous attributes; or in the *Canon Yeoman's Tale* by showing men working a kiln with lists of ingredients pointing to the various vessels; and in the *Reeve's Tale* by including a diagram titled "That Night" showing labeled beds and numbered arrow paths (34). The comic book *Canterbury Tales* may lack the rhetorical nuance and philosophical complexity of the original poetry, but what is gained by virtue of the "amplification through simplification" characteristic of the art form is a sense of comic absurdity.[38]

Chwast's comic book version reflects the cultural updating common to adaptations. Chaucer's language is thoroughly modernized, the pilgrims ride motorbikes and often wear historically neutral costuming, and Chwast incorporates contemporary iconography.[39] Although comics are not necessarily a juvenile art form, the book seems designed in part with a youthful audience in mind. The spare imagery, representational rather than realistic, and the quick narrative clip provide some distancing and distraction from the brutality and vulgarity exposed by the loss of both impersonated artistry (the pilgrims are only sketchily described) and Chaucer's characteristic rhetorical embellishment. Chaucer, often represented as a talking head on various panel margins, warns that readers of the *Miller's Tale* "should be eighteen or older" (24) and shuts down the *Cook's Tale* next to a panel that provides a logical conclusion to the tale with a ménage à trois. The daughter's rape in the *Reeve's Tale* is minimized by leaving her unnamed and including the simple caption "Aleyn slept with the daughter" accompanied by an image of the smiling couple in bed (34). And the occasional use of the modern vernacular in disturbing junctures (Constance's rapist says, "Hey, babe, let's party" [45]) produces a sense of comic disjunction.

The extreme narrative compression and bare visual imagery also have a flattening effect that produces an absurdist form of humor. Abrupt, punctuated resolutions produce a sense of comic understatement given the protracted suffering of the main characters (in the *Clerk's Tale* Griselda responds to Walter's confession of his duplicity with a deadpan, "I'm speechless"; Cecilia's prolonged tortures in the *Second Nun's Tale* are concluded with the simple and anticlimactic statement, "she went to heaven — a martyr" [76; 132]). And there is characteristic Chwastian incongruity — of logical sequence and realistic emotional reaction — producing a comic effect throughout. The *Man of Law's Prologue*, for instance, is managed in one panel focused on an image of tattered trousers and two unshod feet: "Poverty is hell. If you are poor your own brother hates you. No one respects you. You are despised by your neighbor. It is better to die" (37). But this maudlin moralizing serves as a non sequitur, with no bearing on the subsequent tale of Constance's travails. And the bare recounting of Constance's prolonged sufferings, when stripped of the sermonizing and digressions and accompanied by a lack of expressive detail in her facial features, becomes a form of absurdist repetition eliciting little emotional engagement and lacking any meaningful resolution. The conceptual iteration reinforced by the illustrations can also border on parody, as at the end of the *Manciple's Tale* in which the simplicity of the moral ("Don't be a loudmouth"; "Mum's the word!" [141]) is undermined by the combination of the modern vernacular put in the mouths of ancient authorities and the use of contemporary iconography (i.e., the red circle with diagonal over a mouth and an ear). Indeed, the synopsis on the back cover describes the book as "a delightfully comic version of Chaucer's *magnum opus*—farts and all." The humor arises, however, less from the bawdy or scatology, which Chwast tends to minimize, than from the textual brevity and simple visual language which serve to emphasize and exaggerate — often bordering on parody — the latent comic aspects of Chaucer's tales.

Adaptations of Chaucer's texts to traditional highbrow genres, although also reflecting a modernizing sensibility, often tend to be less faithful and more intent on incorporating the Chaucerian text into the creator's aesthetic vision. Christopher Bruce is known as a choreographer with a social conscience, and in his dancework, *God's Plenty*, he tackles several themes, including institutionalized Christianity and its creation of sexual inequality, love as the driving force for human action for both good and ill, and "man's tendency towards violence."[40] Bruce finds Chaucer's thematic concerns "to be as relevant to today's world as to the fourteenth century," hence his invocation of John Dryden, for whom "mankind is ever the same" and who finds Chaucer's characters "still remaining in Mankind, and even in *England*."[41] The transhistorical relevance of Chaucer's political, psychological, and sexual themes is reflected in the score (by Dominic Muldowny), which achieves an eclectic but nonetheless surprisingly harmonious fusion of medieval, Arabic, and modern instruments and music. The dance itself is an interesting pastiche, combining various styles of dance, song, pantomime, and spoken text (Nevill Coghill's enduring modern English translation), complemented by a stark set design. Opening with a processional masque, Bruce invokes a pre–Christian idyll, with a shamanistic dance suggesting a world of "paganism, nature and rites of fertility."[42] With the advent of Christianity comes "the positive teaching of peace and love but also violence, repression, intolerance, and hypocrisy," represented by a flagellation dance, tussling Crusaders and Saracens, and a sequence clearly inspired by the *Man of Law's Tale*.[43] A narrator on the side of the stage, pen in hand, recites a highly edited version of the *General Prologue*, and in an effort to balance the philosophic with the comedic, the first act concludes with various pilgrims gathering for supper, where they are served by a farcically inept team of waiters. In the second act the dancers perform the narrated *Knight's Tale* (with perhaps the first joust done in ballet), followed by the *Wife of Bath's Prologue and Tale* and the *Miller's Tale*. The choice of tales suggests a thematic continuum of what Bruce describes as "love in its many forms—carnal, courtly, pure, and violent."[44] But the play closes with an emphasis on Chaucer's light-hearted, bare-bottomed bawdy, embracing both the aesthetic and moral contradictions—particularly the *eros/thanatos* duality of human nature—manifested in God's plenty.

Troilus and Criseyde has not proven as adaptable as the *Tales*. Indeed, to my knowledge there have been only three efforts in the twentieth century: Christopher Morley's pre-war novel, *The Trojan Horse* (1937), William Walton's post-war operatic adaptation, *Troilus and Criseyde* (1954), and Alice Shields's feminist chamber opera, *Criseyde* (with a Middle English libretto by Nancy Dean).[45] Shields's opera is a promiscuously intertextual reconstruction of the legend, drawing on the poem's reception history and influenced by 20 years of feminist critical evaluation. While Walton and Morley are concerned with *Troilus and Criseyde* as a war story, in a tradition at least as old as Robert Henryson's *Testament of Cresseid*, Shields is concerned primarily with Criseyde's betrayal and with exculpating her bad treatment of Troilus. From the information available in the public domain, it appears that the opera focuses on the coercion involved in Criseyde's seduction, and in the second act, the practical mechanisms of both her trade (i.e., why Troilus cannot marry her) and her infidelity. In this case, while Diomede threatens Criseyde with rape, a more proactive Troilus (borrowed, perhaps, from Shakespeare's *Troilus and Cressida*) comes to her rescue, killing her attacker only to be cut down by Calchas, who is in turn killed by his daughter. Pandarus is a "sociopath" (11) and incestuous voyeur. Shields appears to be channeling Dryden's *Troilus and Cressida, or, Truth Found Too Late* (his revision of Shakespeare's "heap of Rubbish") in which Criseyde remains faithful to Troilus.[46] But she claims to have been inspired to retell the tale "from a woman's perspective" not only by her "outrage" at "the abuses [Chaucer] heaped upon" his heroine, but also by Chaucer's bowdlerization of Boccaccio which leaves Criseyde "opaque, irrational, and trivial."[47] The changes made to Chaucer, which appear to include, for instance, Criseyde's rather prosaic desire to formally wed before consummation, "reflect Criseyde's conscious struggles for survival, autonomy, self-respect, and love within the patriarchal culture into which she was born" (3). Shields hopes that the set, costuming, and score (interactive sculptures representing "psychological cages," faux-feudal dress created out of "space age and transparent materials," and music incorporating Hindustani melodies) will emphasize the "timeless and universal restrictions of patriarchy."[48]

Adaptation theorists often invoke a Darwinian metaphor, adaptation being a "means of evolution and survival," a process by which the original is adapted not only to a new medium but also to new historical and cultural environments.[49] The implication is that the most fit texts, or the most fit parts of texts, survive. But their survival is predicated on the fitness—aesthetic, cultural, commercial—of the creative mutation to a particular environment. In other words, these adaptations are shaped by a number of factors beyond the adaptor's engagement with Chaucer's text: aesthetic and technical conventions of the genre, production contexts and industrial constraints, and the reception history of previous adaptations. While these factors influence the varying degrees of fidelity, all adaptations, through cultural updating, are intended to make the Chaucerian text appealing to a modern audience—and Chaucer's original language, except in colloquial sound-bites, is clearly not part of that appeal. Hutcheon suggests that the adaptation keeps the "prior work alive, giving it an afterlife it would never have had otherwise."[50] Familiarity with the Chaucerian text is not necessary for commercial success, and part of the purpose of the generic and cultural updating is to capture a broader audience, including those attracted to the genre itself (animation, prime-time television, graphic novel, performance arts). Notwithstanding claims for the artistic autonomy of adaptations, one's degree of familiarity with the Chaucerian text does determine the activation of intertextual play or epistemic dialogue with the original, arguably one of the principal intellectual pleasures afforded by any adaptation.

Appropriation

An appropriation is similar to an adaptation insofar as it is also an announced revisitation of a prior work, with verbal, structural, or narrative echoes. The appropriation, however, is less concerned with fidelity or with revivifying Chaucer's text than with incorporating his text, among others, into something fundamentally new. The impulse of the appropriation is not necessarily to update or reinterpret the original text (through generic, temporal, or cultural transposition) but rather to explicitly assimilate aspects of the prior text into a manifestly different work, or as Sanders suggests, into "a wholly new cultural product and domain."[51] Appropriations of *The Can-*

terbury Tales are most often structural, featuring a first-person narrator and a series of stories, often autobiographical and on related topics, told en route to a common destination. Indeed, this highly durable Chaucerian template is often constructed as a creative space for multivocality, making possible discursive variations on a given topic. A recurring theme, appropriated within a variety of genres, concerns social divisions and discord brought on by ethnicity, class, race, and, most frequently, religion. Indeed, these constructions seem not unlike Paul Strohm's reading of *The Canterbury Tales* as providing an aesthetic paradigm of social relations, conveying "the reassuring message that competing voices can colonize a literary space and can proliferate within it without provoking chaos or ultimate rupture."[52]

Marilyn Nelson's lyrical travel narrative, *The Cachoeira Tales*, for instance, explores the dislocation of identity and the search for spiritual and cultural synthesis. Nelson creates an interesting fusion of Chaucer's pilgrimage frame and the trickster tale, loosely imitating Chaucer's verse form and providing clear verbal echoes:

> When April rains had drenched the root
> of what March headlines had foreseen as drought,
> I invited my extended family—
> with artificial spontaneity—
> to join me on some kind of "pilgrimage."[53]

The "General Prologue" proceeds to offer a series of portraits (a "Director," a "Jazz Musician") partly drawing on contemporary American stereotypes in a method somewhat similar to Chaucer's use of estates satire. The narrator, flush with a fellowship, cajoles some family members and friends to travel with her to a "place sanctified by the Negro soul" (11). In this case that place is Cachoeira, Brazil, home to "the famous Sisterhood of the Good Death,/ founded by former slaves in the nineteenth/ century" (49). The various informal, conversational tales—mostly short personal anecdotes—concern racism and alienation, both at home and abroad. The epiphany in the end is the recognition that Black Americans, notwithstanding their descent from slaves, are alienated from fellow diasporic descendants by virtue of their comparative material wealth and Christian heritage. Nonetheless, a vision of synthesis is achieved, perhaps not unlike the Parson's effort to "knytte up al this feeste and make an ende" (X. 47): Oxala, the West African God, and Christ are twins, "'both Lords of the Good End,'" who seek to comfort "'those who suffer, and to quench/ the fires of greed, injustice, and violence'" (54).[54]

Jerry Ellis seeks for a similar spiritual and cultural synthesis in *Walking to Canterbury: A Modern Journey Through Chaucer's Medieval England*.[55] Having previously retraced the Cherokee Trail of Tears, Ellis undertakes the 60-

mile trek in order to both reconcile his Cherokee heritage and British ancestry and to find the "intimacy" he finds lacking in "the competitive modern world" (120). Details of his travelogue, such as checking in to a hotel or having a glass of ale, invoke comparative disquisitions on similar mundanities in the Middle Ages. The same technique is used to weave Chaucer's texts into his narrative, so that a rooster's crow overheard leads to a summary of the *Nun's Priest's Tale*, or his attempted seduction by a lonely local recalls the Wife of Bath and inspires his own humorous barroom quest to discover "what women most desire from men" (no snoring, among other things [208]).

Ellis constructs the *General Prologue* in the tradition established by Dryden, reading the pilgrims as universal types, several of whose descendants Ellis meets on this trek. The tales are not only "timeless and universal" stories (296) with valuable messages such as the Nun's Priest's warning against pride and vanity, but also reflect the profound paradox of medieval culture. *The Canterbury Tales* offers "stories of rape, love, revenge, deceit, greed, vanity, robbery, and murder" (251), but also has a strong spiritual dimension (which Ellis illustrates with an admirably concise summary of the *Parson's Tale*). As one often finds in imaginative time travel, modern culture is a distant mirror of its medieval past: we're cleaner and lack a visceral terror of hell, but we still fear death and still possess a palpable yearning for "meaning and purpose" (110). Chaucer's fictional pilgrimage represents the intimacy and communion, spiritual needs of most Americans which the goods of capitalism are unable to provide, that are the object of Ellis's journey. Upon the accidental discovery of a pilgrim's shell, which joins the snake rattle and feathers in his hatband, Ellis is finally able to reconcile his dual heritage with the recognition that these talismanic relics represent a universal quest for spiritual enlightenment.

Dan Simmons's Hugo Award–winning *Hyperion* reflects a similar interest in the sociocultural effects of capitalism. The sci-fi thriller, however, is less concerned with the conjunction of capitalism and social alienation than the relationship between free market ideology and the destructive proclivities of modern religions.[56] Borrowing *The Canterbury Tales* frame, the story involves seven people chosen to make a pilgrimage to a mysterious shrine, the Time Tombs, presided over by an enigmatic blade-wielding deity known as The Shrike. The pilgrims meet on their intergalactic journey and each has a brief descriptive portrait that is filtered through the point of view of one of the participants. After a communal meal, they decide to share their stories — each autobiographical and each involving the purpose for their dangerous pilgrimage — in the hope that finding the common thread that binds their experiences might foster their mutual survival. Lots are drawn, and each of the stories provides details about the destruction of "Old Earth," the technological and political changes of the past 700 years, and the causes for a final looming interstellar war engineered by computers to protect what's left of the uninhabited universe from human destruction. Chaucer's frame lends a unifying narrative and thematic coherence to a series of independent yet interconnected narratives. The stories, reflecting the diverse social and religious backgrounds of the tellers, cover a range of stylistic genres, including diary entries, detective fiction, thriller, war story, hubristic tragedy, portrait of an artist. But the primary concern in each case is the destructive psychology of human aspirations and desires—for immortality, fame, love, and wealth.

As is characteristic of science fiction, Simmons's concern is less with the future than with the present. In addition to the familiar sci-fi motif of the uneasy relationship between human beings and their technological creations, he targets a number of problems arising from unregulated capitalism, including the depredation of the environment, globalization as a form of neocolonialism, and the cancerous need of capitalism for cheap labor. The novel also provides a meditative allegory on the spiritual instinct in human beings, deconstructing the desire for immortality and questioning why humans habitually construct vicious, death-dealing deities. Other concerns are there as well, reflected in various literary allusions, including the existential absurdity of human existence (Joseph Heller's *Catch-22*; John Gardner's *Grendel*; Shakespeare's *Hamlet*) and the moral and material decline of Western civilization (Ezra Pound's *Hugh Selwyn Mauberley*; William Butler Yeats's *The Second Coming*). The most important intertext, however, is clearly John Keats's *Hyperion*, whose epic showdown between the Greek Olympians and Titans mirrors a cataclysmic battle between man and machine, and which also embodies some queries—particularly the relationship between suffering, truth, happiness, and aesthetics—that permeate the individual stories.

A topical political critique of institutional religion, colonial imperialism, and social injustice is also found in Paul A. Freeman's *Robin Hood and Friar Tuck: Zombie Killers—A Canterbury Tale*, in which the Greenwood gang has an adventure with the undead.[57] Framing his gory thriller as the "Monk's Second Tale," Freeman's nocturnal narrative is told not for "sentence" or solace but to "terrify and make the blood run cold" (1). His parody of Chaucer is primarily stylistic, with the tale constructed in iambic pentameter couplets and sandwiched between a brief prologue and epilogue. The story is told against the familiar fictional backdrop of John's seizure of power and Robin's activities to ease the tax burdens on the poor while the good King Richard is away on crusade. That crusade, a thinly veiled excuse to simply "terrorize and thieve" (10), proves to be a disaster. After the English troops are decimated by zombies and transport the infection back home, Robin and his gang are reluctantly recruited to combat the "unholy beasts" (60). As is characteristic of the early Robin Hood ballads, Freeman's version is highly critical of the venality, hypocrisy, and greed of the upper echelons of the ecclesiastical hierarchy. Zombies have been variously interpreted as embodying an array of signifiers, representing a register of social criticisms (consumerism, economic inequality) and various kinds of fears: of difference (cultural, sexual, racial), of ourselves and our own desires, and of the mindless, dehumanizing conformity of modern life.[58] In this case, one need not seek far for the contemporary anxieties or the social critique. The zombies are Muslims ("Musselmen"), infected by a necromancer working with a "Dark Caliph" who deprives them of their free will and uses them as cheap labor and disposable infantry (16). The arrival of these "ghoulish cannibals" to the shores of England reflects a fear of the spread of religious fundamentalism and terrorism which the so-called war on terror was meant to localize. Reflecting a critique of American- and British-led wars in the Middle East, the spread of Zombieism is seen as a punishment for military crusade, here portrayed as a mercenary action fueled by the greed of the aristocracy, grossly violating the dictates of chivalry. For Friar Tuck, the illness is "A penalty, perhaps, for wicked crimes/ Committed by our own crusading knights/ Against the local people's human rights" (7).

Appropriating *The Canterbury Tales* frame as a useful model for showcasing a diversity of marginalized voices, Karen King-Aribisala also examines the corrosive effects of the legacy of European colonialism in her verse novel, *Kicking Tongues*. The host and authorial narrator ("The Black Lady The") foots the bill for a group of Nigerians, ranging from a wealthy tribal chief to a gas station attendant, to travel to Abuja, the new federal capital, for a governmental conference on the future of Nigeria.[59] The personal stories shared on the bus ("The Tale of the Woman in Purdah: Under cover"; "The Tale of Oyinbo Maclean: The umbrella business") frequently return to a number of themes—the treatment of women, education, religion, class, and race relations—providing a microcosm of the challenges facing Nigerian society: "Bus is stage of country Nigeria./ Nigeria is bus is stage" (163). The individual testimonies revealed in the tales reflect the hard truths needed to kick the tongues (i.e., perverse lies) of corrupt political authorities. While an entrenched culture of governmental corruption keeps the country teetering on failed statehood, the frame narrative reveals the fundamental and deep-rooted social and sexual inequality that contributes not only to suffering and instability but to a vicious cycle of violence and revenge. That is, the pilgrimage to Abuja represents a larger penitential and spiritual journey that needs to be made by Nigerians themselves. The overbearing narrator, who initially appropriates the individual narratives into her own voice, models the kind of transformative journey that is required in order to recognize the "otherness" and "Third Dimensions" (7) necessary for national healing.

American class tensions are the focus in *St. Dale*, in which Sharyn McCrumb uses the pilgrimage motif to explore both the psychology of fandom (with Dale Earnhardt, Jr., as the eponymous celebrity) and what she sees as a stark American cultural and social divide.[60] Harry Bailey, the enterprising owner of a travel agency, concocts an Earnhardt Memorial Tour catering to the driver's followers who still mourn his loss and seek "closure." The tour includes a stop at Daytona International Speedway, "The Mother Church of American Racing" and the site of Earnhardt's death. McCrumb mimics the *General Prologue* in bringing together a collection of followers from all classes, from socialite to mechanic, and includes skeptics who are ultimately converted to the imaginative power of "St. Dale." Each of the participants has an autobiographical story ("The Knight's Tale: February 18, 2001"; "The Bride's Tale: Honky Tonk Truth") that explores the psychology of hero worship, found here often to be the result of psychological trauma. As an avatar of the American Dream, "The Intimidator's" appeal lay in his unpretentiousness and humility, notwithstanding his secure membership in the Fortune 500. Indeed, McCrumb imagines Earnhardt to be a modern St. Thomas Becket, "a poor boy who made good in a system stacked against him, and who retained his humility to the last" (392). His modesty is in apparent contrast to the "wine-and-cheese" crowd, "the self-appointed cultural elite," who, indulging in "hillbilly stereotyping," malign both NASCAR and its fans (252, 393). McCrumb's appropriation of *The Canterbury Tales* frame ensconces Chaucer, notwithstanding his own high-culture status, as the common man's poet, lending some canonical pedigree both to the social critique and the exploration of modern secular sainthood.

Ronald L. Ecker's *The Evolutionary Tales: Rhyme and Reason on Creation/ Evolution, with Apologies to Chaucer and Darwin* also explores the distinctly American intersection between religious faith and social class. Composed in iambic pentameter couplets, the parody combines Ecker's two passions: Chaucer and debunking creationism.[61] Ecker adopts the narrative frame of the *General Prologue*, substituting a description of natural selection for Chaucer's meditation on the physical and spiritual regeneration of spring (and even outstrips Chaucer's long opening periodic sentence):

> When in their own sweet time all species tend
>   To over-propagate, then comes the end
>   For many individuals who find
>   That they are not among the fittest kind;
>   For as resources then are limited,
>   Survivors are those born to get ahead,
>   Selected through genetic variation [1–7].

The "General Prologue" consists of an outline of the history of the creationism

1. Modes of Intertextual Engagement 41

movement, from the 1920 Scopes Trial to the landmark *Kitzmiller v. Dover* decision in 2005. Like *The Riverside Chaucer*, the text is footnoted to help neophytes with the more technical vocabulary. The narrator, a spokesman for evolution, decides in April to travel to Dayton, Tennessee (site of the Scopes trial) for a seminar on creationism ("The seminar turned out to be a bore" [213]). His fellow travelers include eight scientists and a philosopher, traveling incognito in order not to lend scientific credence to the proceedings. They gather for a memorial Coke at Robinson's, "that drugstore ... where Scopes first planned his crime" (174). Each tells a tale on the evidence for evolution (and the fallacies of "intelligent design") from the perspective of his or her specialization, with the closing [Bible] *Scholar's Tale* making a case for the compatibility of evolution and religious belief. There are a few portrait sketches in the "General Prologue" ("There was a BIOCHEMIST on the scene/ Who'd come to life if some protein or gene/ Popped up in conversation" [105–7]), and some feint at providing dramatic links (a dalliance, for instance, develops between the Paleoanthropologist and Biologist), but Ecker is less interested in characterization or impersonated art than in providing a relatively in-depth discussion about the evidence for evolution. While adopting the style and structure of *The Canterbury Tales* in support of scientific rationalism might simply be attributed to authorial idiosyncrasy, Ecker does nonetheless fit in a long tradition of appropriating Chaucer within a context of humanistic secularism and social satire.[62]

While Chaucer's frame is most often put to service political and social commentary and to explore class tensions, *Broadcast* (1999), a live one-day event associating the sixth centenary of the poet's death with the revival of the Tate, appropriates Chaucerian pilgrimage as an icon of London's communal artistic heritage.[63] Conceived by Nina Pope and Karen Guthrie, the Chaucerian narrative template allows a diversity of voices to explore modern conceptions of pilgrimage and the artistic possibilities of modern media technology. Twenty-nine artist-pilgrims provide both a brief prerecorded "portrait" and a live account of their journey to an audience gathered in Borough Market. Participants were drawn from a wide range of British society, from Management Consultant to Poet, Van Driver to Scientist. The pilgrims visited the grave of a World War I poet, a childhood home, Southwark Cathedral, a clairvoyant, Freud's house, the Thames Barrier, Canterbury Cathedral, and the Ashmolean Museum to see the Stradivarius Messiah violin. The motives for the journeys are as diverse as the destinations, but a recurring motif is a return to a place that will evoke childhood memories—out of a desire for, or a way to exorcise, nostalgia, or in the hope of simply remembering. Although Chaucer functions to commodify Southwark as an artistic center, to invoke London's literary heritage, and to promote a sense of urban community, one is left with a sense of cultural fragmentation rather than collective identity. For Jonathan Jones, *Broadcast* is "about solitude ... you get a sense of a fractured world where these people are all glad to have a forum in which to tell their tales, down a phone, to someone they can't see."[64]

Finally, in the spirit of Gavin Douglas's image of Chaucer as "evere ... wemenis friend," but nonetheless probably one of the oddest examples of appropriation, the collaborative *Insomniac Tales by Chaucer's Women* illustrates "the universality of Chaucer's tales and those of his 21st-century women."[65] The Tabard Inn is reimagined as the Women's Wellness Spa, the starting point of a pilgrimage to self-renewal:

> It is in this regeneration time — this season we call spring — when within each of us stirs our own need for rebirth. The pounds must be shed. The impurities must be purged. The skin must be tanned, and the muscles must be toned. There must be a revival on the inside, just as there is a revival on the outside ... in the budding trees, the yawning perennials, and the lengthening days. An equinox of the soul, if you will [4].

On a proverbially "dark and stormy night," the visitors gather in the lobby after a power outage; to pass the time, the night clerk plies the customers with wine, suggesting a tale-telling contest with the winner getting "a most coveted prize": a Hostess Ho-Ho. Clearly mimicking Chaucer's narrative portraiture, the plucky night clerk, "who just happens to be a student of English literature," describes the various dieting insomniacs. Like Chaucer's estates satire, the characterizations are based on common contemporary female stereotypes and clichés (the cougar, socialite, desperate housewife, etc.) with the descriptive language drawn from popular romance fiction. The mysterious and menacing Ileana Knight, for instance, has "malachite green eyes, alabaster skin, full rubicund lips, and waist-length hair as black as a raven's feather"; there is a version of the Prioress, a disapproving Mother Superior (with "flawless and ivory" skin, "naturally deep red lips," and "crystalline blue eyes") whose repressed sexuality is manifested in her extreme fondness for cats; and there is the Wife of Bath, Ernestine Daly, "a plastic surgeon's dissertation" and the owner of a large lingerie franchise "that provides women with all they'd ever need to enslave a man" (10).

Some of the tales do clearly echo Chaucer in an effort to update his material, but with a queer slant. And just as Chaucer's tales are commonly read as characterizing the tellers, many of these sensational yarns are cast as autobiography, revealing character in the sense of an alter ego or hidden persona. "The Reeve's Tale," for instance, told by Olivia Reeve, a lesbian, substitutes John and Aleyn with Jane and Allen, summer practicum students who try to expose the snobby Simon Simpkins's crooked construction contracts. Having failed to expose the swindler, they vow revenge, with Allen gradually seducing, impregnating, and reluctantly wedding Simon's daughter, and Jane teaching Simon's wife "how good sex could really be." In the tradition of the fabliaux, the moral is that "everyone got what was coming to them ... and cleverness was rewarded as it should be" (31–2), with the cleverness in this case wholly on the part of the women and with both males punished for their vanity. One of the better contributions is "The Prioress's Tale," composed in rime royal and providing a Swiftian allegory on the modern abortion debate. Those who Row and those who Wade reside on either side of the "River Choyce." One of the hip-boot wearers who crosses over to the oar wielders is horrified to discover "How each of those who would Row was a staunch member/ Of the belief that the unborn child we could dismember" (58). He proceeds to murder several Rowers and is subsequently executed. Like Chaucer's tale, the morality is muddled in the end. While the Rowers (and the State) consider the Wader to be a mass murderer, his "martyr's" soul ascends to heaven and is eternally ensconced next to the Virgin Mary. As for the literary prize, in the spirit of collective transgression that runs throughout, 13 sexually excited, sleep-deprived, and hungry women pounce on the narrator and democratically share her secret box of contraband Ho-Ho's.

Approaching these appropriations as creative interpretations of *The Canterbury Tales* one finds several recurring features: the journey, the collection of voices representing social types, the generic variety and polyvocality, and the destination that has both communal and thematic significance. Indeed, these appropriations improve upon their unfinished model, constructing a symbolic site — a convent, Canterbury Cathedral itself, Daytona International Speedway, an alien deity's tomb, a women's spa — that has thematic resonance, uniting the various tales. Edmund Reiss suggests that *The Canterbury Tales* is "a perversion of the true Christian pilgrimage" since the pilgrims lack a sustained "search for understanding" or any kind of "real development or maturation."[66] In contrast, contemporary appropriations of the pilgrimage frame — very often concerned with forms of modern spirituality and social division — tend to focus on the individual and communal transformative potential of the journey. That potential is less a product of penitence, however, than actuated by the ritual of storytelling itself. The shared experiences, often cathartic confessions and often involving cultural dislocation, alienation, or secret transgression, allow either the narrator or the group to move toward some sense of social synthesis or collective identity.

A second kind of appropriation is in the form of historical mystery fiction, a major trend in Chaucer's popular reception examined more fully in Chapter Two. These novels take two forms, in which either a murder is housed in the pilgrimage frame with the investigation replacing the formal tales, or in which the poet himself is put to work as a detective within the context of Chaucerian biographical fiction. Mary Devlin's *Murder on the Canterbury Pilgrimage: A Geoffrey Chaucer Murder Mystery* reimagines the poem as a convoluted murder mystery involving allegorical clues and the machinations of a secret heretical group, a successful formula realized most lucratively in Dan Brown's blockbuster, *The Da Vinci Code*.[67] Devlin fleshes out the links, individualizes the pilgrims, and reflecting an interest in recreational medievalism, sketches in the practical topography of the pilgrimage. In keeping with her evocation of the Middle Ages as a time of rampant corruption and hypocrisy, the pilgrims are almost uniformly bad; indeed, even the Second Nun's piety is "overblown and ostentatious" (107). But Chaucer is inspired by this motley group of "volatile, high-strung people" and composes his poem while on the journey (summaries of the tales are provided) in the spare time he has between clearing his own name and solving a mysterious string of thefts and homicides. Indeed, Devlin's Chaucer is particularly suited to the task, given his work as a spy and, more importantly, his facility with astrological charts and tarot cards. The poet's passions, including an intense fondness for cats, suspiciously mirror those of his New Age author's; but notwithstanding the transparent emotional investment, Devlin clearly fits into a long critical tradition of imagined empathetic identification with Chaucer. Less imaginatively idiosyncratic, however, is Devlin's concern with exposing the hypocrisies and shams of institutionalized religion and its acolytes.

In his six-installment Canterbury Tales series,[68] Paul C. Doherty adopts a somewhat different premise, with each of the pilgrims telling two tales; the one during the day ought to "instruct or amuse" (and is not recounted in the narrative), but the one at night should have the effect of Hamlet's-father's-ghost on its audience ("to chill the blood, halt the heart and curl the locks upon our heads.").[69] The pilgrims are largely skeletal reincarnations of their originals, here filtered through Harry Bailly's bourgeois point of view: the Miller, for instance, is a "loud-mouthed bastard," built "like a battering ram" and handy with the bagpipes.[70] Doherty is less interested than Devlin is in fleshing out Chaucer's character; he remains a shadowy figure, an "influential" court dignitary who has a "penchant for marking people's foibles with a gentle mockery" (although oddly enough, given the change in narrative point of view it is Harry Bailly himself who marks and mocks those foibles).[71] Roughly in keeping with the tradition that the tales characterize the tellers, the thrillers are autobiographical, with the links ("Words between the pilgrims") chiefly devoted to ferreting out the veracity of the narrator's story. Not only does the Knight, for instance, play the leading role in his own supernatural spine-tingler about the living dead inhabiting Oxford (with one of these bloodsuckers—Chaucer's Monk—still on the loose), but he also reveals that his daytime story is autobiographical as well, and Emily is revealed to be the mother of his son, the squire "Alexander." The conception of tale telling as confessional autobiography is found throughout the popular corpus, quite different from the critical approach to Chaucer's impersonated art in which the tales are read as a metaphorical, rather than a literal, revelation of character, and with truth associated with something other (e.g., "sentence") than factual autobiography.[72] But in Doherty's case the tales are intended less to provide realistic characterization than to ameliorate an apparent aesthetic lapse in the original poem in which Chaucer characterizes the pilgrims as strangers who simply fall together by happenstance.

The medievalism of Doherty and Devlin emphasizes the grim barbarity of the age, providing a fitting fictional context for their interest in exploring the "the darker side of human nature," and reflecting a conservative ideological orientation common to the genre (i.e., moral certainty, defense of the existing social order, the necessity for state oversight and policing).[73] Peter Ackroyd's *The Clerkenwell Tales* gives us a similar setting with an accompanying gallery of grotesques but instead provides a contemporary political allegory addressing domestic terrorism.[74] The title is a misnomer, for no tales are properly told, and London is a setting rather than a destination. Ackroyd borrows the estates of Chaucer's pilgrims, here presented as dramatis personae, but his characters, all drawn into a labyrinthine plot involving the machinations of a Lollard-like heretical group, often have little resemblance to their originals. The Prioress, Dame Agnes, has a pet monkey, and the hygienic cook has a clean kitchen. The intention is to animate Chaucer's portraits, but given the large cast, Ackroyd is himself often unable to get beyond the preliminary character sketch. Dialogue is frequently drawn from *The Canterbury Tales*, and part of the pleasure for students of Chaucer is in detecting the rather discordant contexts in which the quotations appear. However, apart from overtly invoking Blake's notion that Chaucer has created ageless types, Ackroyd is less interested in commenting on Chaucer than in invoking a superstitious, squalid, and sinister Middle Ages whose atmosphere of conspiratorial paranoia has some frightening political parallels to our own time.

Philippa Morgan (a.k.a. Philip Gooden) adopts a different premise in three titles (*Chaucer and the House of Fame, Chaucer and the Legend of Good Women, Chaucer and the Doctor of Physic*), taking advantage of biographical gaps provided by Chaucer's various diplomatic missions abroad to put the poet to work as a detective.[75] While ostensibly conducting mundane governmental business, Chaucer pursues some secret royal commission, which inevitably involves him in aristocratic intrigue. Similar to Ackroyd's practice, Chaucerian allusion is sprinkled throughout, especially the ubiquitous favorite, "murder will out." Although the crimes tend to reveal an entrenched culture of aristocratic corruption and socioeconomic injustice, like Devlin, Morgan is more interested in developing Chaucer's character rather than indulging in ideological critique. The poet is well suited to sleuthing, gifted with an uncannily reliable "sixth sense" and an ability to project a "bland absence of curiosity" that makes his nemeses inevitably underestimate him.[76] His sense of chivalry (stopping a gang rape, e.g.) makes him quite enticing to the opposite sex, and Morgan imagines Chaucer's erotic poetry as at least partly inspired by personal experience. In *Chaucer and the House of Fame*, for instance, Rosamond is the wife of his captor at Poitiers, inspiring Chaucer's wistful amorous lyric. But the duplicitous beauty does more harm than simply doing the poet "no daliaunce," and is representative of Morgan's favorite theme, namely, the atavistic corruption and social insecurity of the upper echelons.

Garry O'Connor goes further in *Chaucer's Triumph*, constructing most of Chaucer's oeuvre as thinly veiled erotic autobiography.[77] The intrigue is set against the backdrop of John of Gaunt's protracted funeral cortege, and the narrative is told from several narrative points of view. Adam Scriveyn's voice dominates, and he seeks to solve several mysteries, including the murder of Chaucer's former mistress and Cecily Champagne's charge of rape against his master. But the biggest mystery of all, given the incessant amorous shenanigans of Chaucer's courtly circle, is the paternity of Chaucer's children. Chaucer is cast as a lecherous reprobate — although not without his occasional lucid moments— married to Gaunt's pawned-off mistress, acting as pander in Katherine and Gaunt's affair, and whose closest autofictional analogue is January. Chaucer is representative of a conventionally sensational Middle Ages— people are licentious, emotionally volatile, and violent. But O'Connor's real interest is in the mysterious alchemy of art, the ability of Chaucer's poetry in particular to transform what Scriveyn calls "smut" into chivalrous sentiment. As important is O'Connor's concern with family values, that is, the relationship between sexual morality and political stability. Indeed, it is Gaunt's sexual escapades that have "have torn the country apart" (203), leading to political instability manifested most alarmingly in the revolutionary potential of social justice unleashed in the Peasants' Revolt.

Chaucerian mystery fiction — a strange brew of biography, fiction, history, and genre conventions— attests to a conspiratorial, and sometimes lurid, fascination with gaps in Chaucer's biography and to a desire to creatively revise and update the truncated pilgrimage. While the genre often has a conservative tenor, portraying crime as an anti-social anomaly and as a product of individual pathology, all of these writers portray the Middle Ages as a time of gross and intransigent socioeconomic inequality, leaving the reader with some sense of unease with the restoration of the status quo. Chaucer's character largely reflects the conventions of mystery fiction in which the hero works to maintain social stability. But reflecting a long critical tradition, Chaucer is also imagined to be a marginalized figure with modern sensibilities whose anomalous social position allows him insight into the highly provisional nature of medieval civil justice. And while these appropriations update the pilgrimage to fit a contemporary popular genre, they are also critical readings of *The Canterbury Tales*, ameliorating what are seen as aesthetic lapses in the original: realistic descriptive settings, relationships among the pilgrims, developed characterization, action within the links, and, perhaps most importantly, Chaucer's political engagement with some of the dramatic political events of his age.

Invocation

The last two types of Chaucerian intertextuality are forms of allusion. The terms *invocation* and *citation* are here distinguished, however, by both the explicitness and the potential thematic function of the allusion. An invocation involves an overt Chaucerian reference (in the form of an epigraph, internal quotation, or titular reference) that lends conceptual coherence to the modern text. Substantive knowledge of the signified Chaucerian text, while not required, will indeed enrich the reader's sense of literary interplay. In contrast to appropriation, which is most often structural and has the potential to produce various levels of thematic resonance, Chaucerian invocations serve as a form of semiotic shorthand: for social and cultural satire, gender politics, and the symbolic capital of Western literary tradition.

Those works involving social or cultural satire often invoke Chaucer within the context of pilgrimage or some form of communal peregrination. John Guare's *Chaucer in Rome*, for instance, a satire on contemporary art and institutionalized religion, follows the careers of three students studying at the American Academy in Rome during the 2000 Jubilee.[78] Pete Shaughnessy, an art historian, and Sarah, a curator, seek to help their friend Matt, an artist who has contracted cancer from the arsenic-based paints he uses for his brilliant landscapes. In the quest for a safer medium for Matt's message of the environmental and spiritual toxicity of modern existence, Pete suggests videotaping confessions of Holy Year pilgrims desperate for absolution. But what begins as a cruel joke on Pete's parents becomes an international sensation. The stunt has tragic consequences, however, leaving Pete plagued by a desperate need for the same "peace" and "forgiveness" that the videotape project was meant to mock. Part of Guare's purpose is to give us some sense of what's wrong with contemporary art. Matt is a self-absorbed narcissist, an artist who seeks celebrity and fame at any cost; Pete, the art historian, has a research project clearly meant to parody semiotic art history ("Gender issues *slash* class issues *slash* post–Marxism as revealed in the iconography of the — yes — fingernails of the crucified Christ" [11]); and Sarah's profound discovery that painting is "phallocentric" targets the trendy frivolity of aesthetic discourse.

More important, however, is what is wrong with contemporary Catholicism. Guare is clearly irritated not only by the chaotic religious hysteria created by the Church but also by the commercialism, profiteering, and blurring of pious pilgrimage and recreational tourism that characterizes the Jubilee experience. His implication is that the Catholic Church has created an artificial "Holy Year Shuffle" without the means to satisfy either the spiritual or material needs of the pilgrims: "We take no responsibility for your travel plans.... You can sue the Vatican all you want. The Vatican will not pay" (15–16). Father Shapiro, the sunny representative from the Vatican Public Relations Office, is a modern reincarnation of the Pardoner and the Friar, inverting the spiritual and the material ("take a T-shirt"), contemptuous of the faithful ("greedy pilgrims"), and more interested in fraternizing with the rich and famous ("What Marty [Scorcese] wants, Marty gets" [18]) than in ministering to his flock. On the one hand, the invocation of Chaucer's name simply evokes images of pilgrimage and confessional tale telling. But just as Chaucer saw and exposed the ecclesiastical abuses in his own age, Guare, in invoking his name in the title of his play, positions himself as a similar censor, a latter-day Lollard, condemning the superficiality and crass materialism that modern institutionalized pilgrimage entails.

Black humor and social satire similarly infuse *Two Caravans* (titled *Strawberry Fields* in the United States) by Marina Lewycka, a modern *Grapes of Wrath* in dark comic mode, involving a multinational crew of foreign workers hired on to farm the strawberry fields in Kent.[79] The pastoral idyll does not last, and as the group of nine migrates north, we hear their stories — told in a mix of stylistically distinctive first and third person narratives, and including a canine point of view — of past hardships and future fantasies. Their Candide-like optimism in the social and economic possibilities England promises, especially in the face of exploitation, xenophobia, and injustice, can be heartbreaking. But Lewycka deftly keeps the mood light, maintaining focus, for instance, on a romantic comedy between two of the characters. *The Publisher's Weekly* describes the novel as "Chaucer-inspired," and *The New Yorker* suggests that the characters "narrate their journeys in the spirit of Chaucer's pilgrims."[80] Lewycka too fosters the comparison, stating that she found inspiration in Chaucer "for the disparate ensemble" found in *Two Caravans*.[81] Notwithstanding their profound faith in social possibility, it is hard to see much Chaucer in the crew of desperate immigrant itinerants. Lewycka does quote several lines from the *Wife of Bath's Prologue* in her epigraph ("taketh not agrief of that I seye/ For myn entente is nat but for to pleye"), however, and the Chaucerian aspect perhaps consists in her use of humor to cloak some serious political concerns, namely the exploitation of foreign workers and, more broadly, the human cost of the global economy.

Similarly utilizing the point of view of domestic outcasts and foreign travelers, Jim Jarmusch's film, *Mystery Train*, described as "a minimalist's version of the *Canterbury Tales*," explores the tawdry remains of the American cultural landscape.[82] Set in Memphis, Tennessee, the film features three stories that appear to be episodic but prove to be simultaneous. In the first segment a Japanese couple is on a touristic pilgrimage to sites associated with the early history of rock and roll (Sun Studios and Graceland in this case). At the beginning of their exploration of Memphis, the couple passes by a "Chaucer Street" in a run-down and decayed neighborhood. As is often the case, the intertextual mileage afforded by the invocation depends upon one's familiarity with both *The Canterbury Tales* and the modern artist's oeuvre. Approaching the visual allusion from the latter viewpoint, Bennet Schaber suggests that "there is some fundamental relation between the 'fathers' (or 'pops') of rock and roll and the 'father' of English poetry; and that relation is the vernacular, the 'mother tongue.'"[83] For Jonathan Rosenbaum the reference reflects Jarmusch's "sense of history," and for Peter Quartermain, it's an example of the auteur's habit of "deprivileging or perhaps reprivileging cultural icons."[84] On the other hand, approaching the film as a postmodern continuation of *The Canterbury Tales*, Peter Conrad finds the notion of pilgrimage to be the central motif throughout the film.[85] While Conrad finds the single Chaucer reference to be a "semiotic joke" representing the vacuity of cultural signs, Chaucer nonetheless invokes associations of spiritual pilgrimage and salvation, highlighting "the country's need for gods and its craving for miracles" (42).

While Chaucer is most often invoked within a context of social satire, several examples of invocation also construct Chaucer as the iconic fountainhead of a canonical literary tradition that, however contested, retains its acolytes. James Hynes's campus novel, *The Lecturer's Tale*, is a promiscuously allusive and farcical academic lampoon whose several allusions to *The Canterbury Tales* underscore his critique of contemporary academia.[86] The eponymous visiting adjunct — a modern-day clerk — is miraculously given the Midas touch of mind control. He uses his extraordinary gift to get himself a three-year appointment in an English department, to humiliate tenure-track job candidates, and to inflict revenge on his insufferable colleagues. In the epigraph, Hynes cites several lines of the Pardoner's faux sermon from his *Prologue* ("O cursed synne of all cursednesse"), and it seems clear that Hynes views his English academics as contemporary pardoners, hawking their fake wares — in the form of cultural studies and critical theory — and neglecting their undergraduate flocks. Hynes's hobbyhorse is not simply the familiar and easy target of narcissistic, posturing, and back-biting academics, but also the tyranny of theory and the concomitant neglect of both the traditional literary canon, and, most importantly, excellence in teaching. The book is dedicated to his "first and best teacher" who embodies Chaucer's Clerk's finest qualities: "gladly wolde he lerne, and gladly teche."

Chaucer has a different kind of canonical significance — representing the grail of linguistic assimilation — in David Dabydeen's *The Intended*, his fictionalized autobiography about a group of adolescents coming of age in London's Asian immigrant community.[87] The Indo-Guyanese narrator wants to "be somebody and the only way to achieve this was to acquire a collection of good examination results and go to university" (113). Mastering the English literary canon, possessing Prospero's (or Chaucer's) books, will, he thinks, exempt him "from the normal rules of lineage and privilege" (195). Hoping to "make a good impression" on his Asian landlord, he tells him that Chaucer was "especially" concerned with "the love of God," and that *The Canterbury Tales* is "about a group of religious people going on a pilgrimage to a holy shrine just like Muslims going to Mecca" (96). For the landlord, "Saucer ... the man from Canterbury," has a talismanic aura, representing the epitome of the perversely difficult language the immigrant community seeks to master. Dabydeen's title invokes Joseph Conrad's *Heart of Darkness*, the intended being Kurtz's beautiful but naive fiancée to whom Marlow chivalrously lies about her suitor's black mistress, malefactions, and madness. Similarly, the narrator idealizes his own privileged female intended, imagining himself as her "dark secret" and her "medieval knight" (244) in much the same way that Troilus idealizes Criseyde. As they are both studying for their A-levels, he hopes to talk to her about *Troilus and Criseyde*, Conrad being unsuitable because "the sex there, and the description of the blacks in the bush, were too shameful for me to contemplate in her company" (121). He puzzles over Criseyde's betrayal, assuming that there "is some higher quality that we can also possess if we willed it" (173). Both Troilus's language and his emotions are incomprehensible to his friend, enterprising amateur pimp and sex magazine aficionado: "I knew what Shaz's response would have been: she [Criseyde] was only a cunt that Troilus dreamed over and his imagination refashioned into a pool of pure rain-water.... In the end she wanted to be frigged, not fondled by a gentle Troilus or smoothed at with his wet words. What Troilus needed was to catch a rash and be a man" (173). Chaucer, in short, as the canonical father of English poetry, represents for the young narrator both the power of artistic illusion and the linguistic grail of cultural assimilation.[88]

In *Birthday Letters* Ted Hughes provides the tantalizing prospect of one of the more celebrated poets of our time including both a poem titled "Chaucer" and another with Chaucerian allusion in one of the most anticipated poetry collections of the decade.[89] Chaucer here is constructed as the patriarchal fountainhead of an English literary tradition presiding over the two latest additions to the canonical pantheon. "St. Botolph's" describes Hughes's first meeting with Sylvia Plath at the launch party for the *St. Botolph's Review*. Considering his horoscope for this fateful day ("disastrous expense"), he knows, "Our Chaucer would have stayed at home with his Dante./ Locating the planets more precisely,/ He would have pondered it deeper" (14). With Plath ascendant "In my tenth House of good and evil fame," Chaucer's facility with the astrolabe would have told him (as Hughes knows in retrospect) that the romantic union is fatal, that is, both inevitable and mortally flawed: "Our Chaucer, I think, would have sighed./ He would have assured us, shaking his sorrowful head,/ That day the solar system married us" (14).

Turning from Chaucer's association with the archaic art of the astrological forecast to his affiliation with vernal promise, the poem "Chaucer," in which Plath declaims Middle English to a herd of cattle, also invokes the aesthetic spirit of the poet over the early halcyon days of the doomed couple. The poem begins by quoting the opening lines of the *General Prologue*, providing a fitting canonical allusion to accompany the rural spring setting with its "flying laundry" and "new emerald" (51). The Chaucerian lines are recited by Plath, inspired by one of those emotional "bumpers of champagne" made of "pure spirit" (51). The cows, like Hughes, look on, "enthralled," "hypnotized," and "astounded" as Plath continues her exuberant recitation:

> the cows
> Watched, then approached: they appreciated Chaucer.
> You went on and on. Here were reasons
> To recite Chaucer. Then came the Wyf of Bath,
> Your favorite character in all literature [51].

Plath continues until the rapt bovines are shooed away by Hughes: "But/ Your sostenuto rendering of Chaucer/ Was already perpetual" (52). The humorous anecdote illustrates not merely Plath's affection for Chaucer (whom she was studying at the time) but also both her recitative powers and her idiosyncratic literary vivacity, traits that Hughes, and apparently the cows, found highly appealing. Although Lucas Myers "can't imagine any other British student spectator responding the way Ted did" to a "display so obviously calculated," he suggests that the poem nonetheless sustains the memory of Plath's "spontaneity" and "innocence."[90] Attesting to the fluidity of the intertextual play afforded by these conceptual categories, however, Wallace reads the poems as "a sign of powerful poetic engagement with Chaucer ... not just with the texture of Chaucer's language but also with his multiple, nonlinear temporalities."[91]

Finally, Chaucerian invocation is also commonly found within the context of gender or sexual politics, his characters having become archetypes of abused and rebellious women. Caryl Churchill resurrects the figure of Griselda in her stage play, *Top Girls*, a critical look at second-wave feminism, whose "agenda of social and political equality has been achieved in the West" but which is "blind to the everyday struggles of women still mired in poverty and fighting social injustice."[92] Through the character of an ambitious professional, Marlene, who manages a women's employment agency, Churchill explores the emotional and social costs of socioeconomic success. The first act, offering "a fleeting fantasy of transnational, transhistorical sisterhood," features a celebratory dinner for Marlene's recent promotion.[93] The guests include historical and fictional top girls (Pope Joan, Lady Nijo, Dull Gret, Isabella Bird), and Griselda is grossly out of place among these women who outrageously transgressed existing gender restrictions. Part of the humor in the scene is derived from the diners' reactions to Griselda's tale: her husband is variously described as "bonkers," "barbaric," and "a bastard"; a disgusted Marlene leaves in the middle of Griselda's story to go "for a pee"; and Joan puzzles over the logic of Walter's tests ("He killed his children/ to see if you loved him enough?" [I. 23]). Churchill does have Griselda tentatively question the legitimacy of Walter's patriarchal prerogatives: "I do think — I do wonder — it would have been nicer if Walter hadn't had to" (I. 27). Each of the women, however, has her own inner Griselda. Despite their courageous defiance and "enormous achievements" they are collectively "miserable" given the psychological costs, particularly their sacrifice of motherhood, for their social subversion.

Susan Swan's *The Wives of Bath* invokes another female Chaucerian archetype within a similar thematic context of mutiny against conventional gender expectations.[94] Told from a first-person point of view, the coming of age novel is set at a girls' boarding school in Canada in the early 1960s and includes a cast with a number of characters whose sexual identities don't fit patriarchal norms — with tragic consequences. One of the so-called wives is the headmistress, a closeted lesbian who looks "the way Chaucer's Wife of Bath might have looked if she had stepped into the twentieth century: broad in the behind and out for herself, and the rest of the world could go hang" (22). But her school, Bath Ladies College, simply serves to reproduce repressive gender roles prescribing passivity, deference to authority, and both physical and mental inferiority. Jettisoning girdles, nylons, and bras and participating in cross-dressing with her roommate, Paulie, the narrator comes to recognize that gendered behavior is constructed, and constructed to perpetuate the social subjugation (and extreme physical discomfort) of women:

1. Modes of Intertextual Engagement 53

> ... we were all Wives of Bath —from the teachers who terrorized us with their bells and gatings to the overfed boarders and snobby day girls, to Paulie and me who tried to play by our own set of rules. But no matter how hard any of us struggled we still looked dumb ... because Bath Ladies College was only a fiefdom in the kingdom of men [217].

Swan constructs Chaucer's Wife of Bath as an early voice of dissent; but notwithstanding Alison's pioneering protest against masculine power (represented by King Kong in the novel), her Canadian reincarnations are still unable to successfully challenge the prerogatives of patriarchy.

Gloria Naylor's *Bailey's Café* represents a dilemma (examined more fully in Chapter Four) insofar as her novel has no immediately apparent relationship with Chaucer's text beyond the possible invocation of Harry Bailly in the title.[95] The owner of the eponymous café who is also the first-person narrator is in fact unnamed. His restaurant, a surreal greasy spoon, provides a temporary refuge for a collection of grossly abused and psychologically broken customers who come to tell their stories as a form of atonement. A neighboring boardinghouse provides a home for some, while others leave through the café's back entrance into an eternal void. In finding the cafe and cathartically sharing their stories, these characters are seeking a form of salvation. Griselda and the Wife of Bath might be seen as pale archetypes for some of these victims who are cruelly maltreated by various patriarchal figures. But those who find the titular reference to be Chaucerian find less thematic resonance within the novel itself than the idea of the novel as a canonical challenge, a parody that serves as what Hutcheon calls an "ironic visitation" that both inscribes and subverts canonical literary inheritance.[96]

Citation

Citation is an inert allusion, involving those cases in which Chaucer is overtly signified, often in the title, but in which the reference serves little or no apparent further symbiotic or hermeneutic function.[97] What I am calling citation would probably come under Juvan's umbrella of "intransitive textual elements," that is, those allusions that are a semantic or symbolic dead-end. Juvan suggests that sometimes writers cite texts hoping either to enhance their own literary status or to establish a rapport with the reader:

> Thus they lend their texts certain stylistic coloration, add exoticism of difference, point out principles of eternal return (i.e., repetition of the same model in different times and settings), demonstrate their erudition, or through a quotation's phatic function build solidarity with their readers since the latter, insofar as they recognize the allusion, belong to the same group, cultural level, and value system as the author.[98]

Often the citation involves the vague association of a "tale" with fictional and/ or historical (auto)biography in the well-entrenched critical tradition in which the tales are thought to characterize the tellers. Ellis suggests that these "traces" of Chaucer sometimes provide "handy titles and headings for fiction and journalism of a confessional bent ... the interest of such lives often lies in the isolation from community they represent."[66] Recent examples—all of which focus on the eponymous subject—would include historical fiction set in the Middle Ages such as Nicole Galland's *The Fool's Tale* or Bernard Cornwall's *The Archer's Tale*. One might also include A. S. Byatt's *The Biographer's Tale*, concerned with the intersection of fiction and historiography.[100] Wendy Holden, who has a habit of punning on canonical texts in her fictional titles, calls her contemporary social satire and domestic comedy *The Wives of Bath* and includes a single allusion to Chaucer's Wife of Bath: "Next came Laura. Hugo looked at her with interest. Besides thick makeup, she had a wide gap between her front teeth, giving her smile a bawdy appearance. She was wearing a lot of hot pink."[68] Although Holden's Chaucerian title is based largely on the geographical setting, it does nonetheless accurately hint at a story involving the tribulations of modern marriage. On the other hand, the citation in a non-fiction title such as Thomas Augst's *The Clerk's Tale: Young Men and Moral Life in Nineteenth-Century America* is less explicable and somewhat of a red herring since these clerks are not scholars but business apprentices.[102] Augst's topic is "how the moral ambitions of ordinary people were both fostered and frustrated at the onset of the modern era of American capitalism" (3). One enterprising reviewer suggests that the Chaucerian tie-in is the Clerk's theme of constancy in the face of adversity.[103] But monotony is the primary adversity, and the point seems to be how young men in an emerging middle class fostered their creativity, used their leisure time, and maintained a sense of ethical well-being within the confines of market culture.

Constancy in adversity also seems to be the theme of Wendy Cope's "The Teacher's Tale," commissioned for the 600th anniversary of Chaucer's death.[104] Cope is known for her playful poetic parodies, but in the case of this "chalkface Chaucer," as one reviewer describes the narrative poem, the tribute is less to Chaucer than to the teaching vocation.[105] While Cope does deliver a Chaucerian cautionary tale via cliché ("Family life can be a blessing: true/ But don't forget the damage it can do" [56]), the mimicry is primarily stylistic: "In London SE5 there lived a boy/ Called Paul. He was his mother's pride and joy/ When he was born in 1961—/ Best baby ever, Mrs. Skinner's son" (55). Despite the auspicious beginning, Paul is burdened by the great expectations and solicitous psychological abuse meted out by his parents; his dire childhood and quiet despair are ameliorated only by the occasional observant and empathetic teacher. He himself becomes a teacher—as "you'll have guessed" (76) — whose specialty is working with troubled children. Teenage angst is the focus too of Roger Stevens's *The Journal of Danny Chaucer (Poet)* which chronicles a year of high school life in a series of self-contained poems.[106] While creativity perhaps provides some consolation in the face of adolescent adversity, as is the case with Cope, the Chaucerian citation warrants little intertextual engagement nor does it appear to have thematic bearing within the contemporary text beyond the association of the Chaucerian with poetic verse.

But the difference between invocation and citation is especially dependent upon one's familiarity with both the source and the appropriator. One might consider, for instance, Sting's *Ten Summoner's Tales*. The cover art features the edifice of Wardour Old Castle, with the singer in contemplative pose accompanied by his unbridled horse. The lyrics are loosely concerned with erotic entanglements and violations of the sort Chaucer's Summoner might have prosecuted. The title also acts both as a pun on Sting's surname (Sumner) and, depending on the perspicuity of the reviewer, "a deft way for Sting to get some distance from his do-gooder image while sustaining the resonance of his larger social concerns" (*Rolling Stone*), an expression of his "literariness" (*Q Magazine*), or a manifestation of his "pretensions" and "aimless erudition" (*Daily Telegraph*).[107] Similarly, *Canterbury Tales: The Best of Caravan* (1976), a compilation of the progressive rock band's music, has nothing to do with Chaucer per se, reflecting instead both the band's Kentish roots and their occasional incorporation of medieval melodies and instruments in their music.[108] But the original double album cover (replaced in the 1994 rerelease with a photograph of the band members in late-60s period clothing) is a charming parody of Thomas Stothard's colored engraving, "Procession of the Canterbury Pilgrims" (1806–7), substituting the medieval pilgrims with members of the band and, presumably, identifiable contemporaries.[109] If there is an intended Chaucerian resonance, one would guess that the implication is that these are musical pilgrims on their way to "the Canterbury Scene," the center of "the Canterbury sound," a rock, jazz, folk, and psychedelic fusion that flourished in the late 1960s and early 1970s.[110]

Neil Gaiman includes Chaucer in "Men of Good Fortune," an issue of his magnum opus, *Sandman*, in which a medieval commoner is given immortality and returns to the same tavern every century.[111] Chaucer provides some local color for the 1389 setting, sitting in the tavern as he is gently upbraided by a drinking companion for writing in English ("the langue travaillistes") and eschewing both the native verse form (i.e., the alliterative long line) and the popular subject matter found in *Piers Plowman*: "That's what people want. Not filthy tales in rhymes about pilgrims" (103). Chaucer defends his practice of art for "solaas" sake: "But I enjoy rhyming Edmund. And I enjoy tavern tales told of an evening." The background chatter provides a snippet of the kind of primary material that presumably inspires Chaucer's poetry: "up her dress, and she says 'Are you hunting for rabbits again friar?'" (103). Gaiman often indulges in intertextual allusion, and Chaucer is perhaps included here in his capacity as a familiar historical figure. But as a common man whose celebration of common pleasures has achieved for the poet a form of immortality, his presence is also thematically fitting in a story that affirms the value of human life despite the haunting limitation of human mortality.

There are also cases of silent invocation or critical citation in which the text is touted as signifying *The Canterbury Tales*, but in which there are no obvious textual signs that this is necessarily the case. Juvan suggests that "motifs and themes are interpretive constructs that situate a literary text in the universe of discourse, which means that readers judge its relevance by the frames and scripts or categories that obtain in other texts of the culture."[112] Indeed, it has become boilerplate marketing to invoke the poem any time a text involves a group of strangers telling stories—again, usually veiled autobiography—while on some journey. The strategy is intended to foster brand recognition, to trigger generic associations as an aid to readers for categorizing the text, to provide some symbolic capital to a lesser-known author, or to capture a more diverse audience. Karen Maitland's *Company of Liars: A Novel of the Plague*, for instance, is reviewed as "a diabolic take on *The Canterbury Tales*" (*Marie Clare*) and being in "the storytelling" tradition of *The Canterbury Tales*" (*Metro*) and marketed as such with these excerpts appearing as testimonials.[113] Invoking a superstitious and highly parochial milieu, and perhaps best described as historical mystery fiction (with a healthy dose of magical realism), the story involves a group of social misfits (a rune reader, a conjurer, a man with a swan's wing) thrown together by chance as they flee across England in front of the plague. The skeletal plot would suggest a greater debt to Boccaccio rather than to Chaucer, but the story is relayed in the first person (by a "camelot" or seller of fake religious relics) and pit stops do include a pilgrimage shrine (chosen as a potential source of revenue rather than as a source of repentance or renewal). And a particularly vicious and anti–Semitic pardoner has a walk-on part. As we have seen in many examples of modern tale telling, rather than metaphorical extensions of character, the stories are confessional autobiographies. In this case, the company of liars tells tales that manifest some secret to their identity (incest, homosexuality) which act as final confessionals before each character's brutal atonement.

Similarly, Rana Dasgupta's *Tokyo Cancelled* is hailed on the back cover of both the U.S. and U.K. paperback editions as, respectively, "a *Canterbury Tales* for our times" and "a kind of *Canterbury Tales* for a sedentary, globally savvy era."[114] Most reviewers, in addition to the author himself, invoke

Chaucer in the effort to categorize the novel. The primary motif in this case is not so much a journey as simply the Homeric desire to get home. Their flight cancelled, 13 stranded and largely anonymous passengers (there is a Japanese man; "a big man") pass the night telling stories in a generically nondescript terminal "in the Middle of Nowhere" (1). The stories begin grounded in realism with fairy-tale motifs (a tailor makes a coat for a prince; a Japanese man falls in love with a doll) but invariably careen into urban magical realism and social allegory. Characters are not only emotionally transformed, but also literally metamorphosed, sometimes as a result of simple inadvertent human cruelty but also in response to the dehumanization wrought by technology, bureaucracy, capitalism, and consumerism. These various transmutations are clearly psychological metaphors but also represent the vitality of imagination and creativity even in the most stultifying and sterile environments. Although both Dasgupta's social criticism and fiddling with genre might be considered Chaucerian, the marketing allusion is odd since there is no pilgrimage, no first-person narrator, no character portraits, no contest. In this case at least, the citation of Chaucer is an effort to place this first novel within the British literary tradition. But more importantly, perhaps, the citation reflects an effort to grace with a coherent frame what is really a loosely related series of narratives (i.e., a collection of difficult-to-market short stories).

One might include here those cases in which professional readers find intertextual resonance although the work in question lacks overt citation to the Chaucerian text. John Fowles's *A Maggot* (1985) has been described as many things: revisionary historiography, metafictional and hypertextual parody, dialogic postmodernist pastiche.[115] Pertinent here, however, is Carla Arnell's reading of the novel as "a modern metamorphosis of *The Canterbury Tales*," an analysis based on the initial claim that Fowles had been reading some Chaucer "for whatever reason, in the early 1980s, the period during which *A Maggot* was being conceived."[116] Fowles does seem to echo the *General Prologue* in his opening: "In the late and last afternoon of an April long ago, a forlorn little group of travelers cross a remote upland in the far south-west of England. All are on horseback" (1). The parody, however, if such it is, immediately takes on a modernist tone: the landscape, "a waste of dead heather and ling," has "an aura of dismal monotony," and ravens with a foreboding, "watchful hostility" (2) replace the frolicking nightingales of the original. And what turns out to be a pilgrimage, of sorts, to a mysterious cave, ends with an aristocrat's mysterious disappearance and what appears to be a close encounter of the third kind. The subsequent narrative consists primarily of the depositions of the survivors as an investigative lawyer attempts, without any success, to piece together a record of the bizarre events. Arnell argues that the bullying lawyer's inquisition of the principal character — a Quaker maid, turned prostitute, turned Dissenter — embodies a number of themes found in the *Wife of Bath's Prologue*, including the ingrained misogyny of patriarchal authority, the conflict between individual experience and textual authority, and the validity of experiential knowledge. Arnell concludes that while the Wife of Bath is unable to bring "forth a truth that was personally and politically transforming" (946), the Quaker maid is radically transformed and liberated by her strange experience (hence, the maggot).

Many critics have also found Graham Swift's *Last Orders* to be "faintly haunted by Chaucer."[117] Loose structural similarities are perhaps there: four characters travel from a pub in Bermondsey, with a stop at Canterbury Cathedral, carrying out their friend's last order to have his ashes scattered at Margate Pier. Several chapter headings mark the geographical progress with alternating and interwoven short first-person narratives constituting the tales told on the funeral cortege (the dead man himself tells a tale as well). For David Malcolm the intertextuality in *Last Orders* "suggests that there is, at some level, a culture that is shared between past and present, between the poorly educated and high art."[118] The intertwined narratives reveal domestic intrigues, failed dreams, and quiet tragedies, but the central concern is one of Swift's persistent themes, namely, the claims of the past on the present, the sins of one generation visited upon the next. Although Malcolm suggests that Swift's characters "retrace the literary steps of Chaucer's storytellers" (173), a more obvious influence here is William Faulkner's *As I Lay Dying*. Indeed, so obvious, that Frow found cause to censure Swift — for parasitism, if not plagiarism — for his apparent failure to provide "a simple acknowledgement" or "even a passing allusion" to the canonical text.[119] More resonant perhaps is the single allusion to Chaucer found in Swift's *Ever After*, a first-person novel concerned with an intellectual's Hamlet-like quest for meaning in the face of mortality. Having recently weathered not only the deaths of his parents and wife, but also his own suicide attempt, the narrator says, "I feel like the ghost of Troilus at the end of Chaucer's poem."[120] Like Troilus, he suffers from a *contemptus mundi*; but unlike Troilus, he does not laugh at the futility of earthly happiness or find consolation in heavenly contemplation, instead reaffirming the sanctity of earthly love.

Conclusion

One might conclude that the popular corpus often presents the reader with simulacra, superficial and distorted representations that serve less to illuminate than to obscure the original referent. But rather than subverting or threatening the cultural authority of the literary original, reproduction in popular genres perhaps reflects the cultural viability of the canonical source.

Juvan maintains that "a pre-text's primacy ... is constituted only by the later text's speech acts."[121] These speech acts—found in various modes of intertextual engagements—attest to Chaucer's adaptability to new cultural environments. That is, following the Darwinian metaphor, these popular progeny are a manifestation of Chaucer's continuing cultural and ideological fitness.[122] At the same time, Chaucer's cultural fitness is to some degree dependent on the success of such popular adaptations, appropriations, and allusions—mutations that adapt Chaucer to new cultural and artistic milieu. The mutations of Chaucer and his texts are as variable as the media and genres in which he is invoked: dance, opera, film, stage play, musical, rap, poetry, horror, science fiction, academic satire, historical fiction, romance, travelogue, scientific treatise, and detective fiction. And because Chaucerian reproduction is in part dictated by generic environment, that is, by genre conventions and expectations, the authorial functions are by no means coherent, with Chaucer variously associated with social satire, egalitarianism, bawdy, Western literary tradition, British nationalism, proto-feminism, archaic patriarchy, social conservatism, scientific rationalism, and democratic inclusiveness.

Nonetheless, there is a principle of thrift in this proliferation of meaning, and Chaucer's intertextual encyclopedia does afford a few recurring motifs.[123] If one were to play a popular culture word association, the stimulus "Chaucer" would most often elicit "pilgrimage" as a response, probably followed by "satire." It's obviously not surprising that *The Canterbury Tales* is most commonly invoked within a context of pilgrimage, albeit usually lacking a penitential mood and institutional affiliation. As is characteristic of contemporary secularized pilgrimage, the purposes for the journeys are as variable as the geographical destinations, ranging from simple nostalgia, to the search for cultural identity, to efforts to recover a sense of spirituality, to acts of homage. But by far the modern concept is secular, concerned with the transformative potential, or the identity-forming power of the journey itself.[124] Some cases concern individual identity, but more commonly the focus is on the group as a representative social microcosm of a divisive macrocosm. The perceived cause of social fragmentation and discord is often the target of popular Chaucerian satire, namely social pretension and exclusion of any kind. Indeed, one of the primary paradoxes of the popular corpus is that Chaucer is so often invoked within a context that is either suspicious or disdainful of intellectualism and cultural elitism.

Chaucer's structural frame is constructed as an inclusive discursive platform, allowing a diversity of voices on a variety of topics—gender, race, class, religion, sexuality, ethnicity. Unlike Chaucer's version, modern manifestations have a more coherent relationship between the frame and embedded stories, with the destination acting as a thematic touchstone. The movement is often from social antagonism to comity, toward a sense of collective identity based on a synthesis of opposing viewpoints. Michaela Paasche Grudin suggests that "the geography of Chaucer's discourse" tends toward open, "social interactions."[125] Indeed, the modern mimetic temper is inherently optimistic, with Chaucer's iconic function most consistently associated with a narrative structure affording the communication necessary for a sense of community and social communion.

2
Chaucer the Detective

One of the stranger manifestations of Chaucer's recent popular afterlife has got to be his prominent presence in medieval mystery fiction. One finds an embarrassment of creative riches, and genre conventions have bled into the margins of academia, with Chaucer's own mysterious demise recently reconstructed as a crime scene. This chapter thus examines how Chaucer and *The Canterbury Tales* are imaginatively reinvented in both detective and historical mystery fiction, approaching these texts as appropriations of *The Canterbury Tales* and as creative responses to Chaucer's poetry. Whether reflecting the influence of Chaucerian criticism that often perceives the poet's aesthetic work as serving dominant social interests, or reflecting ideological conventions characteristic of the genre, Chaucerian mystery fiction is largely conservative, privileging the maintenance of social stability over questions of social justice. Like many classical detectives, Chaucer inhabits a socially anomalous position yet nonetheless works to preserve the status quo. But like crime fiction detectives of the hard-boiled variety, he is not naive, recognizing the depravity of social elites and the partisan nature of the justice served. Indeed, since most of the crimes in Chaucerian mystery fiction spring from blatant socioeconomic inequities, a subtext of political and social tension infiltrates the conservative ethos characteristic to the genre. Mystery fiction is often found to be responsive to contemporary concerns projected onto an imaginative landscape, but Chaucerian brand of the genre can also be approached as creative and critical responses to Chaucer's fiction and biography. Characteristic of popular culture genres is a resistance to a dominant discourse, and one detects in the consistent desire to read Chaucer's poetry autobiographically, to have Chaucer interact with his fictional creations, and to involve the poet in some of the turbulent political events of his age, a rejection of highbrow interpretive and biographical criticism that insists on the fundamental textuality of Chaucer's poetry.

Why Chaucer and his pilgrims have come to feature so regularly in historical mystery fiction is itself a mystery. Medieval Europe, consistently imagined as a dangerously violent place with an intractable social hierarchy, does provide an ideal imaginative setting for the ideological narratives—particularly policing and class resentment and insecurities—encoded in the genre.[1] But neither Chaucer as protagonist, nor the setting, structure, or cast of *The Canterbury Tales* would seem to be an obvious vehicle for mystery fiction, whether of the classical detective variety—with its mannered ratiocination and focus on the domestic sphere and middle-class anxieties—or of the hard-boiled tradition with its urban moral decay, literary realism, and cultural skepticism.[2] But the association of Chaucer with crime may be a logical choice, for, as Patricia J. Eberle suggests, "a very high proportion of the [Canterbury] tales deal, in one way or another, with the subject of 'crime' ... treason, murder, and rape appear, together with various forms of theft and assault."[3] Chaucer may be also generally associated with the question of justice owing to his broad thematic interest in human suffering, as reflected, for instance, in the first fragment of *The Canterbury Tales*, a concern that, for some, encompasses all the tales.[4] Detective fiction generally defends the existing social system, neutralizing those who try to disturb the established social order, serving as cautionary tales and modeling acceptable social behavior, similar to much of Chaucer's oeuvre from the sociopolitical conservatism of the *Knight's Tale* to the penitential *Parson's Tale*. One might detect ideological similarities between Chaucer's poetry and some classic detective fiction in which, for Lee Horsley, "reluctance to comment on contemporary affairs is in itself, of course, an ideologically loaded decision."[5] And Chaucer's reincarnation as an amateur detective may also owe something to his narrative persona in the *General Prologue*. The portraits themselves can be seen as clue-puzzles, with the pilgrims presenting a deceptive appearance, or being guilty of some "crime"—ranging from venality to extortion—that the reader must discover (aided by the clues provided by the "Explanatory Notes" in *The Riverside Chaucer*). One might also suggest that the estates satire in the *General Prologue* is not unlike the conservatism found in much detective fiction in which it is individual deviation rather than the failure or corruption of institutions that is the cause of criminal behavior.

Murder on the Pilgrimage

The two dominant motifs in modern Chaucerian mystery fiction involve either a murder on the Canterbury pilgrimage in which Chaucer often interacts with his characters in solving the crime, or, within the context of Chaucerian fictional biography, engaging the poet in a murder investigation, usually during one of his missions abroad. The former has a long pedigree, distant cousins to the various fifteenth-century continuations and additions to *The Canterbury Tales*. Gertrude and Joseph Clancy pioneered the murder-on-the-pilgrimage conceit in *Death is a Pilgrim* (1993), in which the Pardoner is murdered during an overnight stop at a priory along the Canterbury route.[6] With Chaucer officiating, an informal inquest is conducted by the Man of Law, and the individual tales of each chapter constitute the pilgrims' alibis during the time of the crime. The priory setting invokes the country-house murder motif common to classical detective fiction, in which the crime both tests communal solidarity and reveals social tensions and anxieties.[7] There are a number of suspects since several of the pilgrims have reason to hate the Pardoner: the Plowman has been relieved of "most part of my stock and store" (134) by purchasing a fake relic to cure his wife; the Pardoner is blackmailing the bigamous Wife of Bath; and he has debauched two of the pilgrims' sons. The solution of the crime restores the contingent authority of the privileged class in the name of social stability. But the Pardoner is a sympathetic character, creating a sense of unease rather than satisfaction in the successful detection and punishment of the crime.

The Clancys' forte, especially compared to subsequent examples of this murder-on-the-pilgrimage model, is their success in animating or vivifying the pilgrims, that is, in providing psychological motivation in place of estates satire. Chaucerian mystery fiction often provides a pseudo or mock General Prologue, featuring familiar leitmotifs: a canophiliac Prioress, libidinous Wife of Bath, lecherous friar. Rather than imitating Chaucer's *General Prologue*, however, the Clancys use action and dialogue to reveal character. They have Chaucer himself comment on the unreality of his tale-telling premise, and there are only glancing references to the original tales. The *Wife of Bath's Prologue*, for instance, consists of her brief discussion over some late-night ales about how she schooled her first three husbands; the Pardoner's boasting about his shameless chicanery is distilled through the Miller's point of view; and the Miller is given the Host's insult at the end of the *Pardoner's Tale*, literally wielding a knife to make good the threatened castration.

In keeping with the tradition that the tales characterize the tellers, the narratives of the informal inquest are used as revelatory confessions, and the tendency is to mitigate the pilgrims' flaws exposed in Chaucer's satirical portraits. The Clancys have a soft spot for the Prioress; in this case, she has been forced into religious life, and although she might shower inordinate affection on her dogs, her anti–Semitism is transferred to her sub-Prioress. It is, however, the oft-reviled Pardoner ("Nicholas de Bury") who is given the most psychological depth. Having a genuine spiritual calling, but cruelly hindered by his social class from taking orders, "Nick" has become a cynic. His pardons are real but his relics are fake, not because of his venality but because he retains a sincere awe for the sacred:

> I could not hold up true relics for folk to kiss. I'd fear that I'd be blasted on the spot. This way, I keep things square with God.... He knows I'm out for naught but

my own profit when I cobble up a relic; He knows I don't believe a word I tell the lackwits who come up to buy them, about miracles and such.... I don't pretend to Him that I'm about His work. I won't deceive myself that *I'm* doing good to folk, whatever good it pleases Him to make of it [171].

And unlike in the original, in which he concludes his sermon with ambiguous sincerity before pitching his wares to the pilgrims, here it is to his friend the Summoner—to whom he refuses to sell a pardon—that he tells the truth: "There's only One can pardon—look to Him when you have honestly repented, and not just had a mite too much of wine" (170).

The crime in mystery fiction can often be iconic, bringing "ideological positions more sharply into focus."[8] In the classical detective tradition, crime is often an aberration that threatens the established social order, and the corresponding punishment customarily receives the approbation of the reader. Although the Pardoner's nihilism and homosexuality would doubtless be perceived as transgressive and destabilizing, his offenses against individual pilgrims clearly constitute threats to their social status. The Franklin, for instance, who considers himself part of the nobility, has tried to raise his son as a "gentleman," only to have him "debauched" by the Pardoner and left "broken by his excesses" (163). The Yeoman's son follows a similar trajectory. And his threatened charge of bigamy against the Wife of Bath imperils the marital prospects upon which her socioeconomic status depends.

The point of view is conservative insofar as the Pardoner is constructed as an anomaly: he makes the individual moral choice to commit his crimes and his punishment provides satisfaction. But the Clancys complicate the reader's complacency since the Pardoner himself—restricted by his social status from a passionate vocation—is a victim of a rigid class structure and prejudice. Indeed, Christianity provides a thin veneer of cultural unity over lingering class suspicion and resentment. The Miller, for instance, vociferously objects to the Man of Law's proposal for a closed "committee of enquiry" to ferret out the killer: "How like are gentry to put blame on their own—when common folk are at hand?" (85). And when the Plowman (appropriately named Will) defies the committee on a point of order, the Man of Law "saw in that face something of the quality he had seen in others six years before" (86). Chaucer, ever "cautious" and "wary" (24, 202), is clearly part of the gentry and assists in the investigation in his capacity as Justice of the Peace. And while he is no disciplinary authority, judging his fellow pilgrims "kindly-like, no malice in it" (113), he does, nonetheless, silence the scandal and shelter the aristocratic culprit under the guise of maintaining social order.

Paul C. Doherty's six-installment Canterbury Tales Murders (*An Ancient Evil; A Tapestry of Murders; A Tournament of Murders; Ghostly Murders; The Hangman's Hymn; A Haunt of Murder*) is probably the most well-known series in this genre. While the Clancys' main interest is to endow the pilgrims with some psychological depth, Doherty takes advantage of the expansive narrative opportunities afforded by the episodic pilgrimage frame, to replace Chaucer's tales with autobiographical supernatural thrillers. *An Ancient Evil: The Knight's Tale of Mystery and Murder as He Goes on Pilgrimage from London to Canterbury* acts as prologue to the subsequent installments. In a parody of the *General Prologue*, not unlike T. S. Eliot's modernist inversion, Doherty gives us a spring in which the sweet April showers are a boon to "the black, long-tailed rats," who "knew the rain had softened the mounds of refuse piled high in the sewers" (1). The pilgrims gather at the Tabard, and abbreviated portraits relying on one or two traits are filtered through Harry Bailly's point of view. The Prioress, for example, speaks "in nasal French" and fingers her "love locket" while feeding her lapdog, and the Franklin, "a lover of good food," has a "daisy-white beard" (2–3). Doherty also adds traits, having the Squire, for instance, admire his father's magnificently scarred body, or, in an appropriate metaphorical extension of his profession, putting the Summoner to work as a pickpocket. The Host suggests an addendum to the diurnal storytelling contest; Hamlet-style tales of terror that "freeze the blood" (4) will be reserved for the evenings, with the best to be rewarded with a far more attractive prize — a bag of silver — than a mere supper back at the Tabard.

The central conceit is that the pilgrims' sensational stories do not simply characterize the tellers but, as is common to the popular corpus, are literally autobiographical. The thrillers ultimately reveal not only the character's secret, sensational past, but also, correcting a perceived aesthetic lapse in the original, prove that the pilgrims are not simply "by aventure yfalle" but are instead intimately connected. In the Knight's case, the ancient evil (dating to the Norman invasion) comes in the guise of vampires — disguised, suggestively, as clergy — who dine on the local Oxonian population. The Knight is the heroic slayer in his own tale which also incorporates elements from his Chaucerian romance. He has, for instance, a friendly rival for the affections of a beautiful Emily; echoing Palamon, the Knight describes her upon their introduction as "a veritable Venus" (26); and like his fictional counterpart, he wins the rivalry (accounting for the Squire's paternity). Similar to the original *Knight's Tale*, the nocturnal thriller offers a critique of chivalry, a theme that runs throughout Doherty's series. Not only is keeping one's word both an outmoded and dangerous liability (especially when dealing with vampires, or commoners), but the violence used by knights — ostensibly to maintain civic order — can be as destabilizing as the predatory antics of their undead doubles. Similarly, in *A Tournament of Murders: The Franklin's Tale*, chivalry is both an antiquated peccadillo for the "foolish" (231) and a last resort for scoundrels, the joust representing simply a ruse to evade civil justice.

Doherty often touches on the hypocrisy of class-based semantic ambiguity of the kind found in the *Manciple's Tale*. But his impulse is also nonetheless fundamentally conservative, less comfortable with relativism than moral absolutes, and with crime having less to do with political economy than individual pathology. We're all potentially evil, a reassuringly egalitarian notion, but the actualization of that evil is presented as an individual choice — as sin, motivated by greed, passion, and envy — unblemished by institutional or social forces. More threatening is that a disregard for the established moral order unleashes a "deep antagonism" within the community (*Ancient Evil* 157). That is, the breakdown in moral values leads to social unrest, disturbing the social hierarchy so that even "beggars" who can customarily be treated "with contempt" become a potential menace (*Ancient Evil* 196). In *The Hangman's Hymn: The Carpenter's Tale*, jealousy and resentment within the ranks of the gentry threaten their control and domination over anarchic have-nots. And in *A Tapestry of Murders: The Man of Law's Tale*, it is Edward II's profligate homosexuality that is found to be ultimately responsible for the wasteful Hundred Years' War.

Doherty often uses red herrings that appeal to readers' presumed prejudices and his denouements inevitably provide a comforting affirmation of the status quo: the vampires are vanquished, the homosexuals (and the Jew) expelled, the ghosts put to rest, the witches exorcised, and the impoverished outlaw "wolfsheads" eliminated.[9] But while such elements that threaten the establishment are caricatured and demonized, motivated simply by "evil," Doherty does nonetheless maintain a background of stark inequality that remains an unresolved subtext. His disquieting distant mirror is heavy on hygiene horrors and a panoply of corporal punishments that make even witches tremble in terror, providing a fitting context for the cruel social inequities that precipitate crime. Although obviously loathing gangs, in which almost all of his villains travel, Doherty does hint at the socioeconomic injustice that makes such alternative familial structures both necessary and inevitable. In *The Hangman's Hymn*, for instance, an incestuous and homicidal coven originates with orphaned children, who, having been neglected by their community, are adopted by a witch, "the only parent we knew" (201).

A blithely sunnier medievalism is found in Devlin's *Murder on the Canterbury Pilgrimage*, a modern retelling of *The Canterbury Tales* spiced up with intrigue and romance — two ingredients ostensibly missing from the original links. Devlin adopts a narrative structure similar to the Clancys,' involving the pilgrims in a murder mystery en route, but in this case weaving in secondary narratives—consisting of summaries of the original tales—that Chaucer busily scribbles down, usually under a tree. Like the Clancys, she is also interested in animating the pilgrims and provides the characters with a modicum of psychological realism. The Knight frets over the Squire's socially inappropriate love interest, and the Clerk is a breathless admirer of Chaucer's early dream visions. Devlin also interweaves some critical commentary, sensibly suggesting, for instance, that Virginius's puzzling behavior in the *Physician's Tale* is the product of the father's social ambition and fear for his own reputation. Most conspicuous, however, is Devlin's imaginative identification with Chaucer, whose elvish character is remade in the author's own image.

In keeping with a soft-focus feminism that runs throughout the novel, the story is filtered through the point of view of a Wife of Bathesque innkeeper who invites Geoffrey to join the eclectic pilgrim group "to widen his horizons and give him more material for his ever-increasing volumes of poetry" (15). The poet agrees to go as a form of primary research, but not before consulting his astrological chart which assures him that "strange goings-on" are imminent (16). Reflecting the popular preference for experiential over textual inspiration, the "fascinating cross-section of humanity" (19) Chaucer encounters immediately inspires him to take a quill in hand and begin the *General Prologue*. Chaucer himself becomes a suspect in the goings-on involving several deaths within the pilgrimage group, and no less a personage than "Johnny" Gaunt — with whom the poet shares a breezy amity — lends his hand in the investigation. The crime, providing an analogue to the *Physician's Tale*, involves a concoction of Lollard heresy, thwarted religious vocation, and Lancastrian imperial ambitions. The common ingredient is an indictment of institutional Catholicism as paternalistic, materialistic, and perverse. This familiar Chaucerian theme is supplemented by another Chaucerian conceit — namely, a fear of fickle mobs, the kind of "stormy people" found in the *Clerk's Tale*, but in this case blinkered by religious superstition (147).

Devlin's real interest, however, is in Chaucer himself, who is made in the New Age author's own image: he is adept at astrology, possesses a deep affection for felines, and is devoted to Tarot cards. Some traits are familiar — his general geniality notwithstanding his loathing for ecclesiastics, his keen "powers of observation" (52), and his insights into human character. The latter two characteristics are of course common to detective protagonists, although he is afforded these talents thanks to his glamorous work as a "spy" (14). His other professional positions, including his current work as Controller of the King's Petty Custom, are merely sinecures allowing him to indulge in his more passionate vocations:

> Both the king and Chaucer knew, however, that the purpose of the position was less to use Geoffrey's accounting abilities than to provide him with an income so that he could indulge his penchant for writing poetry, composing music, and reading astrological charts. Even at a young age, King Richard was a devout worshipper of the arts, both creative and occult. In fact, Robert Willard [an Oxford mathematician on pilgrimage] and the King himself were the only ones still living with whom Chaucer felt comfortable discussing such matters [14].

Breezily oblivious to the rigid social hierarchy that precipitates the murder, Chaucer is intimate with both royalty and Roma. In addition, because unlike "most men of their time" he "genuinely liked, respected, and understood the female species," the poet finds himself inexplicably attractive to women (perhaps, Chaucer reasons, because word is out that he's "a skilled and sensitive lover" [22]). And he owns a cat named Troilus. Devlin's affectionately drawn fictional creation is far from what has become Chaucer's conventional biography; but she certainly represents a contemporary popular example of trends that Trigg traces throughout Chaucer's early reception, including not only a sense of "identification and affinity" and "congenial communion" with the poet, but also "the relatively uninhibited ease with which ... writers and critics can 'speak' and write in Chaucer's place and in Chaucer's voice," fulfilling a desire that professional critics pursue by other means.[10]

Historical Fiction

The second most common form of Chaucerian mystery fiction is part of a trend since the 1980s that, in the wake of Umberto Eco's *The Name of the Rose* and Ellis Peters's Brother Cadfael series, has seen "the veritable explosion of crime fiction placed in an historical setting."[11] These texts take advantage of lacunae in the poet's professional and romantic biography to involve Chaucer in fictional intrigues involving social elites who are, with few exceptions, consumed by greed, ambition, and petty, ancestral jealousies. Two recurring features in these texts engage Chaucer, however circuitously, in some of the great social upheavals of his age — Schism, Peasant's Revolt, Black Death, Lancastrian usurpation — while providing his poetry, particularly those verses concerning courtly love, with an autobiographical foundation.

The innovator of this form is Duane Crowley whose *Riddle Me a Murder* (1986) involves a young Chaucer in a conspiracy superficially concerning a murdered royal consort but revealing the deep political rivalries between the aristocracy and the Church.[12] In a pseudo hard-boiled tradition, our hero is socially marginalized and anti-elitist, but nonetheless possessing latent social aspirations. Crowley uses his mystery as a vehicle for populist social commentary, emphasizing radical socioeconomic inequities and manifesting an almost masochistic fascination with the imagined sadistic perversities and rapacity of the aristocracy, both secular and spiritual. The representatives of the higher estates are cartoonish in their villainy, the clergy gleefully violating the sanctity of confession or poisoning sacraments and sanctimonious nobles given to casual murder while eloquently enumerating the scriptural warrants for serfdom. As in the case with Doherty, chivalry is shown to be a sham, the same violence differentiated only by class and locution: mounted knights on a policing mission and marauding Genoese brigands are all butchers (155). Crowley emphasizes a similar hypocrisy on the part of the Church, especially the tendency to manipulate people's fear of damnation for its own material ends, or its insistence on a divinely sanctioned social hierarchy. In sharp contrast, our hero, despite his own desire for social distinction, is a protodemocrat ("he knew that every man had a life worth living and a tale worth telling" [49]), advocate of social justice, and enemy of feudalism.

Although Chaucer is constructed as a liberal humanist, Crowley is conversant with conventional Chaucerian biography and weaves some erstwhile critical conundrums into his portrait of the poet. Aristocratic ladies, for instance, prove to be an appreciative and enthusiastic audience for the fabliaux (Chaucer accompanies a command performance of the *Reeve's Tale* with a lute); the *Retraction* is the product of blackmail, although Chaucer concedes his artistic integrity on this point knowing that his testament will read as satire; and Speght's suspiciously apocryphal anecdote proves accurate with the poet's anticlerical bent manifested in his giving a Friar an innocuous "knock on the head" in Fleetstreet (76). Most titillating, we find that the *Book of the Duchess* is no mere official Lancastrian commission but an expression of the poet's despair for the loss of his own true lover, Blanche of Lancaster.

The latter tidbit is a manifestation of Crowley's interest in both Chaucer's sex life and his relationship with John of Gaunt — both common topics of speculation in Chaucerian historical fiction. Both, in this case, are united by the issue of class and serve to highlight Chaucer's marginal and tenuous position within the social hierarchy. His wooing of Philippa, for instance, is complicated by what she calls his "prickly" anxiety over their "difference in station" and what he imagines to be the gross disparity of a "vintner's son" pursuing "the daughter of a landed knight" (37). But his anxiety is warranted, and the poet's social ambition compromises both his integrity and his dignity. He is consistently reminded that "he was raised up to stand where he was on the whim of a powerful man and could just as easily be cast down to the bottom of the heap where he had begun" (71). That powerful man, the somewhat obtuse John of Gaunt, is ostensibly his "friend," but their lop-sided amity is based on Chaucer's role as his personal and legal lackey, whose service extends to the poet's marrying a pregnant Philippa and claiming Gaunt's bastard daughter as his own. In the end Chaucer is successful in his quest for truth, but, as in the hard-boiled tradition, justice is more elusive. There is no sense of satisfaction in a restored social order since the Machiavellian architect of the crime is not punished, protected by the power of his political position. Although this is partly due to Chaucer's inferior status, there is also a fatalistic acceptance that existing law is unable to address entrenched institutional corruption.[13]

Morgan (a.k.a. Philip Gooden) constructs apocryphal diplomatic missions for Chaucer — on behalf of Edward III to negotiate a loan to finance the Hundred Years War (*Chaucer and the Legend of Good Women*); to elicit the political allegiance of a powerful count to the English crown (*Chaucer and the House of Fame*); or to maintain trade relations with Genoa (*Chaucer and the Doctor of Physic*) — during which a crime occurs that elicits his reluctant involvement. Morgan's mysteries reflect motifs from the English countryhouse and gothic traditions, featuring an exclusive social setting (usually an ancestral house) ostensibly representing civilized order but concealing "powerful men with guilty secrets," and involving crimes usually committed for property and revenge.[14] While Morgan's sensibility also tends to be conservative, the purpose of detection being to expose and expel threats to established social order, as in the case with other examples of Chaucerian mystery fiction, Morgan maintains throughout a latent theme of social unrest. The resolutions often have lingering ambiguities, and one is left with the sense that for the "little ones" justice remains elusive. But while social injustice is recognized, and individual cases are rectified on an ad hoc basis, Morgan's mysteries end with a restoration of the existing social order. Chaucer does facilitate this maintenance of the status quo, but he is no disciplinary authority, more prone "to let sleeping dogs get on with their sleeping, to let the world roll by in its own sweet or soured way" (*House of Fame* 192).

Like Crowley's hero, Morgan's Chaucer has a combination of traits drawn from his poetry, biography, and the classical detective tradition. He is an adept diplomat because of his "skills of rhetoric," "gift for persuasion" (*HF* 69), and ready "silver tongue" (*Doctor of Physic* 50). Chaucer's instinct for survival is afforded by his war service and by an innate sixth sense, which alerts him, for instance, when he is being stalked. Like the Clerk, he owns 20 books, including his Boethius, which provides consolation during a rough Channel crossing. And like the Reeve, he is "white only on the top of the head, green elsewhere" (*Legend of Good Women* 242). The green is not manifested in his relationship with Philippa, however, which is at best described as "not unharmonious" (*DP* 57). His wife finds something inherently comic at the idea of Chaucer as a love poet, but he does prove attractive to the opposite sex. He is seduced, for instance, by a camp follower after he discards "common sense" and follows the dictates of chivalry in protecting her from a gang of mercenaries (*LGW* 24). But Morgan is most at pains to make Chaucer a common man: "quite unremarkable" (*HF* 153), "average," "ordinary" (*LGW* 37), "bland and incurious" (*HF* 53). Like Sherlock Holmes, he is equally at ease with high and low, whether roving thieves and mercenaries or members of a powerful banking house. And he is a true believer in gentilesse: "True gentilesse can emerge from the lowliest or most unpromising of backgrounds" (*LGW* 69).

The concern with gentilesse is often code for a larger subtext of class insecurity. Although showing superficial signs of being within the classical detective tradition (in which one might expect a conservative exposé of threats to the social order), many of Morgan's crimes are also gothic in nature, occurring within a privileged family circle usually to protect some secret whose exposure would threaten the villain's social identity and status. In *Chaucer and the Legend of Good Women*, for instance, the murder is committed to maintain a family's socioeconomic position, perceived to be threatened by a fellow member's impecuniousness. Similarly, in *Chaucer and the Doctor of Physic* the crime is intended to disguise the villain's collaboration with, and economic dependence upon, a band of feral outlaws. What the novels have in common is that Morgan's elites are largely predatory and ruthless in defending the prerogatives of their class. For instance, a Florentine banking family is obsessed with maintaining its social status, going so far as to commit iconic murders to serve as a political warning to restless commoners (*LGW* 125). Similarly, the social elite in *Chaucer and the Doctor of Physic*, when given the chance, easily match the brutality of the frightening "landpirates" that ostensibly threaten their security (*DP* 242). Regardless of the simmering social tensions, felicitously symbolized by gripping, interlinked hands in one of the novels (*LGW* 155), these mysteries are ultimately comedies, ending with marital unions and with the social hierarchy intact.

The most engaging aspect of Morgan's series for readers familiar with Chaucer's texts is her practice of Chaucerian intertextual pastiche. Quotations from and allusions to *The Canterbury Tales* are liberally sprinkled throughout, and both the characters and omniscient narrators use Chaucerian proverbs: a pass phrase is taken from "Truth" (*HF* 87); a knight's son carves before his father at the table; "They say that pity runs soonest in a gentle heart" (*HF* 278); "The smiler with the knife" (*LGW* 163), etc. As we've seen previously, a consistent feature in the mystery genre is to provide the poet with experiences that inspire his poetry. Here, for instance, the *Reeve's Tale* is based on a "bawdy fabliau of bed-hopping and mistaken identities" involving Chaucer's traveling companions during their journey to France (*HF* 69), and Chaucer's "Rosamond" is based on the poet's experience as a hostage following his capture at Rheims (*HF* 79).[15] More interesting is Morgan's habit of rewriting Chaucer. A vile January figure, who is also blind, jealous, and dependent upon herbal aphrodisiacs, plays a villainous role and is poetically done in by his own pear tree in *Chaucer and the Legend of Good Women*. During the lull in the action in *Chaucer and the House of Fame*, Chaucer entertains his companions with a new version of the *Franklin's Tale*, providing a happy ending in the form of a proper love object for Aurelius (215–220, 331–338). Indeed, Morgan almost achieves a sort of postmodern pastiche in this novel, having the poet, for instance, play a Gawain figure in a scene with a flirtatious Rosamond (hunting, alas, only for gossip). Indeed, recognizing the many Chaucerian allusions provides an intellectual pleasure for the reader not unlike the pleasure associated with "the sheer act of solving ... the puzzle of detection."[16]

Devlin's *The Legend of Good Women: A Geoffrey Chaucer Murder Mystery*, which brings us up to date on the adventures of "Geoffrey Chaucer SmartPants," is an embodiment of the curiously contradictory ideological discourses often found in Chaucerian mystery fiction.[17] Two unrelated crime plots allow Devlin to combine and invert fictional topographies—and the attendant ideologies—of classical detective and crime fiction. The crime committed at a country manor is represented not as an anti-social anomaly as is often the case in the classical detective tradition, but as endemic of a pattern of social corruption and injustice. In contrast, the urban crime, which in crime fiction often reveals the ingrained corruption of the privileged, is here the product of individual pathology rather than institutionalized inequality. Similarly, although in the "Historical Note" Devlin claims to represent "strong and determined" (313) women of the middle class, those women who transgress traditional gender roles are consistently punished. Peasantry and commoners are alternately pitied for their poverty and condemned for their improvidence. And the pervasive contradictions are reflected in the process of detection itself, with the crime solved not by rational deduction but by intuition and astrology.

The urban crime involves a renegade royal magistrate turned serial killer who preys on women in the environs of Aldgate. While Chaucer is preoccupied in the country with a plot to recover the king's tax revenue from an embezzler, Philippa and a local female innkeeper are among the good women who, in a show of proactive feminism, collar the killer. The problem is that his victims, vulnerable because of their independence, and whose fear and weakness excite the murderer, all violate conventional gender roles, especially regarding female sexual modesty. Unlike many antagonists in crime fiction, however, our killer is simply insane rather than the casualty of adverse social conditions. In contrast, the crime at the country manor house that captures Chaucer's attention, while ostensibly involving a simple case of a steward's stealing his lord's revenues, is mirrored by an institutionally sanctioned form of embezzlement—the sale of indulgences—sold to finance both John of Gaunt's imperial ambitions and the Hundred Years' War. The criminal steward himself is a victim of Gaunt's Castilian campaigns, a veteran who has been handicapped and left "without a way of winning lands of his own" (303).

Chaucer dutifully works on behalf of the king, ensuring that the Crown gets its cut of the recovered manor income. But he easily straddles the class divide, having free access to Richard II, but preferring to be at home with his pets, charting horoscopes, and helping his servant clean the house. Philippa is similarly uncannily protean, moving easily from the Savoy to a local tavern to "help with the cooking" (68). But both are made to recognize the extreme class divide they transcend. Philippa understands her neighbors are "too busy trying to survive to care about the welfare of others" (226), and Chaucer knows that a peer's outerwear and casual jewelry could feed three poor families for a year.

In spite of such glimmers of insight, one finds competing ideological discourses throughout. The demands of the peasants are found to be reasonable until Wat Tyler violates decorum with his "outright arrogance" in demanding a flagon of ale (38–9); a good steward (in contrast to the bad) suggests that while some tenants exhibit the appropriate gratitude and loyalty, others "were never happy and always wanted more" (243); and Chaucer recognizes that while the poor often work hard, they also "have too many babies to keep track of them all" (254). Chaucer only laments the latter because lacking a birth date makes an accurate horoscope more difficult; but he can sagely predict "an early death, health problems, and no strong indication of material security" (256) for all of the tenants' children. Notwithstanding this empathetic observation, the narrative ends with an aristocratic marriage, signaling a reaffirmation of the status quo. Gaunt, who has precipitated the crimes that leave corpses representing each estate, will continue to pursue his own royal longings and desires ("Well, it's all been very tragic. But I still have a campaign to organize" [309]). And while even the immature King Richard recognizes Gaunt's responsibility for his steward's malefactions, Chaucer reassures his monarch with an impotent philosophical fatalism: "Be fair ... misery and greed exist even where there are no dukes, no kingdoms!" (310).

O'Connor's *Chaucer's Triumph* (subtitled, *Including the Case of Cecilia Chaumpaigne, the Seduction of Katherine Swynford, the Murder of her Husband, the Interment of John of Gaunt and Other Offices of the Flesh in the Year 1399*) exaggerates to the point of caricature some of the trends we've seen previously. The structure is nominally that of a murder mystery, but as the protracted title suggests, O'Connor also has a number of other interests in his exploration of the intersection of Chaucerian and Lancastrian biography. While the primary focus is an almost prurient fascination with the sex lives of John of Gaunt and Chaucer, O'Connor's larger concerns are the conjunction of sexual immorality and political instability and the paradox of poetic genius arising from the lurid imagination of a licentious reprobate.

Told in a series of flashbacks and from multiple points of view, the primary action takes place during Gaunt's 40-day funeral cortege. The murder of two commoners is informally investigated by a nosey Adam Scriveyn and attended by a bemused Chaucer. The murders, however, have only a tangential relationship to a series of sensational revelations: we learn that Philippa is Gaunt's cast-off mistress, Chaucer is in love with both Blanche of Lancaster and Katherine Swynford, and Thomas Chaucer is Gaunt's son. Chaucer's poetry provides a contemporary diary of these liaisons: *Troilus and Criseyde* is inspired not only by Chaucer's pandering for John of Gaunt but also by his own passion for Katherine; Philippa is the Wife of Bath, while Chaucer is a willfully blind January, resigned to his wife's many lovers; and Chaucer, Blanche's one-time paramour, is the chief mourner in the *Book of the Duchess*.[18] Indeed, the latter poem gets a lot of interpretive mileage; Gaunt suggests, "I would swear that the poem was about the young woman, Katherine, and how through her Chaucer wanted to keep Philippa away from my intemperate desire. Yet the subject was Blanche my duchess!" (55). And Chaucer's description of "the loving tenderness of the knight" acts as an aphrodisiac for Philippa, leaving her "in a state of exquisite and extreme desire" (56). His poetry is not, however, all ludic erotic diary; Chaucer loses his job as Comptroller of Wool because of Anne of Bohemia's anger at Criseyde's character (175), and his life is in danger because of the cautionary sentiments found in "Steadfastnesse" (193), here commissioned by Gaunt.

Chaucer's portrait, as filtered through the somewhat priggish Adam Scriveyn's point of view, is quite different from the detective hero found in most Chaucerian mystery fiction. Consistent with his detective persona, O'Connor does imagine the poet as intimately connected to the center of power, but rejecting the offer of a manorship because he's "a bourgeois through and through" (140). But unlike in any other example from this genre, he is a largely unattractive character: he exudes an "odour of lust" (44), is a submissive cuckold, anti-feminist, and bawd. Curiously, his amorous adventures are not hindered by his "slovenly" appearance (151), let alone the "bags under his eyes, double chins and ... gammy leg" (184). And he can be "sottishly taciturn," or worse, given to moralizing after his frequent heavy drinking (98).

But was he a rapist? This question is Adam's raison d'etre, and perhaps the reason also for the incoherence of O'Connor's Chaucer. In the "Endnote," the author puzzles over the possible connection between the charge of *raptus* and the *Retraction*. O'Connor sees a pattern of mitigation on the part of professional Chaucerians, quoting a conversation with Sheila Delany:

> "To ignore biographical probability in relation to an author's work is to commit an offense against history." She went on, "This is collective censorship — repression — such as several generations of Chaucerians have already committed, on behalf of posterity, in the interests of preserving this purified, moralistic view of a great English poet" [290].

The central mystery—for O'Connor, and presumably for many Chaucerians—is "how a man who wrote the poems we know ... [could] have been guilty of committing rape under any circumstances" (289).[19] O'Connor himself is unable to untangle the ostensible enigma and, apparently like several generations of Chaucerians, tends to mitigate the *raptus*. In the process of pressing a suit on behalf of another party, Chaucer inadvertently seduces Cecilia ("She most loved me kissing her thighs, which while resting would be open and soft, and that which lay between" [258]). Piqued by the poet's refusal to divorce Philippa, whose social connections have afforded Chaucer his social status, the "poor deluded soul," who "loved the poet to distraction" (259), concocts the rape charge and dies following the birth of the enigmatic little Lewis. But if Chaucer remains a paradox, the deleterious social effects of sexual license do not. Drawing a correlation between sexual morality and political stability, O'Connor suggests that Gaunt's serial adultery has led to civil war, the Peasant's Revolt, and the decline of chivalry. Worse, Gaunt's "concupiscence" encourages in "common folk" "the concupiscence of violence" against their betters (203–5). And over this millennial venereal carnival resides its "chief clerk," Chaucer, the inadvertent instigator of incipient social and religious revolutions that blossomed over the next two centuries.

Chaucerian mystery fiction, whether dominated by classical detective or crime fiction conventions, largely reproduces what Stephen Henry Rigby accurately characterizes as the contradictory critical approaches to Chaucer's ideology:

> Firstly, there are those who interpret Chaucer as essentially "conservative" in his social outlook ... and who present his social thought as an expression of the dominant spirit or ideology of his day. Secondly, there are those who see Chaucer as possessing a more heterodox voice, one which in some sense questions or challenges the official world-view of his age and which reveals, as perhaps does all "authentic" art, the processes by which ideology attempts to pass itself off as the expression of eternal truths or as self-evident common sense.[20]

John Cawelti suggests that in the classical detective tradition, sociological explanations are generally eschewed and crime is usually attributed to individuals with transparent, personal motives: "the detective reaffirms the fundamental soundness of the social order by revealing how the crime has resulted from the specific and understandable motives of particular individuals; the crime represents a situation that is possible but not fundamental nor endemic to that society."[21] Morgan tends to adopt this conservative ideological conceit most consistently, leavened with some recognition of a socioeconomic basis for crime. Her theme is the unrelieved greed and ambition of social elites who use and abuse the lower classes and who consider themselves to be above the law. While these elites are usually killed by their victims, none is tried or turned over to civil authorities. Similarly, Doherty's villains, inhabiting a dark medieval landscape that spawns the corresponding supernatural horrors, tend to act out of simple moral depravity. His vampires (*An Ancient Evil*) are, tellingly, immigrants, but are also spiritually weak, manifested in their failure to attend mass regularly. His human villain in *A Tournament of Murders* is driven by a baffling implacable resentment, and a string of murders in *A Tapestry of Murders* is orchestrated by the Sheriff of London whose ludic malevolence is nominally in the service of the king. On occasion there is a hint at the socioeconomic basis of crime, and Doherty can tend toward the conspiratorial, representing the governing estates—both secular and clerical—in league with the criminal underground, implicitly equating the two. But with the elimination of the grossly aberrant villains, justice is perceived to prevail and there is satisfaction in the restoration of the social order—perhaps flawed and abysmally unfair, but nonetheless functional.

All other cases reflect the reigning ideology of crime fiction in which crime is often contextualized within a larger pattern of institutionalized social corruption: "the detective is called in to investigate a seemingly simple thing, like a disappearance; his investigation comes up against a web of conspiracy.... Finally the track leads back to the rich and respectable levels of society and exposes the corrupt relationship between the pillars of the community and the criminal underground."[22] Devlin's crimes are seemingly committed for recognizable localized motives: reputation, social ambition, greed. Common villainy, however, is associated with Devlin's favorite historical motif, the competing interests of "Johnny" Gaunt and Henry Despenser, who are seen as manipulating and abusing their authority for their own personal ambitions, pushing indulgences and fostering heresy for political ends. In the Clancys' *Death is a Pilgrim*, the Pardoner's duplicity and nihilism mirror the same qualities in his employers, the Lords Appellant, and Chaucer's cynical suggestion that the priory turn the Pardoner's murder to their own profit mirrors the efforts of the Lords to manipulate the Archbishop of Canterbury's death for political ends. And in Crowley's *Riddle Me a Murder*, a murderous cleric mimics the greed and ambition of his prominent ecclesiastical and secular employers. While these too have a conservative strain, with crime represented as a product of individual depravity, the resolutions have some degree of moral ambiguity, leaving the reader with reservations about the efficacy of existing law to ensure civil justice. But the presiding ethos nonetheless peddles an impotent fatalism not unlike the problematic Chaucerian dictum advocating the passive acceptance of political expediency: "'Thanne is it wisdom, as it thynketh me,/ to maken vertu of necessitee/ and take it weel that we may nat eschue'" (I. 3042–43).

Two other contributions that resist formula and easy categorization might be included in the genre of Chaucerian mystery fiction. Ackroyd's postmodern gothic thriller, *The Clerkenwell Tales*, is sui generis, involving neither a pilgrimage nor Chaucerian biography. But in keeping with the tendency of mystery fiction to be broadly responsive to contemporary social and cultural preoccupations and prejudices, Ackroyd offers a veiled political analogy to international political events of the early twenty-first century. The title is derived from the gentrified area of London — Clerkenwell Green — today lacking the clergy, the well, and the grass, but, Ackroyd is intent to remind us, long associated with sexual intrigue, gastronomic excellence, and political radicalism.[23] In place of a pilgrimage and tale-telling contest, the central plot concerns a mad nun and her relationship with a secret heretical group known as the "Predestined Ones" (i.e., the Lollards) whose terrorism is ostensibly justified by the venality and corruption of the Church. Drawing on the always malleable incoherence of apocalyptic symbology, the group hopes to usher in a new spiritual era by torch-bombing five parish churches, represented by a covert sign of five interlocking circles (the Olympic trademark?). This aspect of the plot seems to be subtly cashing in on the popular fascination with quashed medieval heresies. But these violent and self-righteous fanatics, bolstered by their belief that they are predestined for salvation and therefore "absolved from all sin" (37) and showing a predilection for suicide bombing, will also strike some as uncomfortably familiar modern figures. The sect, however, acts as a front for a chosen few, known as "Dominus" (reminiscent of the Lords Appellant), who have more secular and political ambitions associated with Henry Bolingbroke's eventual succession. One does not need to search too deeply for the contemporary resonance: the powerful use a radical religious group to foster fear in the populace (specifically their fear of incendiary weapons such as "Greek fire" that cause mass destruction) in order to win popular support for regime change. Indeed, for Barry Lewis, "the entire novel is testament to the cycles and repetitive patterns of history."[24]

Most of Chaucer's characters (missing only the Plowman, Harry Bailly, and Chaucer himself) are either part of or come in contact with this nefarious group. Although he does draw on Chaucer for his description of the principal characters, Ackroyd is less interested in social satire than in providing the intellectual and cultural accoutrements that might accompany each estate. For instance, Dame Agnes de Mordaunt, the eponymous character of "The Prioress's Tale," maintains the "dazed demureness of her childhood" (2), has an infirmaress named Sister Eglantine, and overhears one of her nuns singing "O Alma Redemptoris mater." The table manners of the nuns are described, but the focus is on the rule of silence and the sign language used in the refectory rather than the niceties of aristocratic decorum. The most allusively complex chapter involves the Merchant, here a haberdasher named Radulf Strago, who "married a much younger woman two years before," and whose misogyny is entirely justified. He has an apprentice named Janekin, who seems to be a composite of the Wife of Bath's fifth husband (his "slender legs were shown to best advantage in scarlet hose" [29]), Perkyn Revelour from the *Cook's Tale* (he plays dice and hazard), the Miller (he engages in "a violent game known to them as 'breaking doors with our heads'" [30]), and the *Miller's Tale*'s Nicholas (he uses mock courtly language to seduce the Merchant's wife). The Merchant's disgruntled wife echoes the Wife of Bath ("'Other women ... go gayer than I'" [30]), and, recalling the *Pardoner's Tale* (or closer, William Faulkner's "A Rose for Emily"), buys arsenic from an apothecary ostensibly as a "'poison needed to kill rats'" (33), but instead which she uses on her husband.

Unlike William Blake (who is invoked in the epigraph), who found many of Chaucer's portraits appealing, Ackroyd presents us with a gallery of rogues. Indeed, according to one reviewer, if the original pilgrims resembled Ackroyd's incarnations, "it's likely that the band Chaucer followed from Southwark to Canterbury would have mortally knifed one another before they'd reached the Shooter's Hill roundabout."[25] Among this cast of reprobates is the one-time infanticide, "Dame Alice, familiarly known as the Wife of Bath ... the most notorious a procuratrix in the city" (141), whose name is synonymous with the *balneolum* or "bath-house" she runs. Her clients include Miles Vavasour, a Sergeant-at-Law, to whom she offers an 11-year-old virgin ("'But you must pay. Empty fists retain no hawks'" [143]). The Canon, William Swinderby, while not an alchemist, does nonetheless misuse his Yeoman in a customary sadomasochistic ritual in which he suffers some familiar insults he himself has taught his servant ("'Your breeches are stained with your arse'"; "'I will enshrine you in a hog's turd'" [54]). Indeed, Lewis accurately suggests that "Most of Ackroyd's characters, in fact, bear an ironic relation to their originals.... At other times, the memory of the Chaucerian prototypes serves to interfere with our apprehensions of Ackroyd's counterparts. The effect is deliberate and serves to limn a medieval world far darker than that of Chaucer's jolly pilgrims."[26]

The cover of the Anchor Books paper edition, featuring an enlarged manuscript illumination depicting the Lover from the *Romance of the Rose*, seems to promise a pastoral of courtly love, chivalry, and aristocratic privilege. This odd disjunction between form and content is perhaps a misleading marketing ploy (the more staid hardcover offers muted and sober illuminations of clergy and Richard II), promising a nostalgic return to Merrie England but instead giving us a medieval version of "Ellroy's L. A."[27] But it also serves to highlight what Hutcheon calls the "postmodern contradiction" insofar as Ackroyd indulges in "the use and abuse of the conventions of both popular and elite culture," invoking generic expectations in order to subvert them.[28] Ackroyd's genius is imaginative historical reconstruction, and as a jacket blurb blazons, the primary commercial appeal of the novel is Ackroyd's ability to "sharpen one's sense of late 14th-century London as squirmingly alive" (*The Spectator*), a feat achieved by providing brief disquisitions on subjects such as astrology, pharmacology, and iconography, and imparting useful and colorful euphemisms for genitalia and pederasts. And his liberal quotation of Chaucer's pithy and proverbial sayings, which Wallace describes as "a kind of voguing in Chaucerian language," lends an idiomatic authenticity to the dialogue.[29]

However, judging by the series of parodic footnotes in "The Author's Tale," Ackroyd's purpose seems more complex than fitting into the niche of period crime fiction. Laura Marcus suggests that Ackroyd's "urban gothic" works to open up "hidden spaces within the city ... uncovering patterns which are both spatial and temporal, palimpsestic layerings of past events."[30] Indeed, Ackroyd seems intent on reanimating Clerkenwell Green itself, providing a psycho-geographical sense of place for the newly fashionable neighborhood, reminding patrons of the world-famous St. John Restaurant, for instance, that Radulf Strago died on site while using the privy (footnote 5). The purpose here is to mock the academic annotation and our romantic touristic fantasies of a lurid cultural landscape lurking beneath the trendy shops of Islington. In other words, Ackroyd both partakes in, and subverts, what Hutcheon calls "the myth- or illusion-making tendencies of historiography."[31] In playful postmodern fashion, Ackroyd also indulges in "historiographic metafiction," manifesting a "theoretical self-awareness of history and fiction as human constructs."[32] For instance, the masochist William Swinderby, a leading member of Ackroyd's fictional Dominus, was an historical Lollard, an associate of Wyclif, persecuted and forced to publicly retract his heretical preaching in 1389, and possibly later martyred. The historical record is silent on his taste for the whip. Similarly, although footnote 21 in "The Author's Tale" claims that "the connection between Dominus and the predestined men" is revealed in a letter from William Exmewe (housed "in a bundle of ecclesiastical documents in the library of Louvain Cathedral"), Ackroyd's conception of Dominus is probably derived from Wyclif's conservative theories of *dominium* taken to a pathological extreme.[33] Thus, Ackroyd participates in Hutcheon's notion of the postmodernist project, playing with the margins of genre and invoking conventions in order to subvert them. The problem is that, as Umberto Eco acknowledges, for this kind of ludic scavenger hunt for allusions and quotations to be successful, "The dialectic [between "order and novelty"] must be perceived by the consumer who must not only grasp the contents of the message, but also the way in which the message transmits these contents."[34] The game, and no doubt, the fiddling with formula, clearly irked some reviewers who were otherwise taken by Ackroyd's wry commentary on contemporary political events.[35]

A similar blurring of the generic conventions of history and fiction is found in Terry Jones's rhetorically titled *Who Murdered Chaucer? A Medieval Mystery*, an energetic bid to make Chaucer "a political animal" whose work was "inextricably bound into the political and social web of his age."[36] It may seem odd to include a text packaged as academic biography in an overview of historical mystery fiction; but with its curious blend of expertise and speculation, the book certainly represents a hybrid, a convergence of fact and fiction, a commingling of "the study of the medieval and the practice of medievalism" that Trigg sees as a trend in the popular understanding of the Middle Ages.[37] Jones utilizes the silence of the historical record, messiness of the textual tradition, and scholarly disagreement to make a case based on *argumentum ad ignorantiam*. The plot, in short: "Arundel wanted to silence the critics of the church; he knew that there was no one who could match Chaucer; and that is why Chaucer had to die" (283). A primary assumption is that Chaucer was not only "famous" but "one of the most prominent members of his society," "the intellectual superstar of his time," admired, and read, by both royalty and aristocracy: "He was certainly celebrated by his contemporaries as their greatest living poet, rhetorician, and scholar" (3). To support this claim, Jones must account for several puzzlers like the lack of record of payment (Chaucer would have refused remuneration to distinguish himself from professional minstrels; Richard's chamber accounts are missing), or the lack of manuscripts dating to his lifetime (they were deliberately destroyed), or the lack of evidence that he enjoyed royal patronage (Richard II's library is lost). The assumption that Chaucer had a high social profile feeds the necessity for conspiracy, reflecting the logic of cultural celebrity narrative in which, Joli Jensen suggests, for "posthumous celebrity, part of the story is about tragic outcome."[38]

For evidence, Chaucer's poetry is reread within the biographical and political context that the poet did not "survive the events of 1399–1400" (7). The "Complaint of Chaucer to His Purse," for instance, is an insulting "tongue in cheek eulogy" mocking Henry IV's tripartite claim to the throne (a joke Henry IV apparently missed, granting Chaucer his annuity). More importantly, *The Canterbury Tales*, with its mockery of pilgrimage, excessive clerical satire (particularly concerning relics and indulgences), and coded Lollard sympathies, proved to be Chaucer's "death warrant" (183–227). The incompleteness of the manuscript record provides physical proof of the strenuous efforts to obliterate the poet's literary output, including the lost "Book of the Lion," which Jones posits was a political allegory "which made Richard look good" (331).[39] Professional Chaucerians, Jones suggests, have been blinkered by the success of the "Lancastrian propaganda machine" (104). And his book is, in the end, a challenge to scholars to jettison the "traditional image" of Chaucer's quiet end which divorces "the man from the political context and dangerous times in which he lived and worked" (360). Although it is difficult to tackle an argument based on the assumption that a claim not proven false must be true, the book has received little professional notice — and one assumes the silence is not necessarily a sign of approbation. But Jones's biographical whodunnit, notwithstanding its hyperbole, is certainly part of a continuum of a conspiratorial strain that sometimes surfaces in the critical tradition, particularly concerning the confusing state of the early manuscript witnesses. Patterson, for instance, pondering the problematic absence of the epilogue to the *Man of Law's Tale* from the Ellesmere manuscript (in which the Host fingers the Parson as a Lollard), suggests that one can "well imagine why, in the first decade of the fifteenth century, when the alarmed Archbishop Arundel was mobilizing the ecclesiastical and governmental forces of repression against the Lollards, that a scribe or editor putting together a deluxe copy of the *Tales* would skip over a passage that explicitly identified this otherwise ideal figure as a Lollard."[40]

Jones's eagerness to read Chaucer's poetry autobiographically and to involve the poet in the prominent political events of his own time is also quite in keeping with the popular aesthetic of Chaucerian mystery fiction. Certainly the most conspicuous feature of this genre is the consistent fictional conceit that constructs Chaucer's poetry as autobiography, either as a record of his romantic escapades or as a reflection of his "real life" experience. Like the Wife of Bath's insistence on the authority of her experience, the desire to find continuity between art and life is a consistent feature of the popular culture aesthetic. But the propensity to read his poetry within a biographical and historical context has a long critical legacy too, dating back to the sixteenth century when the biographies included in editions of Chaucer's collected works (constructing Chaucer as exile, informant, prisoner, Protestant) were largely based on details drawn from what was assumed to be his poetry. And the connection between the historical and fictional personas clearly continues to generate intense interest, manifested most recently in the renewed scrutiny of Chaucer's relationship with his scribe, Adam Pinkhurst.

Chaucer's reproduction in popular culture also reveals what remains appealing about his poetry. Like stage versions of Chaucer's *Canterbury Tales*, mystery fiction reflects a fascination with what could be called the loosely postmodern possibilities of his narrative, in which Chaucer interacts with his fictional creations. Modern popular readers are also interested in expanding the dramatic narrative possibilities afforded by Chaucer's links and providing more social interaction between the pilgrims, a more detailed setting (particularly the accommodations along the Canterbury route), and more imaginative reconstruction of historic details such as costuming and cookery. One also finds a special interest in Chaucer's source for *The Canterbury Tales*, with the professional consensus on the fundamental textuality of Chaucer's poetry or the influence of his Italian predecessor clearly resonating less with a popular audience than the romantic myth of autonomous creative inspiration.

Chaucer's character as reproduced in the genre of Chaucerian mystery fiction is the product of an odd distillation of his poetic narrative persona, detective genre conventions, and the idiosyncrasies of each author's imaginative identification with the poet. But most aesthetically appealing and ideologically useful is Chaucer's ambiguous social position and concomitant political sympathies. Most strikingly, in what is usually portrayed as a starkly hierarchical social structure, he is happily in the middle, existing in his own bubble of meritocracy and social prestige, with easy intercourse (sometimes literally) between high and low.[41] While his anomalous social status might reflect "a largely middle-class readership's projected fantasies,"[42] the popular and the professional Chaucer also have much in common:

> He is the son of a rich merchant, but one educated in noble households; a king's squire, but one who fulfilled the duties of a clerical administrator; a modest servant of the Crown, but one who numbered among his friends some of the king's closest associates. To specify his social identity with precision and confidence seems impossible. For what the evidence reveals is a Chaucer on the boundary between distinctive social formations. Not bourgeois, not noble, not clerical, he nonetheless participates in all three of these communities."[43]

Patterson concludes that Chaucer's "sense of marginality" is related to his "sense of subjectivity, the sense of selfhood that stands apart from *all* community" (39). This perceived marginality may also explain his adaptability to mystery fiction, in which the detective is often a liminal figure, neither disciplinary authority nor subversive instigator of social justice.

He appears to be, in short, an ideally flexible figure not unlike Strohm's social Chaucer, who works for the "maintenance of social order, but on terms receptive to previously excluded or under-acknowledged ranks and groups."[44] Chaucer's detection does serve to reinforce the existing social system. But he is made cognizant of the obvious injustice and inequality that often serves as a catalyst for crime, and the poet's investigative involvement does often effect instances of justice unavailable to the powerless through institutional means. In those cases, however, in which the upper ranks of royal or ecclesiastical power are involved, he is consistently unable or unwilling to bring the prominent malefactors to justice, often invoking the dubious defense of political inaction in the name of civic stability. Indeed, the pervasive philosophy of impotent fatalism endorsed in Chaucerian mystery fiction is perhaps finally closer to Marxist readings of Chaucer's politics in which the reigning conservative ideology advocates the myth that "questioning established order unleashes anarchy."[45]

3

Chaucer on the TV Screen
The BBC's Canterbury Tales *and Jonathan Myerson's* Canterbury Tales

Given the variety of aesthetic, technical, and commercial challenges to adapting *The Canterbury Tales* to the screen, the poem has not had a prolific filmic afterlife. Contemporary analogues to the *Pardoner's Tale* include *The Treasure of the Sierra Madre* (1948) and *A Simple Plan* (1998), both which adapt the Pardoner's exemplum on greed to critique the corrosive social effects of capitalist ideology.[1] Michael Powell and Emeric Pressburger famously invoke the *General Prologue* and the pilgrimage motif in their wartime *A Canterbury Tale* (1944), a film that uses Chaucer as iconic shorthand for Britain's cultural heritage, and by extension, social and national cohesiveness.[2] And Helgeland's *A Knight's Tale* (2001), which has inspired an astonishing body of professional criticsm, invokes Chaucer as the embodiment of class passing and social mobility. These are not, however, adaptations in the sense of an extended engagement with Chaucer's text, and Pasolini's auteurist and neorealist *I racconti di Canterbury* (1972) remains the only cinematic version of the poem.[3] The two most recent adaptations of *The Canterbury Tales* were produced for British public television, which, allowing the luxury of leisurely serialization and licensing support, has tended to be the venue of choice when it comes to extended creative engagements with Chaucer's capacious poem.

The BBC's *Canterbury Tales* (2003), pitched as a "prestige series" intended to reflect "life in the new century" and "the identity of Britain today," finds modern analogues for Chaucer's tales, translating Chaucer's thematic concerns into a contemporary idiom.[4] Drawing on the conventions of melodrama, the series embodies contemporary social problems—immigration, crime, consumerism, socioeconomic inequality, and bigotry—within sexual and familial relationships.

The three-part *Canterbury Tales* (1998–2000) with a script by Jonathan Myerson, packages Chaucer's bawdiness and adult themes (rape, death, adultery) for a young audience, taking advantage of the visual abstraction and distancing provided by 3D and 2D animation. Generally eschewing the genial proverbial didacticism one might expect, the animated shows are infused both with the comic effects afforded by exaggerated caricature and with the theme of metamorphosis inherent in the artistic medium. The production also has sardonic undertones, mocking class pretensions and manifesting a streak of anti-elitism and anti-intellectualism that punctuates Chaucer's popular oeuvre.

The latest television productions are not ex nihilo, borrowing techniques from earlier BBC-sponsored efforts to visually dramatize the poem. Nonetheless, while the two newest versions retain Chaucer's unshakeable association with bawdy found in earlier incarnations, the tone is decidedly pessimistic, with the BBC series giving "evidence of humanity's continuing inhumanity to humanity,"[5] and the animated *Tales* emphasizing the "dark and disturbing undertones" of Chaucer's tales.[6]

Both screen versions reflect a trend toward stylistic innovation, an "emphasis on high production values," and some degree of fidelity — that is, showing a "*respect*" for the source as well as making an effort to convey the "spirit" of the original — that Cardwell finds characteristic of recent British television adaptations of literary texts.[7] However maligned as a basis for critical evaluation in contemporary adaptation theory, fidelity does have its practical functions. It is obviously a concern, for instance, for those interested in teaching the text.[8] And as Cardwell reminds us, BBC's Reithian remit which dictates that the purpose of public service broadcasting is to educate, inform, and entertain, "still has currency today with broadcasters, critics, and audiences."[9]

The adaptations are loosely faithful, however, because both versions of Chaucer's texts are radically affected by a number of material factors, namely the technical, institutional, and financial constraints of the television industry (including, but not limited to, the exigencies of artistic collaboration, budgetary restrictions, episode length, production code standards, scheduling, and rival programming). A not insignificant factor is an interest in audience share, and producers of commercial media desire to attract an audience beyond the provincial demographic of Chaucer's readers.

While some professional reviewers griped about fidelity, both adaptations might be considered successful in the sense that they were commercially viable and largely critically appraised.[10] And beyond bringing Chaucer to mass audiences, both shows also afford those who are familiar with the Chaucerian text the pleasure of Cowart's literary symbiosis, that is, the conversation with the original text as it is transformed to a new medium and cultural context.[11]

BBC's Canterbury Tales

The six one-offs in the BBC's *Canterbury Tales* series ("The Miller's Tale"; "The Wife of Bath"; "The Knight's Tale"; "The Pardoner's Tale"; "The Man of Law's Tale"; "The Sea Captain's Tale") might best be described as commentaries or creative restorations, retaining the primary characters, basic narrative plot, and broad thematic concerns of the original, but adapting the genre and social context to reflect contemporary interests.[12] The idea of producing a modernized *Canterbury Tales* with the twin appeal of contemporary relevance and relatively low production costs is not new. *Alan Plater's Trinity Tales* (1975), for instance, also transformed individual tales into a contemporary, but largely comic, idiom.[13] Providing a frame story in which tales are told to pass the time on a minivan on the way to a rugby final at Wembley stadium, Plater consistently plays with television conventions and viewers' expectations for dramatic realism. Both the new and older BBC versions are marked by intertextual allusions to visual media and share an emphasis on the tensions and pretensions of social class. Unlike Plater's adaptation, however, the BBC series makes no effort to imitate the *General Prologue* or pilgrimage frame, serving to emphasize the social and cultural diversity of modern Britain rather than the communal camaraderie found in the earlier version. According to the controller of drama commissioning, the decision had little to do with either aesthetics or a cultural commentary of the decline of British communal identity, but was instead dictated by the exigencies of programming: "The obvious thing would have been to put them all on a coach in a traffic jam on the way to Canterbury. But we did away with the idea so that we could be more flexible about the order of the plays and the transmission dates."[14]

The opening credits common to all the episodes consist of a montage of road signs superimposed on the A1, setting the stories on locations along the route from London to Canterbury (Gravesend, Rochester, Chatham). Each episode begins with an epigraphic voice-over that is common to melodrama and also provides an acknowledgement of the impersonated artistry of Chaucer's tale-telling frame.[15] Asked to remain true to the spirit and the themes of Chaucer's texts, the writers often focus on a central incident or motif from the original (for example, imprisonment in the *Knight's Tale*; the Wife of Bath's wayward fourth husband; the mysterious figure in the *Pardoner's Tale*) and retain a skeletal Chaucerian narrative arc. Those cultural and social concerns that are anachronistic or ostensibly no longer operative (chivalry, virginity) are jettisoned, substituted with more contemporary issues: socioeconomic inequality, violent crime, immigration, xenophobia, and the cult of celebrity. And catering to what Hans Robert Jauss calls the audience's horizon of expectations—in this case assuming that "the bulk of the audience ... won't know the original *Tales*"[16]— the writers shoehorn Chaucer's tales into popular visual genres, invoking narrative conventions with which viewers will be familiar (soap opera, the con, horror).

Despite the generic variety, there is nonetheless a sense of visual and thematic unity. A muted, somber palette predominates, with the color red (representing passion and vitality) acting as a linking device. Indeed, marked by editorial stylization and leisurely scripting, the episodes feel more filmic than televisual. The series nonetheless manifests some of the familiar conventions that Fiske finds to be among the hallmarks of television culture: an emphasis on "the contemporary" and the "experiences of ordinary people," realistic characterization (with a heavy emphasis on mid-range and close shots), and a reliance on "familiar interior settings of human domestic scale."[17] The relatively low resolution of television prefers tight shots in static interiors, so it's not surprising that the content emphasis is on close human interaction.[18] Generally dominated by a woman's point of view, the episodes embody conflicts involving female transgression and male identity, reflecting larger social and cultural concerns.[19] And as is common to social melodrama, while it is often romance that precipitates the conflict, love is nevertheless reaffirmed as the "one source of transcendent moral order."[20]

THE MILLER'S TALE

Chaucer's *Miller's Tale*, in addition to involving tricks for sex or revenge, is about mockery, targeting both the genre and language of courtly romance and various kinds of bourgeois stupidity and vanity. The medium reinforces the message — and at least on a microcosmic level, everyone gets what they deserve. However, fabliaux are like long off-color jokes, lacking the character development needed for a one-hour television drama. Moreover, older men who marry young women are no longer considered foolish, but lucky, and cuckoldry often belongs to the genre of tragedy rather than comedy. While crude bodily humor remains au courant, Chaucer's more subtle parody of aristocratic pretense does not. To deal with such anachronisms, Peter Bowker transforms the fabliaux tricks of the original into an elaborate con game and replaces the parody of aristocratic mores with a critical view of the fascination with celebrity and the foolish things people will do for their fifteen minutes of Warholian fame.

Stranded by chance in a picturesque bedroom community, Nick claims to be a producer at a major music label, and ingratiates himself both with Alison, who, with Nick's encouragement, develops some pretensions for a recording career, and with John, who hopes to profit from his wife's talent. Nick also nurtures the romantic hopes of Danny Absolon (the local barber and Alison's singing partner, whom John assumes is gay), and appears to be an energetic altruist to several other villagers. Nick does indeed bed Alison, neutralizing John with a clever trick involving cookies, and we do have the two misdirected kisses. But in the final montage of scenes, Nick proves to be a tremendously "hendy" operator, bilking everyone he comes in contact with and leaving Alison on the side of the road (a nice touch is the geographical marker "Tatling End" behind her), forlornly awaiting their assignation. In the final scene, Nick has begun a new con on two young lovers, posing as a producer for a reality show focusing on newly engaged couples.

The change in plot reveals the change in thematic focus, namely the revelation of Nick's Pardoneresque duplicity as he orchestrates a complex con. The confidence game is an inspired modern analogue of the medieval fabliaux trick, for in both, the con artist's success not only depends upon the gullibility of the mark but also on the con artist's ability to cater to his victims' "fantasye." Slick Nick, like his medieval predecessor, is successful because he is able to appeal to the vanity of his victims: in successful cons, as in fabliaux, the dupes are usually victims of their own delusions. Bowker does seem to suggest that all relationships are to some degree predatory, but he is also concerned with a larger sociological message. The point is not simply a Chaucerian warning of the dangers of trusting outsiders ("Wel oghte a man avysed for to be/ Whom that he broghte into his pryvetee" [I. 4333–34]), but also has to do with the invasive and deleterious effects of the media, especially reality television, on social relationships. The various reality shows that, like Nick, seem to promise either fame or wealth, also con their audiences into accepting and applauding a thinly disguised but nonetheless brutal capitalistic ethos that commodifies human intercourse.

THE WIFE OF BATH

The Wife of Bath may be a textual incarnation of one of Jerome's "wikked wyves," but because she speaks frankly of physical and psychological female desires she is often considered the most modern and appealing of Chaucer's characters. Although her primary concern with how to achieve happiness in marriage obviously still has contemporary relevance, the causes of misery in her own marriages—the oppressive authority of patristic exegetes and *auctoritees* who privilege the sanctity of chastity and legitimize misogyny—are obviously relatively irrelevant at least in industrialized and secularized Western cultures. Her updated version—Beth Craddock—an "international superstar" and executive of her own production company, is as larger-than-life and financially secure as her medieval counterpart. And she deals with some of the more prosaic issues—like infidelity, loss of sexual attraction, aging, and abuse—raised both in the *Wife of Bath's Prologue* and *Tale* and in modern soap operas. But although Beth may be immune to the dour opinion of men who "may noght do/ Of Venus werkes worth his olde sho" (III. 707–8), she must nonetheless deal with her own patriarchal cultural pressures, namely the unreliable and fickle expectations of public opinion (standing in for the exegetical authorities of the original) and a modern ladder of perfection that equates female beauty with youth.

In place of the Wife of Bath's *confessio*, the episode opens with a celebrity exposé, in which, in an obvious echo, Beth declares, "Experience has taught me everything I know." Beth shares her prototype's ostentatious sex drive and crass jocularity; she too has also done much "wandrynge by the weye" but has nonetheless found 16 years of happiness with her current mate, a callow dentist who represents the Wife of Bath's fourth husband and who will prove as false as the front teeth he fashions to fix Beth's gap-toothed smile. Her rebound paramour, Jerome, is a "very pretty boy," and over 30 years Beth's junior. In a clever interweaving of the *Wife of Bath's Prologue* and *Tale*, and blurring the distinction between fiction and reality, Jerome and Beth consummate their relationship on the set while filming a scene in which Beth's character, "Ros," exonerates Jerome's "Gary" for rape in return for a good "shag." The union is predictably moribund although in this case the problem is not Jerome's literary tastes but his assumption that his falling ratings are due to audience perception that he's a "sad git" for marrying an older woman. Beth, in turn, attempts to become Chaucer's magical Loathly Lady — both beautiful and true — and with the help of modern cosmetic technology, does some shape-shifting of her own.

Stam suggests that "aesthetic mainstreaming," in which the literary source is purged of complexity and ambiguity in the name of "mass-audience legibility," is a common feature of popular adaptations.[21] In this case, the writer, Sally Wainwright, reads the central critical crux of the Wife of Bath's character as her "inability to function without a man in her life even though she is very successful economically":

> Chaucer's Wife of Bath was a feminist ahead of her time.... But then she lets herself down by this Achilles' heel of having to have a man in her life. She's one of those women who just doesn't seem to be able to function unless she's part of someone else.... She's very confident, apart from this need for a man.[22]

Substituting the issues of aging women's self-esteem and codependence with the question of exegetical authority, Wainwright provides an instance of symbiosis, what Cowart describes as "a statement about the modern temper as contrasted to the spirit of the age that produced ... the work being refitted."[23] On the one hand, Beth and Jerome live in a rarified world of public opinion and tabloid gossip that is as alien to most readers as the Wife of Bath's preoccupation with textual glossing. Beth, like many women in her milieu, whether celebrities or not, may have little concern about ecclesiastical opinions regarding female sexuality. But she does face a cultural ladder of perfection that is equally pernicious: the Western cult of youthful physical beauty. Indeed, Naomi Wolf's bestselling *The Beauty Myth* interprets the impossible ideal of perpetual youth (in which female desirability is predicated on the illusion of fertility) as a patriarchal backlash against feminism, an exercise in institutional power to control women — not unlike the Wife of Bath's exposure of the misogyny underlying authoritative interpretations of scripture.[24]

THE KNIGHT'S TALE

Like the original *Knight's Tale*, the BBC version is about two prison inmates who fall in love with the same woman and whose frustrated desires raise larger philosophical questions about cosmic justice and the possibility of human happiness. The writer, Tony Marchant, focuses on the motif of imprisonment, the "foule prisoun of this lyf" (I. 3061), as Theseus puts it, not in the Boethian sense in which ignorance and worldly pursuits cloud one's understanding of the workings of the true good, but as a metaphor for the economic, social, and institutional limitations that circumscribe — as surely as the malevolent gods in the original — the efficacy of human will. The anachronistic chivalric culture of the original is replaced with an urban street code of male friendship based on mutual protection. And since God appears to be no longer operative, replaced with ubiquitous security cameras (which, to add to the insult, no one seems to be monitoring), the question of divine justice and how human misery fits in the design of a providential ruler is less relevant than, as Robert Stretter says about Chaucer's *Knight's Tale*, a concern with the "struggle between two competing ideals of affectivity, one a theoretically nonsexual love between men, the other a fundamentally erotic love between the sexes."[25]

Paul (Palamon) and Ace (Arcite), who have been friends since childhood, have been incarcerated for selling reprogrammed mobile phones (an objective correlative for the problem of human communication that permeates the episode). Invoking one of the narrative conventions of the prison movie — escape in the form of mental victory over the system — Ace convinces Paul that his tenure at the facility is an "opportunity" to improve himself, primarily by taking advantage of the literacy program. Both fall in love with Emily, a social worker and prison tutor who "wants to make a difference" and who lives in an apartment that appears to be a converted church, emphasizing not only the prosaic and utilitarian uses to which London's surviving spiritual centers are often put, but also her status as angelic savior to the two inmates. Although this is not courtly love, the romantic assumptions are the same: the idea of love at first sight, that love is a transforming experience, and that love involves suffering and service. Emily inspires both men to become "better people": Ace is given an assignment on gardening which serves as a metaphor for his own emotional and intellectual growth (he is rewarded with a red flower representing the vitality Emily awakens in him) and Paul comes to recognize that his arrested development (which appropriately is also the name of a band he frequently quotes) can be ameliorated through literacy and love. The problem is that since Emily prefers Paul, she excites "a demonstration of their maleness" and "their need to assert their territory," as Marchant phrases it.[26] Lacking whatever conditional order that chivalry affords or any mediating authority to channel male aggression, Paul and Ace must struggle with what they see as mutual betrayal. In a "not very subtle" gesture of his impotent rage, Ace threatens to immolate the three of them. In the end, Ace is afforded an epiphany similar to Arcite's: his friendship with Paul is his highest good and his love for Paul cannot be "unlearned."

In the voice-over at the beginning of the episode, Paul prosaically proclaims that "All is fair in love and war," but it's not, and that's not the point. The updated version is more concerned with "the intoxicating and destructive nature of romantic love, the male ego and sexual obsession" and less with the problem of how to reconcile evil, injustice, and freewill with the existence of a providential ruler, or with the efficacy of chivalry in promoting civil stability.[27] Nonetheless, Palamon's central gripe does linger: "What governance is in this prescience,/ That giltelees tormenteth innocence?" (I.1313–14). Of Chaucer's tale, Collette observes

> ... the emphasis at the end of the tale is not on the joy of union after long striving, but on the price of love, the cost of achieving even transient happiness. The world the Knight creates in this tale is one of limited horizons and even more limited options available to characters who clearly aspire to wider knowledge and deeper understanding than they can achieve.[28]

Similarly, Paul and Ace are both trapped (the numerous shots of bars and screens emphasize their physical, social, and emotional barriers), but their suffering has to do less with a cosmic void, which is simply taken for granted, than with the more mundane but equally stifling limitations imposed by socioeconomic class: education, income, and opportunity.

THE SEA CAPTAIN'S TALE

"The Sea Captain's Tale," although retaining the central folktale motif of "the lover's gift regained," transforms the original fabliau into a short film noir. Although the alienation, paranoia, and fatalism that one generally associates with a noir sensibility may seem a long way from the cheerful amorality usually associated with the fabliaux, the basic architecture is there: the illicit sex, the trickery and betrayal (for sex, profit, or revenge), the cynicism, and the protagonists of dubious moral quality (the duplicitous wife; the jealous husband; the philandering dupe). More substantively, early post–War American noir was, in part, concerned with the corrosive effects of capitalism and excessive consumption; in this case too, the writer, Avie Luthra, examines the economic basis of social interaction, providing a neat, thematic link with the exploration of the mercantile mentality found in Chaucer's *Shipman's Tale*.

Imitating the visual style associated with film noir — low-key lighting, desaturated color, and shadowy interiors — and reinforcing a mood of claustrophobia, secrecy, and intrigue, Luthra sets his adaptation among an insular British Asian immigrant community living at the port of Gravesend: "'You can't make sense of it in the white community. You need to set it among people who make their own laws.'"[29] Jetender is a godfather-type figure with a profitable import-export business, including trade in illicit antiquities; he is older and jealous, in keeping with the fabliaux tradition, and also appears to be the possessive and overbearing patriarchal character common to noir casts. Meena, like many fabliaux females, feels both sexually and financially frustrated (her allowance in both areas being inadequate), and, like many a femme fatale before her, is trapped by a dull marriage and conventional gender expectations. She uses retail therapy as an outlet for her frustrations ("Shopping is one of the few pleasures I get in this marriage"), and in keeping with the original plot, has a large debt she can't pay. Having been refused an advance on her allowance, Meena easily seduces the virginal Pushpinder, acting on the erroneous gossip that the recent immigrant has "made a fortune" selling drugs.

Whereas the *Shipman's Tale* is usually read as an indictment of the proto-capitalist commodification of social intercourse, reinforced by the crass financial and sexual puns ("frankes"/ "flankes"), the focus here is a bit different since it appears to be taken for granted that relationships, whether sexual, marital, familial, or communal — are based on, and defined by, a complicated network of social and commercial transactions and commitments. Luthra is more interested in undermining noir and fabliaux stereotypes by seeing what happens when an emotional component — namely, love — is thrown into the triangular amorous mix. Film noir, like the fabliaux, often betrays a conservative ethic; threats to the nuclear family are often punished or neutralized, as Pushpinder is here. But although the British Asian community is ostensibly like "a large family" as Jetender proudly proclaims at the start, he is sadly disillusioned to find that his family is not beyond blackmail, especially when it comes to gossip concerning his wife's indiscretions. As for Meena, although she appears to be a stock femme fatale, "the evil seductress who tempts man and brings about his destruction" and who uses her sexuality as a bid for independence and power, threatening the existing (patriarchal) social order, like her Chaucerian prototype, she does not suffer the ritual punishment usually meted out to transgressive women in both the medieval and modern genres.[30] The couple appears to return to a sterile status quo based on social status and security, leaving the viewer with the bleak recognition that the pair remains, like many noir protagonists, trapped in a claustrophobic world of their own making.

THE PARDONER'S TALE

The original *Pardoner's Tale*, an efficacious tale told by a vicious man, consists of a sermon on the tavern sins and an exemplum illustrating the Pardoner's favorite theme: *radix malorum est cupiditas*. While the Pardoner, long ago described by Kittredge as a "lost soul," suffers from a whole array of problems—he's fraudulent, cynical, hypocritical, unregenerate, and cupidinous—the sale of phony relics seems trivial in comparison to the sex abuse scandals that have plagued the Church in the early twenty-first century. Moreover, in an age that has Internet poker, an American vice president who settles his differences with a ranking congressman by telling him to "[expletive] yourself," and a magazine devoted to dipsomania (*Modern Drunkard*), the medieval sins of gambling, swearing and drinking are now usually categorized as vices (if that). And in a capitalist economy the popular perception is that, as Gordon Gecko (*Wall Street*) puts it, "Greed ... is good." According to the writer, Tony Grounds, "Chaucer's story is really about three drunken revelers who get their comeuppance because of greed. I've had to make my version a lot nastier.... You can't just kill off people on TV these days for being greedy; our threshold is a lot higher. I needed to make the central characters very nasty pieces of work."[31] The BBC's "Pardoner's Tale," therefore, the loosest of the adaptations (similar to what Wagner would call an "analogy"),[32] retains the popular motif of the discovery of hidden treasure (c.f., *The Treasure of the Sierra Madre*; *A Simple Plan*), but, demonstrating a feature of some adaptations in which "indeterminacies are completed and actualized,"[33] transforms the original exemplum into a ghost story exploring the causes, effects, and civic responses to sociopathic behavior.

The story takes place in Rochester, crowded with tourists visiting the Norman castle and cathedral (providing some gothic atmosphere) who are easy targets for three local hoodlums. Although appearing to be garden-variety thieves, a secondary narrative involving the disappearance of two local female teenagers suggests that these three swindlers may be more sinister than they appear. The narrative focuses on Arty, who shares some characteristics with the Pardoner: they are both eloquent, have delusions of grandeur, and take advantage of people's charitable impulses. Arty too has a penchant for literary citation. And he is clearly disturbed. Through a series of flashbacks to his childhood, it appears that he is haunted by nostalgia, alienation, and an innate sense of depravity. Having aggressively seduced a young girl who is helping search for the latest missing teenager, Arty reveals in his post-coital ramblings that he wants to be famous for doing something "noble," to "do the world a service," to be the "king of the world." The mysteriously passive girl says she can help and directs Arty and his friends to a house where they inadvertently discover the gold, and the predictable conclusion of violent mutual destruction ensues. Suggesting the impotency of spiritual leadership, in the final scene there again appears a clerical figure who first appears in the initial shot — wearing a death's head ring, teeth stained from tobacco, singing a sarcastic rendition of "It's a Wonderful World"— who observes two of Arty's victims ascend a stairway (to heaven?), justice apparently having been served.

Grounds' adaptation lacks any overt treatment of clerical corruption, hypocrisy, or cupidity, and the only apparent thematic connection with the original is the broad theme of the causes of human depravity (or, as the teenage ghost puts it, "Why does there need to be horrible people?"). The adaptation is, however, quite interested in the long-standing critical crux of the old man in Chaucer's tale, here transformed into a ghost, invoking popular motifs derived from the gothic tradition.[34] Ghosts are often a manifestation of subconscious guilt, psychic disorder, or fragmented identity. As the numerous flashbacks attest, Arty is clearly haunted by the unconditional love and admiration he enjoyed as a child; but as a young boy he realizes that "I don't want to be me," and as a man he yearns for the lost innocence of his preadolescence, before he became "nasty." In gothic fashion, this feeling of nastiness appears to be traceable not only to his conflicts with an oppressive patriarchy (his father, Father Christmas, God) but more specifically perhaps to child abuse. Spectral revenants are also sometimes the disenfranchised seeking some form of power or recognition, clearly applicable here. Finally, ghosts can also serve, as in this case, as a deus ex machina plot device to remedy a gross injustice that social institutions are unable to deal with. But we are not left with a simple Manichean conclusion in which evil is defeated; by equally balancing both Arty's angst and the irremediable grief of the victims' families, Grounds offers a complex analysis of the inadequacies of our understanding of, and impotency in dealing with, random acts of vicious crime.

THE MAN OF LAW'S TALE

The *Man of Law's Tale* has traditionally been described as a secular saint's legend in which the prolonged travails of the Christian Custance ostensibly represent the mysterious workings of God's providence. While it is true that Custance never loses the faith that God is guiding her ship and her quiet evangelism, the tale also touches on a bewildering variety of themes, including patriarchal authority, the persecution of early Christians, astrological predestination, the vagaries of religious conversion, multiculturalism, xenophobia, misogyny, the fickleness of earthly happiness, the cruelty and insanity provoked by unrequited lust, and the dangers of feckless messengers. For the writer, Olivia Hetreed, "'What survives from the original is the power of that single character who changes everything around her because she is good without compromise.'"[35]

The updated tale, while dispensing with the digressive editorial matter and focusing on "the conditions in which xenophobia flourishes," touches on a surprising number of themes from the original.[36] The BBC version is, nonetheless, more overtly a cross-cultural love story, with many of the plot devices that inhibit consummation (amnesia, misunderstanding, miscommunication, family, race, and social class) that modern viewers expect from the romance genre. Constance, a Nigerian refugee who is a victim of brutal sectarian hostilities, washes up in a life raft off the Thames estuary in Kent. She is discovered and sheltered by Mark and Nicky Constable, and although she is clearly suffering from post-traumatic stress, she maintains the unshakeable conviction that "God has a purpose for us all" and that "God [is] watching over me." Her quiet self-possession and solid conviction convert Nicky (although her less enthusiastic husband considers Constance to be a "religious fanatic") and attract the agnostic Alan King, who "practices safe religion": "Like safe sex, but not as fun." Constance's faith is again put to the test as a member of her church group confuses their spiritual fellowship with sexual lust. In a fit of psychopathic desire he kills Nicky, and as in the original, Constance is blamed for the crime. In the de rigueur courtroom cross-examination scene common to television dramas in which civil justice and human guilt replace the miraculous interventions in the original, Constance is exonerated; and, despite the meddling of her prospective mother-in-law, the lovers are eventually reunited. Indeed, throughout her ordeals, Constance, like her predecessor, is characterized by her "capacity to endure ... to resist and suffer with patience and fortitude, rather than to confront and conquer with strength and wit," suggesting that these features of female heroism that Mary Beth Rose traces back to the early modern period prevail in the popular imagination.[37]

It is not God, however, who effects a happy ending, and in this case the writer is highly successful in encouraging the viewer to reconsider the moral of Chaucer's tale, sometimes read as a neat allegory of constancy rewarded, although, given the uncertain relationship between virtue, justice, and providence, often viewed as "asking searching metaphysical questions of or about the Christian God."[38] The central paradox here, represented by the bloody gold crucifix Constance clutches in her hand like an anchor, is that religion often causes the very adversity for which it provides consolation. While faith may lead to fellowship, it also incites or is used as an excuse for hatred, violence, and cruelty. Like the original Custance, the Nigerian version passively accepts God's will that her lot in life is confined to suffering. But Constance does have a secular humanist epiphany common to the romance genre, although lacking in the original: much of her misery could have been avoided if she would have simply had faith in Alan and his love for her. Picking up the central image of Constance's boat, ostensibly guided by God in the original, learning to sail serves as a metaphor for human agency and the modern Constance learns, as she puts it, that Alan is her "captain," she is his "crew." The romance ends on a note of promise and hope; nonetheless, the often insurmountable obstacles of race, religion, and social class, and the numerous shots of the dramatic tidal fluctuations of the Thames seem to reinforce Chaucer's concluding sober observation that "Joye of this world, for tyme wol nat abyde;/ Fro day to nyght it changeth as the tyde" (II.1133–34).

"The Pardoner's Tale" and "The Man of Law's Tale" aired last, garnering the lowest audience shares of all the episodes—roughly half that of "The Miller's Tale" and "The Wife of Bath" that led the series.[39] Margaret Rogerson accurately finds in the series a thematic "shading process ... darkening into the madness, depravity, and greed of 'The Pardoner's Tale' and the inhumanity ... of 'The Man of Law's Tale.'"[40] A number of factors, like rival programming, can affect viewership. But the fall-off might have been due partly to the departure from the expected Chaucerian bawdy reflected in the more successful initial episodes; those shows too, focusing on the cult of celebrity and the travails of an aging actress, have less of the topical social realism that infuses the rest of the series. Cawelti suggests that social melodrama eases middle-class tensions arising from perceived "social and cultural changes."[41] The identity of modern Britain today as reflected in the series appears increasingly multicultural and materially affluent but nonetheless not immune to socioeconomic inequality, bigotry, crime, and corruption. "The Man of Law's Tale," like the others, frames larger social issues (in this case, bitter prejudice against asylum seekers) as individual dilemmas, arising from and best addressed within the family. The creed is fundamentally conservative, with the various social ills presented not as institutionally systemic but as personal problems best solved by individual agency and the magically transformative power of romantic love.

The Canterbury Tales: Leaving London; Arriving at Canterbury; The Journey Back

The *Canterbury Tales* trilogy turns to animation in a strategic and aesthetic effort, according to Myerson, to make "Chaucer accessible."[42] Associated with imaginary fantasy and a fabricated world, animation carries "connotations of innocence and undemandingness," providing the distancing that makes Chaucer's adult subject matter more palatable to a juvenile audience.[43] Chaucer is made accessible both by the use of colloquial English (a Middle English version is also available for the subsidiary educational market) delivered via top British actors and Royal Shakespeare Company alumni, and by the massive abridgement, compression, and streamlining characteristic of commercial adaptations.[44] Appropriating a range of animation styles and techniques, from the relatively realistic look of stop-motion 3D to highly stylized 2D drawings, the production foregrounds Chaucer's variety of genres and philosophical moods, ranging here from flatulence to fatalism. The inherent fluidity of the animated image serves to accentuate both the comic and the chimerical aspects of Chaucer's poetry. Add to this an anti-elitist spirit, a consistent exposure of hypocrisy, and mockery of adult pretensions—social, religious, intellectual—and you have a winning formula, with *Leaving London* nominated for Best Animated Short Film at the 1999 Academy Awards.

The animated version has some similarities to the BBC's ambitious 1969 seven-episode *Canterbury Tales* (written by Nevill Coghill and Martin Starkie) done in live action and period costume.[45] The 1969 version also makes an effort to provide an impression of the generic scope and tonal variety of Chaucer's poem, including both a reference to the *Retraction* and the arrival at Canterbury. Bits of the *General Prologue* are interwoven throughout the journey, with the "reality" of the links, which were shot on location, clearly demarcated from the "fiction" of the tales which were filmed in studio. In the new animated version, 3D stop-motion with clay (or plasticine) puppets, effective for more mimetic representation, is used for the frame and for those tales with a contemporaneous setting. In contrast to the "realism" of the pilgrimage and historical setting, 2D "cel" or drawn animation, an older style, more stylized and abstract, is used to underscore the artificial worlds of the fictional tales. Myerson eschews conventional order, an editorial decision justified by the disarray of the scribal record described in Chaucer's brief biography included as one of the DVD extras. The first segment features the most widely taught or most recognizable tales ("The Nun's Priest's Tale"; "The Knight's Tale"; "The Wife of Bath's Tale"), but there are also some subsequent surprises like "The Squire's Tale" and "The Canon's Yeoman's Tale." The selection seems to have been partly dictated by those tales featuring illusion and deception, themes amenable to the inherent metamorphosis of the animated visual image. Like the *Tale of Beryn*, and the 1969 BBC television version, Myerson brings his pilgrims to Canterbury, where a few pray at Beckett's tomb while the rest indulge in some medieval recreational activities (bear-baiting, cock-fighting, visiting a dentist, and attending a mystery). The tease throughout is that the Miller's turn is imminent, and the trilogy climaxes with a masterfully intercut montage of "The Miller's Tale" and "The Reeve's Tale" as dueling performances of "quyting."

Ellis suggests that the animated version accentuates the "dark and disturbing undertones" of Chaucer's poetry.[46] The effect is created in part by the contrast between the ostensible "innocence" of the animated form "making the 'transferred' elements of the text stand in a new relief."[47] A monochromatic palette of somber neutrals predominates, and it is immediately apparent that, notwithstanding the luminous background of green English countryside, the emphasis is on the gritty, benighted Middle Ages. The opening scene at the Tabard, for instance, eschews the theme of vernal rejuvenation, and is Monty Pythonesque in mood, framed with the image of a footless cripple — whom everyone blithely ignores — crawling through the mud with hand braces. Later, the pilgrims witness a sobering flagellant scene (invoking Ingmar Bergman's *The Seventh Seal*). Barry Purves describes how clay is good for representing "oddness," and the emphasis is on the comic grotesque, with the pilgrims possessing the exaggerated physical features (outsized noses, elongated chins, swollen bellies) found in parodic farce.[48] One's first impression is that Chaucer's company consists of a gallery of vulgar type figures: the pustule-ridden Summoner; the ascetic Knight, the prudish Prioress, the vain Squire, and the lisping, lascivious Friar who has an unfortunate predilection for sibilants. Chaucer, whose narrative pose of confidentiality was influenced by Michael Caine's *Alfie*, manifests his stereotypical affability and genial tolerance.[49] He is introduced in a Socratic moment, dodging a thrown chamber pot, the contents of which inspire the sardonic opening lines of the *General Prologue* ("When April's soft showers have cracked the March drought"). He almost makes it to the west wind before he is interrupted, and in an abrupt parody of his protracted opening, simply summarizes, "that's when people get the itch." As for the intermittent farts, inebriation, and vulgarity, Myerson distills Chaucer's disclaimer of responsibility at the end of the *General Prologue* into a simple insistence on verisimilitude: "What can I say? If any of you are too delicate, this is what people are like." While vaguely Chaucerian in sentiment, the tone also reflects a "populist 'folk' sensibility" often associated with animation's reputation as a democratizing medium.[50]

Myerson suggests that "Chaucer didn't have dramatization in mind" when choosing his frame structure. Myerson's method, therefore, was to take "all of Chaucer's lines, jumble them up then stick them back together in an order which would bring the banter between the pilgrims to dramatic life."[51] Dialogue is composed of recycled bits from the *General Prologue*, the links, and the tales, as well as a number of authorial additions reflecting modern critical readings, divvied out to a handful of pilgrims. There is quite a bit of so-called "smart" chatter—"come-backs, put-downs, puns"—associated with comedy.[52] Myerson uses topical streamlining, with most of the chatter involving the miseries of marriage, the virility of the clergy, class rivalry, and the stages of drunkenness. *The Journey Back*, however, is heavy on both class antagonism and a related anti-intellectualism. The Man of Law, declaring his boredom with the Prioress's tale, is reprimanded by the Reeve for his lack of courtesy. The emphasis in the Canon's Yeoman's Tale is on learning as deception and sham, and concludes with the moral that "The greatest scholars aren't always the wisest men." To which the Summoner responds:

I'm safe. Not much Latin down my gullet.
—burps—
Benedicite.

Chaucer sarcastically introduces the Clerk as "The eternal Oxford student": "He hasn't managed to find holy office. He couldn't find it with a map." And in response to the Knight's fear that the Miller's tale "is going to be most unattractive," the Miller retorts with Host-like malapropisms: "Is it my fault I never slept in the Ascropolis? Or read Julius Seizure?"

The characterization of the pilgrims is often only loosely Chaucerian. Some of the anachronistic niceties of topical social satire are often dispensed with, and for comic effect Myerson plays against character type or exaggerates features. The rough bawdy is appropriately filtered through the Miller, who is given the Host's ruminations on the virility of the clergy ("If I was Pope I'd let all you shave-heads marry"), insults Chaucer for his rhyming, and shares the scatological insult delivered to the Pardoner with the Cook. The Wife of Bath, who appears to establish a sexual liaison with the Nun's Priest and lustfully grabs at a startled Squire, insists, oddly, that the Pardoner not speak of anything "uncouth." The Pardoner is asked to "Tell us something funny," and is more of a clown than a pariah. In keeping with the egalitarian spirit than runs throughout, the Squire's ostensible good breeding becomes simple sycophancy; discovering himself being observed by Chaucer, he stifles his high-handed rudeness to a barber, leading Chaucer to describe his courtesy in a mocking falsetto. And the Prioress is bled of bourgeois pretension; she is given the Man of Law's lines ("That man, what's he called? I read all his books. He already tell every story. Chaucer. He leave no stories for us to tell") and is, somewhat surprisingly, a nonnative English speaker. Notwithstanding her affection for her poodle, she exhibits charity that clearly extends beyond weeping over dead mice, and the concluding shrill lines that we overhear of her tale are simply soporific rather than shockingly anti–Semitic.

The ten fully animated tales, each roughly seven minutes, are remarkable for managing the requisite narrative and visual condensation while communicating traditional critical readings and adding novel interpretive touches.

The episodes are marked by the "literalizing" inherent in the medium, that is, the necessity of transforming and compressing both description and abstractions into concrete moving images.[53] The Miller's Alison, for instance, quite economically harbors a weasel in her considerable bosom and John rubs the large knobs on an astrolabe as he expresses his concern for his young wife's safety in the face of the impending flood. Similarly, the Pardoner's sham played on his parishioners is captured quite economically; during his mock sermon, which he performs for the pilgrims at a rest stop, a pauper widow with two young children offers him her only coin and reverently kisses his bogus reliquary containing the "pigges bones" of his leftover lunch. Most prominent, however, is the property of metamorphosis, a feature that Wells describes as the "constituent core of animation itself."[54] Given the "plasmatic potential" of the graphic image, animation is most suited to "changes in characters or situations that may be termed 'magical' or impossible within the concept of the real world."[55] Here the inherent plasticity of the animated image serves to accentuate the motifs of illusion and transformation in each of the tales. More specifically, the animated version emphasizes the mutability of physical reality, the transient nature of happiness, and the illusion of stable human identity.

The first segment, featuring Chaucer's better known tales, is loosely unified by the notion of the fleeting nature of happiness. "The Nun's Priest's Tale" is narrated in a Yorkshire accent, and the fowls are given regional inflections in order to underscore the folk origins of the tale. The rhetorical excesses of the original — digressions, anecdotes, and overt moralities concerning women's counsel, flattery, and self-deception — are streamlined, with the focus on the humorous absurdity of the mock heroic. The artists, Ashley Potter and Dave Antrobus, use bold, nonnaturalistic colors, effective in underscoring the imaginary and incongruous drama of the barnyard (Chaunticleer is befeathered, for instance, in royal purple and blue, and he shares a bright pink and purple boudoir with Pertelote). Jerky movements imitate the chickens' gait, and their circumscribed perspective and short attention span are emphasized by extreme close-ups and flash cuts. The central discussion about dreams (in Chaucer running to some 200 verses) is edited down to a handful of lines, still managing however to showcase the comic absurdity of chickens consulting authorities.[56] The editorial technique, common to all the tales, is to jettison anachronistic cultural allusions, such as Pertelote's discussion of contemporary medical pharmacopeia, to omit all illustrative exempla, and to distill disquisitions into a single summarizing statement. Wells suggests that animation "most properly deals with the *imagist* agenda within literary texts."[57] The emphasis is on concrete language that can be literally visualized; Pertelote's lines are accompanied by images of flames, arrows, and demons arising from an open book; Chaunticleer pulls out a tome for each named authority, using his feathers to flip through the pages; and the tips of Pertelote's wings, held behind her back, are transformed into wiggling worms, visualizing the frightening efficacy of her laxative of choice. As in the case of Barbara Cooney's classic children's version, *Chanticleer and the Fox*, Pertelote does not immolate herself, and in the final scene the two birds are unceremoniously carried home as they discuss the significance of their experience.[58] Chaunticleer naturally blames it on the hen, but Pertelote has the last word ("there must be some moral; you just have to know what"), side-stepping, in good Chaucerian (and critical) fashion, the obvious anti-feminist import of the fable.[59]

Similar methods of compression and a reliance on the visual image to communicate ideas are found in the subsequent tales. The rendition of "The Knight's Tale" is less interested in chivalry, love, or a philosophical exploration of happiness and justice than the lack of human self-determination in a world overseen by meddling but inscrutable gods. Dave Antrobus and Mic Graves use simple, geometric lines, rendering their human characters as almost stick figures, and setting them against vast, largely bare backgrounds to conceptualize the smallness of the human imprint. The assertion that men are nothing more than "sheep cowering in the fold" is represented by the earth encased in a spherical, spinning astrolabe overseen by amorphous, outsized deities. The gods themselves, prevalent from the start, are almost abstractions, drawn in single, simple lines in profile and without expressive detail, emphasizing their impersonality and impenetrability. Reflecting what Wells describes as animation's tendency to enunciate "the conflicts and tensions in the 'serio-comic,'" the gloomy epistemology, emphasized by the use of dark, saturated colors, is leavened with almost incongruous comic effects.[60] Emily's visit to Venus's temple has a quite provocative introduction ("Emily ritually disrobed and ... perhaps I shouldn't go into details right now ... but it'd be fun, eh?") that mitigates the frightening image of blood in her bath betokening her inevitable espousal. And Saturn, stertorously enumerating his cosmic powers ("Mine is the drowning in the limpid sea. Mine is the tightening of the noose"), is at a loss for words to accompany the more mundane manifestation of his might captured in the image of a painter falling off his scaffold. But despite the feints at levity, the animated version maintains a bleak vision of astral determinism and cosmic injustice.

"The Wife of Bath's Tale" is drawn by Joanna Quinn, known both for her concern with contemporary (post)-feminist politics and for her "kinetic sketchy caricatures," appropriate for the exploration of physical and psychological transformation found in the tale.[61] Penciled with fluid, dynamic lines and characterized by a spare use of color, Quinn's "live-wire" drawing style articulates tension and energy. The rape is handled as a blurred tussle, the knight's lust symbolized by his rearing horse and the maiden's deflowering captured in a yellow flower that wilts in her hand (the flower revives after the knight's rehabilitation). Women are clearly in control throughout and the knight himself becomes a sexual object; Guinevere pushes his face into her bosom, and the hag licks her toothless lips in anticipation of the nuptials. In the end, it is clearly shown that it is perhaps only the knight's perception of the hag that has changed (an interpretation that mirrors critical readings). Indeed, the piece ends with a tussle reminiscent of the initial rape, with the Loathly Lady cackling as her physical form fluctuates in the arms of her satisfied partner.[62]

The *Wife of Bath's Prologue* is succinctly summarized with the sound precept, "Don't get married and you won't get deceived," which serves as a thematic touchstone linking the first segment (*Leaving London*) with "The Merchant's Tale," the first tale of *Arriving at Canterbury*. The technique in "The Merchant's Tale" is to emphasize visual puns that serve as fruitful double entendres and provide an ironic subtext. January, who, according to the Merchant, either "got religion or was plain ga-ga," consults with his advisors while they bathe in tubs, prefiguring John's later deception in "The Miller's Tale." His declaration that only a nubile bride will do (based on the assumption that "You can train a young one up, like wax in your hands") is accompanied by the image of his bar of soap leaping out of his grip. Each subsequent contribution to the discussion ("You have to ask yourself — is she a nagger? Does she spend your money? Does she hit the bottle? Can she control herself?") is punctuated by the soap slipping out of the interlocutor's grasp. After the wedding night we see January's cat, legs spread, cleaning itself in serene self-satisfaction, an obvious analogue to his owner's nocturnal exertions. And the pear serves throughout as a recurring objective correlative suggesting sexual desire. May's declaration, "Look at those pears!" for instance, is accompanied by the phallic-looking fruit placed between Damian's legs. The subsequent physical activities in the tree (censored by the image of a large pear) are suggested by pears falling on the ground all around January. In the end, January's "got a son and heir. Someone's son. His heir." As the three principals promenade, all three are shown looking at potential amorous partners as they are gradually frozen into the image of a faded tapestry. The final metamorphosis serves a double purpose, suggesting not only the antiquity of the story but also the artistic parallel between the two visual art forms.

Instead of a reliance on visual motifs, color and line are used for thematic effect in "The Franklin's Tale" and "The Squire's Tale." Stripped of its rhetorical embellishments and exploration of the complexities of medieval notions of "honour" and "trouthe," "The Franklin's Tale" embodies an idealistic literalism bordering on absurdity. Indeed, no one is listening when the Franklin poses his *demande* about who is the most generous. Damian Gascoigne uses minimalist, ink and watercolor drawings with bold, stylized lines for the characters, lending the figures a degree of vacancy, impersonality, and artificiality. The drawings resemble pictographs or flat woodcut engravings, without the shading that lends the illusion of dimensionality.[63] Using limited animation, there is little movement and little perspective, accentuating the static, confined, rule-bound world inhabited by the characters. Dual complimentary color schemes (purple/orange; red/purple) underscore the bold moral contrasts. And the lack of shading suggests the stark choices—infidelity to her promise or to her husband—that Dorigen faces (her even more anachronistic choice between suicide or dishonor is omitted).[64] In contrast, in "The Squire's Tale" Iain Gardner uses vibrant textured watercolor washes, inspired by Oriental design, to emphasize an exotic mood of romance and magic. Following in the wake of Edmund Spenser and John Lane,[65] Myerson completes the tale, transforming the miscellany of genre motifs in the original into a coherent interlaced romance framed by the knight's quest for Canacee's hand in which he must prove that he is no fickle tercelet or dynastic usurper. The focus is on the hazardous geography of romantic relationships, particularly the problem of accurately parsing the appearance of sincerity. To emphasize the themes of deception and illusion, the human figures lack outline; their faces are often transparent and opaque, fading into the background, emphasizing the softened, misty contours of reality. Most prominent, however, is the theme of visual metamorphosis reflecting animation's ability to "naturalize ... magical conditions."[66] As the Red Knight, for instance, describes the power of his bird-shaped ring in conferring the gift of flight on its owner, the ring becomes a flock of birds, which in turn becomes the armor of the Knight. The transformations serve to illustrate at once the physical properties of the magic ring, which provides the possibility and protection of flight, and both the romantic and political aspirations of the knight.

The final installment, *The Journey Back*, delivers on the bawdy promised throughout with a brilliant climactic montage of "The Miller's Tale" and "The Reeve's Tale." A quick cross-cutting of matching scenes both achieves a "hyperbolic comedy of speed," and allows the visualization of incongruities, particularly sudden changes and reversals, associated with comedy.[67] The 3D clay puppets feature huge lips and teeth and are what Wells might call "overdetermined" caricatures. Their exaggerated, distorted features work to dehumanize the characters, blunting their cruelty and humiliation and allowing the vulgarity customarily denied live action intended for a juvenile or educational market.[68] Absalon's effeminacy is manifested in a lisp, and John's impotency by his broken saw. Visual motifs, such as a cat suggesting Alison's sexuality in "The Miller's Tale," and a rat representing Simkyn's mentality in "The Reeve's Tale," provide tonal unity. The rat kicks his droppings into Simkyn's corn, and John delivers his line about God's "privetee" while peering through the cat door and inadvertently inspecting his cat's rear end. The montage maintains the pacing and narrative economy of the originals, managing to capture the humor of the genre as well as the fabliaux philosophy that consistently eschews an "exemplary concluding *moralitas*."[69]

Contemporary adaptation theorists often rightfully minimize talk of fidelity, intent upon both establishing the aesthetic autonomy of the film versions of literary texts and redirecting attention to the many extra-hermeneutic forces that shape the production of screen adaptations.[70] The serial form chosen for the BBC series, for instance, while allowing more leisurely treatment of Chaucer's texts, also makes good fiscal sense since "costs can be spread advantageously over a number of episodes."[71] Similarly, the BBC's decision to jettison the pilgrimage frame was influenced by a variety of technical and commercial factors, including scheduling and allotted episode length. The selection and adaptation of individual tales was dictated by the conventions of one-offs airing during prime-time, expected to be character-driven, one-hour dramas, starring popular actors, and addressing, via domestic conflicts, socially relevant issues. Myerson's choice of tales was probably dictated in part by those that afforded both a linear plot amenable to seven-minute condensation and the visual imagery necessary for a graphic narrative. Since the animated shows were produced, in part, for an educational market, pedagogical popularity was no doubt another influential factor in the selection of tales. And while the traditional association of animation with anthropomorphic animals perhaps inspired the choice to adapt the *Nun's Priest's Tale*, some of the surprising pieces like the *Squire's Tale* and the *Canon's Yeoman's Tale* probably might have suggested themselves given animation's forte in representing both illusion and transformation.

Producers are less haunted than academics by the specter of originary authority, and these shows were marketed as adaptations of Chaucer, whose cultural visibility should provide "a certain amount of built-in insurance": "Insurance derives from the success of the pre-tested narrative, while the title and author of the original provide automatic advertising."[72] The shows were also judged by professional critics according to their fidelity to Chaucer. While the animated production (a pastiche that sounds Chaucerian without actually quoting the poem) largely escaped censure, in otherwise largely laudatory appraisals critics complained that the BBC's modernized adaptation was, as one reviewer puts it, not Chaucer, but "Chaucer Flavoring."[73] And more forcefully:

> "The Canterbury Tales" contain as little Chaucer as permissible under the Sales of Goods Act.... The stories have been detached from their gold setting like old jewelry broken into pieces, and we were left with half-a-dozen modern one-act plays.

Python and scholar Terry Jones, who shed a new and blinding light on *The Knight's Tale*, believes Chaucer was murdered. I see what he means.[74]

But it's arguably the alterations to the text, the changes made to adapt the poem to the aesthetic and technical exigencies of a new medium and to a new cultural environment that made the shows both commercially successful, and for those conversant with the original, intellectually compelling.

Comparative analysis certainly can produce constructive discussions about Chaucer's familiarity and alterity, of those generic and thematic aspects of his work that remain amenable to cultural updating. The connections made, for instance, by the individual BBC writers between the self-serving *confessio* and the celebrity exposé, the didacticism of the exemplum and modern ghost stories, and the vanity and delusion common to the fabliaux and film noir, attest to both the malleability and the modernity of Chaucer's literary materials. Myerson suggests that the movements of the clay pilgrims were modeled on the riders in *The Searchers,* and the animated pilgrimage certainly shares visual motifs and thematic characteristics with both the western and its descendent, the road movie: panoramic landscapes, the flouting of conservative social norms, group bickering and bonding, and the "natural" behavior on the journey contrasted with the civilizing and corrupting influence of spiritual and social life in Canterbury.

As the numerous adaptations and appropriations attest, Chaucer's tales and frame structure have proven remarkably amenable to new artistic genres. Although the Chaucerian retains an unshakeable association with bawdy, it is Chaucer's ostensible social realism, based on the assumption that *The Canterbury Tales* provides a mirror of historical reality, that continues to attract popular audiences. The BBC series transforms *The Canterbury Tales* into working-class melodramas, manufacturing the illusion of realism by the use of frequent location shots. The emphasis is on the function of environment, including most conspicuously the erosion of communal bonds, on the characters' quest for self-determination and social acceptance. Domestic dysfunction — adultery, illiteracy, racism — provides a metaphorical microcosm for larger sociopolitical problems, including the social limitations imposed by gender, race, and class. The animated version is certainly less overtly topical, accentuating instead the paradox of an iconic literary work infused with flatulence and fornication. The emphasis on vulgarity betrays an almost documentary fascination with the fundamental physical grotesquery of medieval life. In addition to providing some authenticity, the groping, farts, and put-downs are also a manifestation of the disdain for social pretension of any kind. Indeed, notwithstanding its consistent critique of institutionalized religion, the animated version is most conspicuous in its scorn of intellectual elitism, including the high-brow text upon which the show is based.

4

The Canterbury Pilgrimage and African Diaspora

In Nelson's *The Cachoeira Tales*, King-Aribisala's *Kicking Tongues*, and Naylor's *Bailey's Café*, The Canterbury Tales is appropriated as a vehicle for exploring contemporary African diasporic identities. Although authored by academics, these texts, like much of the popular corpus, are forms of marginalized Chaucerian discourse insofar as such creatively critical responses to his poetry have traditionally fallen outside normative, institutionalized Chaucerian criticism. Wallace, valiantly casting about for a suitable designation for such "spatial frameworks that are powerfully local, yet global," and that play "to broader publics," suggests the phrase "new Chaucer topographies."[1] But the term "popular" is serviceable here as well. Stuart Hall suggests that "the popular has always been 'the other'" and in "continuing tension (relationship, influence, antagonism) with the dominant culture."[2] These texts in particular can be contrasted with both dominant academic Chaucerian discourse and the Western canonical tradition, constituting both resistant and self-authorizing appropriations of Chaucer's text.

The Canterbury Tales might not immediately strike one as an obvious inspiration for the exploration of displacement, dislocation, or diaspora. True, for two decades Chaucer's engagement with contemporary categories of difference, including most obviously gender, but also race, social class, and sexuality, has been explored through the lens of cultural historicism and cultural materialisms.[3] There has also been some critical effort to historicize Chaucer's own postcolonial literary sensibilities.[4] But as the iconic wellspring of the English literary canon, intertextual engagement with Chaucer's texts within the context of emergent literary traditions has distinct ideological ramifications and can be haunted by the specter of Eurocentrism and cultural normativity. Nonetheless, seizing on the conceptual connection between pilgrimage and diaspora, these writers convert Christian pilgrimage into a transformative quest for black identities and inspirit Chaucer's tale tellers with the voices of the alienated and dispossessed. All seem to value the egalitarian multivocality inherent in the notion of communal tale telling and appropriate this Chaucerian conceit to showcase the cultural plurality of contemporary black diasporic and postcolonial communities.

Each represents an example of "signifyin(g)," the well-known form of intertextuality marked by "repetition and revision" in the rewriting of prior texts. The signifying with respect to *The Canterbury Tales* is certainly what Henry Louis Gates, Jr., calls "motivated," constituting a parodic revisioning of a traditional discourse, or what Hutcheon describes as "a formal repetition with ironic critical distance, marking difference rather than similarity."[5] But the parodies are also "unmotivated," insofar as modern engagement with the medieval text represents an act of homage and renewal. Each undertakes a tropological revision, that is, a repetition of the pilgrimage trope with a difference. All jettison the competitive aspects of Chaucer's frame and replace the tale telling and "quyting" with bonding, communal testimonials. While representing very different kinds of modern pilgrimage — spiritual, political, psychological — each embodies the sense of exile and the desire for understanding and self-transformation inherent in medieval Christian pilgrimage. But more important is the plurality of narrative voices afforded by Chaucer's frame, reconfigured by these writers as a social dialogue essential to the formation of collective identity. Indeed, the assimilation of Chaucer — among many other literary voices— represents aesthetically the cultural and social synthesis that the authors model in their texts.

The Cachoeira Tales

Nelson's neoformalist *Cachoeira Tales* appropriates the structure and style of *The Canterbury Tales* to explore a number of interests relating to pilgrimage: the transformative potential of travel, manifestations of religiosity, the quest for cross-cultural diasporic identity, and most importantly, the synthetic spiritualism of African diasporic religions.[6] Reflecting Chaucer's generic diversity, this meditative travelogue, composed in loose pentameter couplets, is inhabited by a pastiche of discourses, including anecdotes, reminiscences, jokes, folktales, proverbs, idioms, and clichés. The appropriation of Chaucer into what Todd Edmondson describes as "a postmodern pilgrimage of the black diaspora," mirrors, formally and aesthetically, Nelson's thematic interest in the dynamic and inspiring potential of syncretic cultural traditions—literary, musical, and spiritual.[7] Although the subject is serious, involving the dislocation of cultural identity and double consciousness, Nelson seems to adopt the Chaucerian dictum that "A man may seye ful sooth in game and pley" (1.4355), and, by utilizing Chaucerian deference, understatement, and self-deprecation, maintains a deft, comic tone throughout.

Like *The Canterbury Tales*, the poem is named for a pilgrimage site, in this case a small, colonial-era town in the Bahia region of Brazil, home to the Sisterhood of the Good Death "founded by former slaves in the nineteenth/ century ... as a way to serve the poor" (49). In an act of overt invocation, in the "General Prologue" Nelson mimics Chaucer's seasonal opener, here stripped of its elaborate synthesis of plant, animal, and human responses to spring, and transformed into a thematically irrelevant weather report:

> When April rains had drenched the root
> of what March headlines had foreseen as drought
> I invited my extended family —
> with artificial spontaneity —
> to join me on some kind of "pilgrimage."
> A fellowship gave me the privilege
> of offering to cover their airfare
> and several nights in a hotel somewhere.
> Thinking of a reverse diaspora,
> I'd planned a pilgrimage to Africa [11].

As Wallace suggests, in contrast to Chaucer's collection of strangers, here one finds a familial group, reflecting "the endurance and adaptability of family ... one of the great wonders of African American culture."[8] In the spirit of Chaucer's pilgrims' ostensible but unspoken desire to seek out the holy martyr who had helped them when they were sick, Nelson's small fellowship joins her in her fellowship-funded mission to visit a place "sanctified by the Negro soul": "My brother Mel's response was, 'what the hey:/ I'll go to Timbuktu if you're going to pay'" (11). Although the range of qualifying sites is sobering, the sanctified place proves quite hard to find, Zimbabwe being too dangerous, Senegal too expensive, Jamaica too touristic. But the town of Salvador, where Nelson's son is studying, proves to be just right, and has a church "sacred to Christians and followers of Candomble" (12). The latter is significant for Nelson, reflecting her chief interest in spiritual hybridity, particularly the synthesis of Christianity and West African–derived religions. She strives to realize a similar synthesis in her poetry, both adapting the iconic literary expression of Christian pilgrimage to a contemporary touristic "reverse diaspora," and packaging naturalistic speech within the formal contours of iambic pentameter couplets.

Nelson continues to overtly invoke and parody Chaucer in her "General Prologue," moving on to a series of formal portraits: "The following describes the friends who went ... simplifying each to a major attribute" (12). Although portraying the members of her family and her friends (most of whom actively participate in black culture and aesthetics), some of the portraits are stereotypes, in the same way that Chaucer draws on the estates for his characters, but in this case affectionately drawn and without the social satire. The most Chaucerian — using both array and dentition to reveal character — is her sister,

4. The Canterbury Pilgrimage and African Diaspora   109

a "DIRECTOR" of a small black theater whose major attribute seems to be her Clerkish idealism:

> She had decided to be poor,
>   if that's what it would take to live for art.
>   She'd spent three decades following her heart's
>   uncompromisingly high principles,
>   making aesthetic and political
>   choices of scripts and casts ...
>   She was an ample sister, middle-aged ...
>   with one tooth missing from her ready smile,
>   a close Afro, and a bohemian style [12–13].

There is a JAZZ MUSICIAN (her brother, Mel), a "charmer," whose "California cool, go-with-the-flow/ attitude was a most endearing trait" (13). But Nelson soon breaks the mold; the retired PILOT, who, like the Knight, is characterized by a catalogue of his various eclectic accomplishments and interests, cannot be simplified to a major attribute. The "ACTIVIST," who has lost two sons to AIDS, is introduced by a brief meditation on the book of Job, which perhaps links her suffering with Griselda's. Indeed, in a modern analogue to Griselda's obedience, the Activist believes that "By serving is one comforted" (15). But a bit of satire is reserved for the affected antics of two travelers, Harmonia and Moreen, "two sisters from home ... retracing the diaspora" (21). In what Nelson suspects might be a "James Bondian disguise," they wear bright-colored outfits "bought on the continent" and they speak "in some kind of secret code" ("'You know black people always been wanderers/ but God made us too poor to pay the fare'") that they "acted like we were supposed to know" (21).

A temporal transition creates a temporary sense of dislocation, marking an end to Nelson's formal appropriation of Chaucer's *General Prologue*:

> Now I have thumbnail-sketched the company
>   of interesting people who went with me,
>   who are now (a different now) sitting
>   around a table, telling sidesplitting
>   stories, which just unfold in the exchange.
>   I interrupt, suggesting we arrange
>   a little competition, with a prize.
>   Everyone turns, with are-you-kidding? eyes.
>   Then they turn back [15].

In the spirit of Chaucer's bookish naiveté, she pokes fun at her own artificial spontaneity and pretension, suggesting that however convenient as a literary model, the competitive tale-telling trope proves strained and contrived. Nelson does nonetheless prevail in the effort to put the new wine of contemporary poetic travelogue into Chaucer's old structural bottle. Over dinner in "The

Jazz Musician's Tale" the group approaches "the subject of race,/ and how black skin, in almost every place/ we'd traveled, was a liability" (16). Over a subsequent repast in "The Activist's Tale," they discuss "the rich:/ those obscene, greedy children of the Bitch" (19). But neither race nor class—or even the topic of gender—lights a fire. "The Jazz Musician's Tale," for instance, is a short recollection of the musician's arrest and incarceration stemming from an unpaid jay-walking ticket; while the incident was initiated perhaps by the color of his skin, the infraction was nonetheless aggravated by his "laid-back" attitude in settling his debts. And the brief "Activist's Tale" simply provides an apocryphal anecdote illustrating the modern cliché that "need is the mother/ of invention," perhaps a modern version of Chaucer's idiomatic "to maken a vertu of necessitee" (1.3042).

The problem is that in Brazil's cultural milieu, their skin color is only a liability insofar as it has an alienating effect on the quest for spiritual and cultural connection. They find themselves identified chiefly by their nationality—as Americans—and, as Americans, they are both assumed to be—and are, in relative terms—both rich and powerful, "like visiting gods" (50). Nelson also finds her neat project of finding a place "sanctified by the Negro soul" complicated not only by the local exploitation of heritage sites (a pillory where slaves were "tied to posts and flogged," for instance, is crowded with touts) but also by the dynamic complexity of African and New World spirituality. And she perhaps finds Chaucer's structural template inadequate, both for a more casual and naturalistic representation of contemporary storytelling, and for allowing a space for the intimacy of meditative reflection.

Nelson does continue to tell tales, turning to a chronological narrative inhabited by a medley of discourses and framed by the narrator's quest for an understanding of how African tribal spiritual traditions were adapted to Christianity. The longest poem, "Baxia Mall," for instance, recounts a bout of alcohol-inspired "conversation catch" featuring anecdotes, urban legends, jokes, asides, and trickster tales. All relate to both the material and psychological hybridity of cultural identity. Teased by her sister, the Director, for her interest in "monk stuff," for instance, Nelson—in a Wife of Bathesque digressive reminiscence on youth and beauty—recalls teasing her sister about "her black/ favorite doll, which I said was ugly":

> "Look at that spoogly ol' black doll!" I'd scream,
>   with my *Little House* and *Little Women* dreams,
>   my brain washed white as snow...
>   But I digress.
>   Where was I? Oh yes, Africa [28].

But travel produces another kind of double consciousness. Although Nelson compares American consumerism to "self-sold" slavery, the exchange rate makes her feel "rich ... spending money/ like fountains of beneficence" (25). An Anansi story follows, recalling a time that he "switched his tool/ for the tool of his friend, the elephant bull" (25), providing both a lesson about "greed and good sense" and an apt phallic metaphor for the burden of wealth. There are several recollections of the onus of American identity and the sense of cultural and ethnic dislocation experienced during previous trips abroad. The Jazz Musician, for instance, recalls a barroom episode in which, after being ridiculed for his ignorance of the local African dialect, convincingly invents "Creole Swahili": "For several hours I drank their beers/ and taught them a language invented between my ears" (29). In his work with a Christian fellowship, the Pilot is repeatedly asked if it's true that Americans have "twenty-five different kinds of toothpaste" (26). Stuck on a sweltering runway in Burkina Faso during an incipient military coup, he muses, "'Thank God my ancestors escaped'" (29). While there are more heartening encounters, Nelson refuses to lapse into nostalgia, or to gloss over the entrenched socioeconomic inequality and gender discrimination encountered in African and diasporic African societies.

In the end, however, Nelson performs a series of cultural, spiritual, and literary syntheses. Two poems, "Da Blues" and "Olodum" (named after an Afro-Brazilian activist musical group), describe music that was inspired by similar traditions of "despair" and "poverty" but which nonetheless manifest an affirmation of life, a "cyclone of joy," celebrating "life's one-drumbeat brevity" (48). Two scatological stories from very different popular traditions—an urban legend, "The Ski Accident," about a woman skiing backwards with her pants down and a Trickster tale about why "ol' ass can't whistle"— produce libertine laughter.[9] And most importantly, after visiting both the convent in Cachoeira, founded to serve the poor, and the Nostra Senhor do Bonfim church in Salvador, dedicated to both Oxala ("a long-ago king in West Africa") and Christ, Nelson understands how it is that slaves and their descendants reconciled Candomble with Christianity. Both religions grow out of a foundational conviction "to give/ comfort to those who suffer, and to quench/ the fires of greed, injustice, and violence" (54). Poetically too, by signifying on Chaucer, Nelson adapts a dominant literary discourse to her own uses, reconfiguring the iconic expression of Western Christian pilgrimage into the contemporary phenomenon of diaspora tourism. Wallace suggests that the effect is symbiotic; Nelson's integrationist impulse "challenges the imperialist grand narrative adumbrated by Chaucer's *Canterbury Tales*."[10] But the neoformalist poem is also synthetic, a stylistic testament to the multivocal inclusivity afforded by the musical versatility of Chaucer's verse and the conceptual versatility of his structural frame.

Kicking Tongues

King-Aribisala's *Kicking Tongues* features a very different kind of pilgrimage, in this case involving a group of Nigerians traveling from the crumbling commercial center in Lagos to the new federal capital of Abuja. The event is organized by the provocatively named host, "The Black Lady The," whose "vision" is to challenge the kicking tongues—the lies, false promises, and "perversities" of the political and military leadership—"With tongues/ Which/ Kick/ The truth" (242). In what might more accurately be termed "inter-structurality,"[11] King-Aribisala appropriates Chaucer's frame in order to showcase the numerous social, political, and environmental challenges that face the emerging Third Republic in Nigeria, 40 years after the withdrawal of the British. The destructive legacy of colonialism hangs heavy, and one might assume that having provided the "materials of a nationalist English tradition," Chaucer's might be one of the tongues that could use an ideological kicking.[12] Indeed, the felicitous neologistic gerund "Chaucering" ("she begin for to talk ... Chaucering me to stand still and to listen to what she did say" [53]) manages to encapsulate the pedantry of Western linguistic and cultural norms.

King-Aribisala, however, generally eschews conventional responses, taking a "subversive attitude" toward "canonical texts, national leadership, feminist theorizing, and cultural nationalism ... [exhibiting] the utmost irreverence toward established notions about identity."[13] While the appropriation is "motivated" in Gates's sense of parodic revisioning of a canonical representative of cultural imperialism, King-Aribisala nonetheless acknowledges the continuing relevance and durability of a literary model that remains highly amenable to an egalitarian aesthetic. For Sara Upstone, King-Aribisala "seizes upon *Canterbury Tales* because it offers an incomplete potential: a journey filled with hybrid voices that might be reworked from an African perspective to challenge the inequalities of Nigerian society.... Such a journey acknowledges the colonial English culture it is based upon.... Yet ... it also powerfully interrogates the purity of these images with a retelling through African voices and circumstance."[14] But most important is the notion of pilgrimage itself, which, by temporarily suspending social barriers, provides a liminal space allowing the democratic dialogue and social cohesion needed for an imaginative transformation into "other dimensions."[15]

The poetic novel, framed by the geographical movement of a bus journey and the gradual psychological transformation of the first-person narrator, consists of a series of tales, some in poetry, some prose. The tales themselves reflect Chaucer's own generic diversity, intertextual play, and linguistic inventiveness. Indeed, in a complex pastiche, King-Aribisala draws on fable, folklore, myth, and fairy tale. She "plays on" a number of Western and African writers, and she adapts English to the rhythms and cadence of Nigerian dialects.[16] Evan Maina Mwangi suggests that King-Aribisala "extravagantly and self-referentially claims to transpose Geoffrey Chaucer's *Canterbury Tales* to an African context, despite the fact that its link to Chaucer might not go much farther than mentioning him and his *Canterbury Tales*."[17] It's true that in "The Postgraduate English Major: This literature life" among a range of allusions to the Western literary canon, Chaucer is generically associated with humor — with "laughter" and "sounding absurdums" (98–99). But the similarities between the texts arguably go beyond what Mwangi describes as a "distant echo" (141).

The long "General Prologue" is a parodic inversion of the original, the effects of a repressive and violent military regime standing out in sharp contrast to Chaucer's seasonal and spiritual renewal and leisured bonhomie. Instead of spring, "The killing comes again" (1). A mono- and disyllabic staccato drumbeat throughout mimics the "stamp-stepping high ... of army boots," the "rhythms of a mortar's beat," and "the knocking hollow round of/ Skulls" (1–3). These are "Beats/ Not of the/ Heart"(4). Nigeria is a spiritual wasteland, and, perhaps echoing T. S. Eliot's own parodic echoing of Chaucer's opening lines, these travelers are "Departing from their dead-living lives" (9): "Our gods/— Such as they are —/ Have/ Left/ Us" (3). It's not only the violence of military rule and civil strife that has caused a "waking death.... In death of silenced tongues" (2). It is also the eponymous kicking tongues "In politician mouths/ Which open wide in promise/ Deceit coiled tight in bright-red tongues" (4). The host, The Black Lady The (the unusual name variously signifies her skin color, her mourning, her evolving identity, and her aesthetic and ideological aversion to pink), recruits individuals "who cared, really cared about what was happening to our country": "Those were the criteria I used.... They had to be individualistic but they also had to have a sense of unity, however dormant. And they had to have something to say with their tongues or their lives which is of course a kind of tongue" (20).

In a trenchant inversion, this is not a merry company; each of the participants "In spite of differences in sex, in class, in tribe" (6) has "A yearning/ For/ Some other life/ And need" (5). This journey is not made as an act of thanksgiving nor are the tales told for pleasure. Rather, the journey is an obligatory penitential act, an act of "atonement" (9) done "In recompense and shame" (9), reflecting the sense of collective guilt for Nigeria's ills. There is no feast; the group is "wanted-triumph-fasting/ In the wilderness of pain": "Our sustenance/ Shall be the stories/ Which we tell/ And listen to" (7). But the mourning is leavened with the hope that telling tales will lead to "journeys into otherness" (7), or, in The Black Lady The's more colloquial prose: "hopefully, by each and every one of us placing ourselves in another's shoes, so to speak, we shall be able to enter, at least imaginatively, into ... each other's lives" (12).

Reading Chaucer's texts as a "literary response as a postcolonial writer" to Anglo-Norman culture, John Bowers suggests that Chaucer asserts English nationalism by countering "the stereotype of 'otherness' that a dominant culture maintains to render manageable subaltern people."[18] Bowers suggests that Chaucer's nationalist aesthetic is accomplished primarily through the *General Prologue*, which provides not mere English "types" but "a crowded pageant of uniquely crafted personalities" that asserts "an English multiculturalism that is as eclectic as it is eccentric" (56). In her own "truly national fiction," King-Aribisala mimics Chaucer's structural blueprint, providing a wide social variety: milk-maid, soldier, flight attendant, palm-wine tapster, cook, Sultan.[19] The Black Lady The proclaims that she will describe her companions ("Their dress, rank, sex, their placement/ Such as it is/ Their profession" [11]), but foregrounding Chaucer's narrative artifice in the *General Prologue*, King-Aribisala eschews a series of formal portraits.[20] The Black Lady The has pre-screened each of the participants; she puts their "lives into some kind of context in poetry form" (69), often providing a formal poetic prologue preceding the respective tale and emphasizing the sometimes tenuous association found in Chaucer between tale and teller. The autobiographical prologues and tales often stylistically fit the tellers; "The Dentist: The secessioning teeth for pre-supposed sweet," for instance, relies on metaphors of orality and decay to represent the tempting corruption of nationalism.

The tales cover a number of topics—women, colonialism, education, leadership, social class, traditionalism, and spirituality—described as "phases," and addressing "so-called important issues" that plague Nigeria. A short list includes governmental corruption, gross economic inequality, environmental degradation, provincial patriotism, and the corrosive psychology of power. But the most important issue is the "silenced tongues" of women, whose subjection—sanctified by tradition, religion, and tribal custom—is common to each phase. Indeed, many of the women either exhibit Griseldan suffering or are inspired with the Wife of Bath's defiance of sanctioned gender expectations. Men have their share of the blame, relying on outmoded social and belief systems, such as the purdah, polygamy, and sanctioned pubescent conjugality, in order to exercise their power over women. But women too are complicit. "The Tale of the Medical Doctor," for instance, recounts the troubled teller's struggle with the guilt of filial "disobedience" in the face of her mother's insistence that she be "dutiful" and marry the village Chief: "You are a woman; our lot is to be sacrificed and sacrifice is a good thing" (49). Her eventual acquiescence, metaphorically realized in a bizarre ritual that involves imbibing in a gourd of the Chief's urine, has a quite sobering effect on the company: "The coffee which we were drinking grew stale in our mouths in the silence that followed" (50).

As in *The Canterbury Tales*, the company never reaches its destination, the bus breaking down just short of Abuja. The novel does, however, provide both closure and "spiritual hope" (239) for Nigerian solidarity and democracy: "I had a vision when I got these people together for the trip; it was that our love for Nigeria should be 'set in order'; and I think this dream has been realized and that's even before we begin to deliberate on so-called important issues" (240). The Black Lady The, colloquially comic but nonetheless "authoritarian," "monopolizing" (68), and self-righteous, models the kind of transformation needed to get beyond divisive "bickering" and "destructioning/ Divisive-divisioning/ Hate" (75).[21] She is chastened, for instance, by her harsh misjudgment of a British national participating on the trip: "Kicking Tongue/ Mine/ Which/ Lashed Out/ In/ Miss-/ Directed/ Hit/ At/ Things/ Not Under-/ Stood" (188–89). And despite her aversion to both tribal Nigerian patriarchal authority and the gender conformity represented by pink "traditional African dress" (15), she becomes "great friends" with an Oba (a "highest-ranking chief") and has "been known to wear pink on occasion": "I'm even going to change my name I think ... to The Lady" (240).

Jennifer Wenzel finds King-Aribisala's parody of *The Canterbury Tales* "problematic" in part because "the book ultimately sublimates its political protest by turning Nigeria's future over to a decidedly Christian evangelical God" (an interpretation King-Aribisala has reiterated in interviews).[22] And indeed, like *The Canterbury Tales*, which concludes with "som vertuous sentence" (X, 63) in the guise of the Parson's pointing out the penitential path to celestial Jerusalem, it is religious representatives who have the last word in *Kicking Tongues*. The epistolary "Tale of the Deaconess," addressed to St. Paul, describes the teller's struggle to get beyond reading Paul's letters as efforts to subjugate women "under the guise of Biblical injunction" (222), and ultimately finds the essence of the "Spirit of Woman" in Jesus's "humility, compassion, and subjection" (225). The jovial Pastor appears to have some affinity with Chaucer's ecclesiastical rogues; like an updated version of the Monk, he "Could be seen dressed in Yves St. Laurent suits/ His feet sporting well-polished-shiny boots/ In one ear/ A small precious pearl" (216). His prologue, "Heart attack," recounts how his pastoral flock resents his materialism and waits for his divine comeuppance; but they find to their surprise that the Pastor's heart "beats/ With a love/ Jesus love/ For them" (220). His tale — a humorous Nigerian television interview with the prophet Isaiah — is, like Chaucer's Parson's, about personal repentance as a prerequisite for social salvation. Indeed, reflecting King-Aribisala's own sentiments (her book is dedicated to God), The Lady concludes that "everything will be all right with Nigeria once we're right with God" (239).

Bailey's Café

Perhaps a more complex case of tropological revision is presented by Naylor's *Bailey's Café*. Although it is widely suggested that Naylor is "African Americanizing *The Canterbury Tales*," the invocation of Chaucer is certainly playful, more symbolic than substantive.[23] Set within the context of Jim Crow, Hiroshima, and the Holocaust, the novel is narrated by the cantankerous, gregarious, pseudo-eponymous owner whose urban grill provides a temporary rest stop for several grotesquely abused and emotionally destitute women. Rather than a pilgrimage or tale-telling contest, the narratives are structured around a musical motif (invoking lullaby, symphony, jazz, and blues) with Bailey serving as Maestro: "sit back and enjoy the music" (4).[24] "The Vamp" (in jazz, the introduction of a repeating sequence of chords) provides a warm up, introducing two customers—Carrie, a puritanical religious fundamentalist, and Sugar Man, a pimp—from opposite ends of the spectrum of sexual morality. Both are apparently "one note players," "flat and predictable" (36); but "just take 'em one key down" and both are guardians of female sexuality. Paradoxically, but perhaps reflecting the schizophrenic view of women sponsored by the Judeo-Christian tradition, the fundamentalist views her daughter "Angel" as a "bitch in heat," while the pimp works hard "to protect his women" who are "a little like children; but a whole lot like angels" (37).

The predation of female sexuality and familial betrayal provide the harmony for the variable sad melodies played in "The Jam," constituting the individual tales of Bailey's desperate customers. Sadie, desperately searching for love, is a wino and "twenty-five cent whore" (42), "The One the Coathanger Missed" according to her sadistic mother. Eve, like her namesake, is brutally cast out of her home and church by her adopted preacher father ("Godfather") after he finds her unknowingly masturbating. "Sweet Esther" at 12 years old is given by her older brother to his boss to gratify his sado-masochistic fantasies. The beautiful Mary, filled with self-loathing for her sexual desires, brutally disfigures herself in an effort to reconcile her distorted self-image. Jesse Bell, a heroin addict, has lost her husband and son in her efforts to maintain a link with her cultural roots. There is Stanley (a.k.a. Miss Maple), whose preference for the utility and freedom of women's clothes acts as a metaphor for his social emasculation and defiance of gender and racial restrictions. And Mariam, an Ethiopian Jew, whose mother had the midwives "close her up ... tightly" (154) following her purification ceremony, but who becomes unaccountably pregnant at 14 and is cruelly exiled from her community. Although these women arrive at the strange, "mobile" (29) café "from all over" (3), all are at a "hopeless crossroads" (229). The virtual grill provides a "place to take a breather" (29) before either stepping out back to the "void" at "the end of the world" (71) or, for some, finding their way to Eve's boardinghouse, a refuge that provides some chance of recovery and redemption. The thematic harmony of their wrenching testimonies has been variously interpreted, but since several of the women's narratives have biblical resonance, Naylor clearly is chiefly interested in a critique and revisioning of Judeo-Christian myth.[25] The novel nonetheless ends with a communal celebration of the birth of Mariam's son ("the place went wild"), a Christ figure whose "lone cry of new life" (23) mirrors the epigraphic lullaby and temporarily lifts the collective blues with "an explosion of new hope" and the faint possibility of "a whole new era" (162).

Since Naylor has a habit of "signifying" on her canonical forbears—most conspicuously invoking Dante's *Inferno* in *Linden Hills,* and Shakespeare throughout her oeuvre—a number of readers have found, in addition to Scripture, Chaucer's *Canterbury Tales* to be an important intertext.[26] For Donna Rifkind, "If [*Bailey's Café*] reminds you a little bit of *The Canterbury Tales,* it's supposed to: Chaucer's host at the Tabard Inn was Harry Bailly, and Naylor's chorus of tale-telling voices echoes its 14th-century ancestor."[27] Charles E. Wilson, Jr., finds that "the collective pilgrimage highlighted in *The Canterbury Tales* is taken ... inside Bailey's café"; and for Lynn Alexander, "Borrowed from Chaucer, Naylor's unnamed cafe owner links the stories of various women, creating the framework for the individual tales.... It is the narrator who provides clues as to relationships among characters and as to how to read their stories."[28]

But from a Chaucerian's point of view the intertextual invocation might appear tenuous, and perhaps the more pertinent question is how the invocation enhances Naylor's text. There is no pilgrimage, no tale-telling contest, no formal portraits. True, the first-person narrator retains the café's previous name, and "Because of that, folks think my name is Bailey and I see no reason to tell them otherwise" (28). But Chaucer's Harry Bailly is not a first-person narrator, and Naylor's narrator—scarred by his experiences in the Pacific theater of the Second World War who discovers the café when he is "hanging on the edge" (29)—has little in common with his literary forebear (apart from a troublesome spouse). Structurally, the two works are quite different as well; as we've seen, collections of short autobiographical stories on a shared theme are often given the imprimatur of being "Chaucerian," providing an epistemological frame, but in this case it is the blues that provides a thematic, structural, and stylistic unity. (One might add that any number of jazz or blues artists would fit the allusion: Buster Bailey, Deford Bailey, Kid Bailey,

Mildred Bailey, etc.) Indeed, once citing the Chaucerian connection critics often go on to list the fundamental differences between the two works, recognizing for instance that Bailey is an assumed name, or that the café is not a destination but as Bailey calls it, a "hopeless crossroads."[29]

This backpedalling is not simply over aesthetic ground but reflects the ideological baggage — the weight of linguistic, cultural, and aesthetic normativity — that attends Chaucer's iconic canonical status. Dorothy Perry Thompson, for instance, suggests that focus on Naylor's literary intertextuality constitutes one of various "Eurocentric approaches" to her work, less fruitful or relevant than her search for an authentic voice or her African womanist refiguration of myth and gendered ideology.[30] Naylor's engagement with Chaucer's text therefore is often read less as substantive, stylistic, or symbiotic revision than as symbolic reference, with Naylor both indulging in a counter-canonical critique and positioning her work within the master discourse of a Western cultural aesthetic. For Wilson, for instance,

> Without question, Naylor makes a political statement with these gestures. She proves to the literary establishment that she, an African American woman, does know and can emulate the works of the masters. And in so doing, Naylor validates not only herself, but African American literature in general. Instead of displacing the white fathers, she joins them and carves for herself a comfortable literary space.[31]

Elsewhere, Wilson reads more thematically, suggesting that Naylor models *Bailey's Café* on the *Canterbury Tales,* "successfully bridging the African American and European literary traditions and disregarding, in yet another context, formerly imposed boundaries of separation."[32] Similarly, Wood suggests that while Naylor acknowledges "the universal canonicity of Chaucer's work," the use of Chaucer's structure "necessitates her mastery of Chaucer's text to the degree that she can rewrite it."[33] And for Margot Anne Kelley, "through this process of allusion and response, Naylor is able to articulate her own place within the canon, critically examine her precursors, and remind readers that diverse literary texts can represent the multiple truths of our lives in ways that can fruitfully, mutually exist."[34]

While the Chaucerian reference certainly accentuates both the penitential tenor of the customers' sad stories and the quest for spiritual and social renewal, many Chaucerians might agree with those readers who find the ephemeral invocation of *The Canterbury Tales* having less to do with Chaucer than his ontological status as canonical representative. The case of one customer, Jesse Bell, however, does provide some evocative parallels with the Wife of Bath. Jesse Bell, a heroin addict who has been "thrown to the dogs" by her family, has been most conspicuously read as a revisioning of Deuteronomy's Jezebel, the shadowy Phoenician wife of King Ahab and notorious temptress who brings her worship of Baal to Israel, and whose apostasy is as reprehensible as her influence over her husband. She loses in a sacrificial showdown with the prophet Elijah, is murdered, and her corpse ravaged by dogs. Like her biblical predecessor, Jesse Bell marries into the King family and has a two-decade losing battle with an Uncle Eli over her efforts to maintain an emotional and cultural connection with her lower class, "coloured" family: "White folks were Uncle Eli's god. And it was a god I wasn't buying" (128). The collard greens, biscuits, and oxtail soup that she prepares for her husband are denounced as "slave food," and like her biblical and literary predecessors she uses her sexuality, in a quite amusing scene involving a form of culinary cunnilingus, to educate her husband:

> I run me a warm bath.... I go into our bedroom, carrying one of my pies, dressed the same way I stepped out of that tub.... I laid back on the pillows. Took out a slice.... And wedged it right between my legs. It was time for the first lesson. Husband, I said pointing, this is sweet potato pie. Didn't have a bit of trouble after that. Except it was all the man wanted for dinner for the next month [126].

In order to sketch out Jesse Bell's character — she may be a "real nasty bitch" but is nonetheless "a good wife" — Naylor turns to a more familiar figure with the linguistic authority to tell her own tale. Jesse Bell's battle with patriarchal authority and her domestic efforts to educate her husband have obvious Chaucerian echoes. She achieves and maintains her socially advantageous marriage by providing the "best poon tang east of the Mississippi" (124). Like the Wife of Bath, who knows how to manipulate and placate her husbands' egos,[35] Jesse Bell feigns jealousy: "He'd get tickled over my being a little on the jealous side, and if truth's told, I played it up a bit more than it really was. Makes a man feel special that way. And thinking about it, he was special cause I never had a problem about her" (125). "Her" is Jesse's long-time lover; and although unlike the Wife of Bath, Jesse Bell is not concerned with defending her sexuality, she is condemned by the authority of the same patriarchal texts that dog her medieval predecessor. Her divorce and the loss of her son, for instance, are accomplished by a public smearing afforded by Uncle Eli's access to the press: "I didn't have no friends putting out *The Herald Tribune*. And it's all about who's in charge of keeping the records, ain't it?" (120).[36] And even within the refuge of Bailey's café a religious fundamentalist repeatedly wields her "dog-eared Bible" (136), indulging in the same promiscuous and prejudicial exegesis that the Wife of Bath seeks to counter in her *Prologue*:

> Jesse will throw down her fork and start cussing something furious which only spurs Carrie on: And I'm suspicious that she takes a little poetic license with some of those verses:
> And the Lord saith, Yeah, yeah, you're gonna burn and fry because of vile affections...

> I'm not a church-going man and don't want to criticize somebody else's beliefs. But it started becoming clear to me that Jesse's salvation wasn't the thing uppermost on Carrie's mind [136–7].

Whether Jesse Bell will be saved remains unclear, because like all the "folks" in the café, she is "in transition": "they come midway their stories and go on" (223). Although a victim of character assassination, her resistance to Uncle Eli's integrationist ideology and white idolatry is not as self-destructive or hopeless as her biblical namesake's since she survives to tell the tale in her own voice. But neither is she afforded an ostensible fairy-tale ending of domestic accord found in the Wife of Bath's case as her struggle with patriarchy extends beyond gender, encompassing issues of cultural identity and class. Indeed, the lack of resolution is in keeping thematically with the mood of the book:

> If this was like that sappy violin music on Make Believe Ballroom, we could wrap it all up with a lot of happy endings to leave you feeling real good that you took the time to listen. But I don't believe that life is supposed to make you feel good, or to make you feel miserable either. Life is just supposed to make you feel [223].

Naylor's emphasis on the provisional nature of Bailey's name seems to be playfully postmodern, an instance, perhaps, of intertextual tricksterism. Sanders finds it "significant that the name was already there when the host-narrator of Naylor's sequence of tales ... arrived": "the notion that the building, the narrative architecture, in which these stories take place was pre-existent is crucial."[37] Sanders doesn't elaborate, but the implication is that Naylor self-consciously and overtly writes within, and subverts, established Western literary tradition. If so, Chaucer's narrative structure presumably affords a model for plurality and precedent for exploring transhistorical issues of sexuality and patriarchal oppression. And as with Chaucer, notoriously resistant to structural and thematic closure, the mood, in keeping with the musical metaphor that runs throughout, is modal rather than tonal, ending with "more questions than answers" (234).

While Naylor's subtle reference to Chaucer's host in *Bailey's Café* suggests the penitence and salvation of Christian pilgrimage and accentuates the customers' struggle for self-determination and search for redemption, more compelling perhaps is the politics of intertextuality raised by the invocation. Nelson and King-Aribisala, however, more overtly signpost their appropriation of *The Canterbury Tales*, representing physical journeys made by groups seeking a sense of communal identity. In *The Cachoeira Tales* the quest is for the authenticity of a common diasporic heritage. More specifically, Nelson is interested in cultural synthesis, particularly in the adaptation of Christianity to indigenous West African religions. And her appropriation of Chaucer mimics aesthetically the spiritual synthesis that she discovers in her poem. In *Kick-*

4. The Canterbury Pilgrimage and African Diaspora 121

ing Tongues, a political action pilgrimage is made in the hope of the social transformation needed to construct national unity in a country traumatized by colonialism, civil war, and governmental corruption. The bus provides a liminal space where social hierarchies are suspended, allowing the democratic dialogue and individual testimony needed to forge a sense of collective identity.[38] Both types of community must necessarily embrace a multiplicity of identities, and Chaucer's narrative frame lends continuity to the episodic narratives in each text. Both authors also merge Chaucer's first-person narrative persona with the Host, creating deftly comic narrators who are naive alter egos of their authors. While similar to Chaucer's Host, both loquacious narrators provide sometimes suspect interpretive direction, both are nonetheless ultimately crafted to embody the transformative discovery expected of the reader.

All the authors are concerned with cultural, social — and especially female — exclusion and oppression, particularly as it is sanctioned by Christianity. Female subjugation cuts across geographical and social borders and perhaps in an effort to provide a transhistorical perspective and canonical legacy, Chaucer is an obvious choice given his own apparent concern with women suffering under various patriarchal dictates of gender decorum. But all three works are also concerned with spirituality and identity, and certainly it is Chaucer's association with pilgrimage that is paramount. Other literary models might suggest themselves — Dante, Langland, Bunyan. But Chaucer's is, as Reiss suggests, an "untypical" pilgrimage, less concerned with sin and penitence, than with "the fallible human world."[39]

5

The Chaucer Brand

Fiske maintains that those cultural commodities that are relevant, providing meaningful resources out of which social aspirations and identities can be articulated, will be made popular. The various modes of popular intertextual engagement with Chaucer's texts yield a number of functions addressing social relations, and notwithstanding the conservatism of Chaucerian mystery fiction, the prevailing tenor is certainly populist. Across the popular corpus one finds Chaucer repeatedly associated with an egalitarian disdain for pretension and elitism, and the narrative structure of *The Canterbury Tales* is most often appropriated as a democratic forum accommodating the voices of the middle and the marginalized. If Chaucer's reproduction in popular culture thus reflects the continued viability of his texts and persona as meaningful symbolic resources for addressing social relations, Chaucer's name would presumably enjoy some commercial viability for similar reasons. While no commodity fetish, Chaucer's name does nonetheless possess some metonymic power to address consumer interests. And in his capacity as a brand identity Chaucer serves a number of functions that are somewhat different from those who approach Chaucer as a creative resource. As a cultural commodity, Chaucer is most often associated with tradition, specifically, British cultural heritage, historical authenticity, and artisanal craftsmanship. The appeal is to the upscale consumer with a sense of nostalgia, Anglo nationalism, and the distinctive taste for niche commodities. And as the iconic representative of a canonical literary tradition, Chaucer's predominant semiotic function appears to reflect consumer anxiety about the continued efficacy of the social distinction that attends the acquisition of high literacy.

Consumption is often approached as a form of social positioning or social expression. The theory of cultural branding, however, suggests that the most successful marketing associates the product with an identity myth, that is, a simple fiction that addresses cultural concerns.[1] The assumption is that cultural icons, that is, "society's foundational compass points," can be constructed as brands epitomizing compelling myths that palliate collective anxieties and desires.[2] Collective interests fluctuate with historical context, but from his earliest laureation, Chaucer has consistently been a "totem of Englishness, at once linguistic, national, and personal."[3] In order to sell the war cause both to the weary British and skeptical Americans, for instance, Powell and Pressburger's *A Canterbury Tale* (1944), a "Why We Fight" film vetted by the Ministry of Information, invokes *The Canterbury Tales* to promote a sense of national identity and a cultural heritage worth preserving. Andrew Moor suggests that in the film, "'Pilgrimage' metaphorically stands for the pursuit of the war effort itself, while the tightly knit feudal organization of Chaucer's pilgrims is emblematic of the film's ideal community — a mythic model for the nation, bound by common purpose."[4] In the opening sequence, as a voice-over reads from the *General Prologue*, Chaucer's pilgrims appear on horseback; the Knight lets loose a falcon, and in a jump-cut the Knight is transformed into a soldier and his bird becomes a Spitfire. The narrator tells us that while the "hills and valleys are the same" now a "new kind of pilgrim," the kind that rides in armored transports, inhabits the Pilgrims' Way. The film, according to Powell, was intended to explain "to the Americans and to our own people, the spiritual values and traditions we were fighting for."[5] Those values and traditions are embodied in a preindustrial cultural heritage — the countryside, cathedral, and village community — for which in the opening sequence Chaucer serves as iconic shorthand.

The images of the cratered city of Canterbury itself, especially contrasted with the monumental majesty of the cathedral (which escaped serious damage in the 1942 Baedeker bombing raid), provides a visceral and shocking reminder of what was at stake beyond spiritual traditions. Amid the ruins, however, are signs that both identify the shops that once stood on the rubble and direct passersby to the sites where the businesses have relocated. In other words, although representing a rejection of "consumerism and materialism in favour of transcendental values and social cohesion," the film ends fostering an image not only of native resilience and fortitude, but also of the indomitable strength of British commercial enterprise.[6] Today, the city is the center of the Chaucer commodities industry and the newest kind of pilgrim is the tourist seeking a heritage experience. But for Douglas Caulkins, Canterbury continues to represent a form of "resistance to European dominance," and an important contribution to national identity politicking is "The Canterbury Tales" visitor attraction: "Strategically located on the rail line to the continent, Canterbury, and the heritage site, are part of the defense of English language and literature within the EU. While the designers of the attraction may not have had ... the politics of the EU in mind, Canterbury Tales is an important representation of Englishness for visitors from the continent."[7]

"The Canterbury Tales" visitor attraction offers a form of cultural tourism, seeking to satisfy the contemporary touristic desire for casual education and a sense of historical authenticity. The venue offers a "staged authenticity," that is, a performed simulation of a fiction that presumably embodies historical realism.[8] Costumes are provided for children, and authenticity is performed insofar as visitors become, for about 30 minutes, a group of pilgrims, part of a constructed, closely-packed mock *communitas*, armed with hand-held speakers, reenacting the fictional pilgrimage (followed ten minutes later by another group). Staged authenticity is often judged by pre-existing expectations and seeks to satisfy projected stereotypes. Inside, in stark contrast to the commercialized modernity of St. Margaret's Street, one encounters a series of tableaux drawing on a range of popular sensational associations. The Tabard is dark and dirty, its scruffy grotesques passed out by the hearth. Rats and thrown slops add to the atmosphere of cramped and dirty streets, and the visitor is assured that fleas and thieves lurk in a dormitory scene. Chaucer himself is represented as an unusually sober and serious figure — goateed, black-robed, and carrying a crooked walking stick. As the pilgrims are horsed, he provides brief snarky glosses on the *General Prologue*: he hopes that the journey is "not too parochial" for the well-traveled knight (who holds his short straw and wears his rust-stained gypon); the Prioress he finds "insufferably vain"; and the Wife of Bath's dentition, we are told, is a sign of "lewdness."

    The handful of tales themselves are by necessity schematically summarized (and available in a variety of translations), complemented with visuals in the form of projected slides and pop-up flats. There is a hint at Chaucer's narrative links: Harry Bailly, for instance, praises the Nun's Priest's virility, and a great periodic fart by the Miller provides a dramatic end to the *Knight's Tale*. Reflecting a desire for closure that is found throughout the popular corpus, the pilgrimage is completed, bringing us to the two highlights of Christ Church Cathedral: Becket's reconstructed shrine (with a string of pilgrims' offerings) and the colorful tomb of the Black Prince (with whom, Chaucer informs us, he fought in France). Ellis accurately describes this as "a rather bizarre doubling of the original monument that is only a few hundred yards away," but the fabricated tableau offers a more authentic imaginative medieval experience than Becket's actual sanitized shrine with its dramatic, modernist sculpture (three jagged iron swords, one broken, poised over the site where Becket was murdered) or Edward's tarnished tomb surrounded by protective fencing.[9] We are told that the "spirit of St. Thomas lives on," one assumes in the healthy tourism of Canterbury rather than in the issue of ecclesiastical privilege and civil authority revived in recent scandals. Tourism has been compared to secular pilgrimage, constituting a quest for authenticity and for a sense of genuine society, often located in the past, or at least somewhere else.[10] Commercialism and obsolete technology can undermine the perception of authenticity, and some might experience the simulated historical venue as artificial kitsch.[11] But consumer evaluation provided by TripAdvisor suggests that the attraction is perceived to be a worthwhile diversion, the gripes largely reserved for the cost and dated audio-visual effects, suggesting that what is desired is a more authentic mimesis for the money.[12]

Since souvenirs both prolong the immediate heritage experience and certify the authenticity of one's visit, the gift shop provides tourists' transhistorical desire for commemorative tokens. Here one finds a plethora of commercial, pocket-change products offering everything from pencils and erasers to tea cozies and tie clips, usually branded to validate one's visit to the "The Canterbury Tales" attraction itself and clearly targeting school children, and, at the risk of stereotyping, the more senior traveler. Alcoholic beverages figure predominantly in a Chaucer mythology of convivial social inclusion. Latter-day customer-pilgrims are sometimes offered a complimentary beverage after the rigors of the simulated pilgrimage, and the gift shop offers a whole line of artisanal spirits (mead, sloe gin, old jenny) bearing the Geoffrey Chaucer label. Should one overindulge, there is "Chaucer's Hangover Cure," an inefficacious concoction "prepared and blended using the traditional apothecaries knowledge from medieval times." The cure is packaged with a colored woodcut of the Friar (from Caxton's second edition of *The Canterbury Tales*) with the motto, "He knew the tavernes well in every town." And if you are looking for something more substantial, like a biography, there is G. K. Chesterton's *Chaucer* (1932), underscoring the impression that what is being marketed here among the sachets, pencil pouches, and kitchen towels is a romantic nostalgia not only for domestic simplicity but more importantly for a sense of communal inclusiveness, largely secular and desaturated of Chesterton's sense of the unifying force of transcendent spirituality.[13] Chesterton might also be serviceable in promoting the nationalist self-assertion that Caulkins detects. Chesterton's Chaucer (in particular, his native traits of modesty, "self-effacing sociability," broad humor, "irresponsible individualism," and "abstract liberality underlying concrete conservatism") is not only the father of English poetry but also the "Father of his Country," an "emblem of England," "as large as the land and as old as the nation."[14]

While cultural branding seeks to construct simple fictions that address consumer desires and concerns (i.e., for an authentic touristic experience of British cultural heritage and its recreational accoutrements), brand associations can also be self-expressive, invoking a number of lifestyle orientations. The Chaucer brand is largely affiliated with upscale products, targeting the consumer with the leisure time and distinctive taste for preindustrial artisanal products. The Bargetto Winery, appealing to consumers with a relish for the organic quality of domestic craftsmanship, sells mead and dessert wines under the Chaucer's Cellars label ("without the addition of artificial flavors"), meant to "be enjoyed in the tradition of Medieval England" and offering "a pilgrimage in sensory delight."[15] Tapping into the association of poetic inspiration with drink, Wedgwood's Canterbury Pilgrims' Mug features a reproduction of Blake's "Canterbury Pilgrims," and on the bottom, we are given Chaucer's two most significant biographical attributes: "Poet Laureat, in the twelfth year of Richard II, 1389, obtained a grant of an annual allowance of wine." The oddest item associating the poet with alcoholic inspiration is the limited edition Royal Doulton "Geoffrey Chaucer Toby Mug" featuring the poet's bust with pilgrims on the handles (modeled on the Ellesmere images) as though sprung from Chaucer's imagination.[16] The drinking mugs are also a manifestation of Chaucer's relation with quality manual arts and several British pottery and fine china manufacturers carry a "Chaucer" style or have produced commemorative plates, tiles, or figurines of the pilgrims. Similarly invoking ideas of quality and traditional styling, a number of furniture and household fixtures carry the Chaucer name, including the Tempo Chaucer Pub Collection ("hand-crafted iron work"), Klaussner Georgian-style tables, rustic furniture made from solid oak (Oak Furniture Land), and Quorum art-deco light fixtures. One also finds Chaucer's name associated, not surprisingly, with upscale travel accessories (Dr. Koffer Fine Leather Accessories Chaucer Travel Bag). Such products attest to the Chaucer brand as a free-floating signifier for quality craftsmanship, comforting domesticity, traditional design, reliability, and trustworthiness. But brand associations are not necessarily coherent. Perhaps by virtue of the Host's characterization of his fellow pilgrim as a "poppet," or a long tradition of construing Chaucer's poetry for children, "Chaucer" also appears as a frequent name for collectible plush toys (e.g., Boyd's Bears "Chaucer the Cat"; the "Chaucer Bear" by Russ Berrie and Co.; Jellycat's "Chaucer Dog").

The logos available on a variety of so-called lifestyle products (e.g., casual wear, coffee mugs, book bags) available from online merchandisers for niche-market commodities attest to the range of eclectic, sometimes contradictory semiotic functions that Chaucer serves. Diana Crane suggests that T-shirts, the most common Chaucer-branded product available, act as vehicles for expressing identity politics and lifestyle orientation.[17] Perhaps the most common T-shirt — featuring a version of what has become Hoccleve's iconic illustration of Chaucer — packages the poet as a purveyor of innocuous, pithy proverbial lore[18]:

"Ful wys is he that can himselven knowe!"
"That he is gentil that doth gentil dedis."
"There's never a new fashion but it's old."
"The guilty think all talk is of themselves."

Chaucer has long been valued as an observer of human nature and mild moralist, and the fondness for the Chaucerian aphorism has a long history, dating back at least to the Renaissance with Thomas Speght's 1602 edition of Chaucer's works which included marginal fists noting "Sentences and Prouerbes."[19] Presumably reflecting the fatalist perspicuity of the wearer, Chaucer here is the common man's philosophical poet, pious but not didactic, with benign, paternalistic insights—rendered quaintly archaic, if not comic, by the faux Middle English — into the venial flaws of human nature (i.e., gossip, hypocrisy, self-delusion).

But by far the most common refrain in self-expressive lifestyle products is a curious mix of symbolic associations embodying both an assertion and disavowal of social distinction and exclusivity. There is, for instance, the privileged burden of Chaucer as an educational requirement:

"Student of Chaucer/ Have somme pitee."

A related theme is what Andrew Ross sees as staple popular culture resentment or disrespect for the intellectual[20]:

"'The greatest scholars are not usually the wisest people'
Geoffrey Chaucer."

One also finds a prominent strain of assertive and self-aggrandizing cultural literacy:

"The Renaissance is a lie some old dudes made up to make the Middle Ages look bad."

"CHAUCER. Because Shakespeare was too easy."

Industry gripes embody a self-conscious irony of disaffection and distinction:

"Save the Holidays: Move the MLA Convention"

"When Adam delf, and Eve span/ Who had to publish two books to/ get tenure?"

And then there is the bizarre confessional, a bit of high-minded vulgarity which requires a modicum of Chaucerian literacy to recognize its apocryphal status, and whose humor depends upon the incongruity of the sentiment and the attribution:

"'I don't jerk off in my parents' basement anymore'
Geoffrey Chaucer"

As leisure clothing that blurs social differences, T-shirts may express mass informality, but because textual knowledge of Chaucer retains vestiges of educational privilege and the attendant sociocultural capital, the T-shirts serve to both assert and disavow status.[21] One might consider, for example, the "Chaucer is my homeboy" T-shirt with its odd combination of elite assertion and erstwhile retro urban street credibility. Such a familiar sentiment of amity has a long pedigree and is in the spirit of Dryden's declaration that he has "a Soul congenial to" Chaucer's.[22] In this case, approaching the product as an example of popular culture consumption, the linguistic dissonance of the logo partakes in the paradoxical interplay of ideological domination and subordination that Fiske finds in the field of popular culture: "Popular culture is the culture of the subordinated and disempowered and thus always bears within it signs of power relations, traces of the forces of domination and subordination that are central to our social system.... Equally, it shows signs of resisting or evading these forces: popular culture contradicts itself."[23] Thus, the logo is at once an assertion of educational status and a concession that the cultural capital which such attainment brings, which once might have carried some socioeconomic currency, is no longer necessarily operative (c.f., "I study medieval literature/ Because that's where the money is"). Those who have homeboys—a term originating in American Black slang of the 1940s, and adopted by Black and Chicano street gangs in the 1970s, then hip-hop, rap, and youth culture in general—are provocatively not part of the socioeconomic elite. On the one hand, we have a concession of cultural impotence and an odd solidarity of the rebellious dispossessed (those who study Chaucer and have homeboys are similarly disenfranchised) at the same time that we have an assertion of low-level defiance, with the Chaucer aficionado somehow in league with ethnic, youth, and musical subcultures.

A similar dialectic—the assertion of social distinction and disaffection, of subordination and opposition—can be found in the semiotic register of products sold through *Geoffrey Chaucer Hath a Blog*.[24] The "marketplace" draws on the rhetoric of resistance, utilizing anticommercial rhetoric that disavows commodification in order to market the products ("If ye fynde it noysome, tel me and ich shal remoue it"). The poet's "liverie" is intended for fans, whose social connection can be expressed through shared consumption:

"Woldstow have a mighti/plowe or a tinye oon?"

"WTS? = whatte the swyve?"

"Swynke, drynke, swyve & aftir, make retraccioun"

"Okaye, so/sometymes it/ raineth in March:/ make notte a chancerye case of the whole mattere."

"Ther sholde be a daunse/ called/ the bradshawe shifte."

"Maketh motor for to runne/ Shoopen us to heigh-waye/ No aventure shal we shunne/In what-evir cometh ower waye" ("Born to Waxen Wood" T-shirt)

Like the blog itself, the livery logos have the appeal of providing the privileged pleasure of a multiple-access exclusivity. That is, the wearer presumably possesses the educational competence allowing access to a number of high and low cultural discourses required to decipher the coded puns (spam, text slang, Chaucer's poetry, Harley lyrics/ Harley Davidson, Steppenwolf).[25] But the pleasure of the popular is by definition oppositive. For Henry Jenkins, fan writing "can be characterized as a type of textual 'poaching' ... a strategy for appropriating materials produced by the dominant culture industry and reworking them into terms which better serve subordinate or subcultural interests."[26] Certainly part of the pleasure here also comes from the poaching and parody of mass media forms and academic discourse (e.g., the professional habit of making a chancery case or fetish of textual criticism). Fandom is finally a form of empowerment, and both the consumption of the livery and the fulsome participation in the blog's textual production represent forms of resistance to the institutional authority of the "sanctioned interpreters" who control Chaucerian cultural production.[27]

One might view the monograph, *Geoffrey Chaucer Hath a Blog: Medieval Studies and New Media*, generated by *Geoffrey Chaucer Hath a Blog* as a manifestation of the inevitable incorporation or containment by the dominant discourse, with the attendant neutralization of the blog's playfully transgressive spirit.[28] Drawing on the assumption that academics are always aligned with institutional power, Fiske argues that the "inclusion of popular culture into academia allows for its conversion into economic rewards and social status for academics."[29] The status is derived from a reappraisal of Bourdieu's conception of cultural capital, with cultural omnivorousness (consumption of both the high-brow and low-brow) conferring the capital once associated with a taste for high culture.[30] Or, perhaps the blog's gentrification reflects a merging of the productivity and pleasure that Fradenburg sees as integral to the enjoyment of our subject. Or, perhaps it's a tangible manifestation of the apparent assumption that "medievalists have more fun than other academics": "Chaucerians are more likely to LOL (laugh out loud) than say, scholars of Gratian or Columbanus. Perhaps papyrologists also chortle, but not in such numbers."[31]

For although throughout this study the popular has been defined in contrast to the professional, with Chaucer's popular reception defined as such both because of its exclusion from and resistance to professional discourse, within the larger context of cultural theory concerned with capitalist ideology, the academic occupies a more uncertain power position. Bourdieu famously describes intellectuals as the dominated dominant in the sense that while possessing the cultural capital that attends higher education, as a group they tend to lack economic or political capital.[32] Fandom attracts groups with a sense of exclusion or subordination, and the rhetoric of marginalization is not unfamiliar to our own particular habitus.[33] Thus the institutional appropriation of popular culture as manifested in this example of new social media is perhaps less containment by the dominant discourse than a sign of affective allegiance between the professional and the popular.

The blog nonetheless reflects the spirit of egalitarian anti-elitism and the resistance to a dominant discourse that infuses the popular Chaucerian aesthetic. In Martin Riley's stage version of the poem, a central conceit is that Chaucer, "one of England's finest half-dead poets"— played by an actor who sits comatose among the audience throughout the play — will be revivified by the fast-paced and farcical adaptation of his poem.[34] Chaucer is roused by the play's end, *"furiously indignant"* and sure that he's in hell, being forced to watch his "sinful" poem performed by inept infernal thespians (98). He is nonetheless "amazed" that he has been brought back to life and the play ends with a raucous, communal recitation of the opening lines of the *General Prologue*. Chaucer's resurrection here is a playful metaphor for his cultural vitality, with the suggestion that it is the popularization itself (rather than his professional interpreters) that lends the poet an afterlife and resuscitates interest in his poetry.

The initial pitch for the importance of the popular was based on the assertion that such popularizations can teach us something about why Chaucer continues to enjoy a vital canonicity. Intellectuals trained in aesthetic and critical discrimination, who prize difficulty and intellectual demandingness, might remain dubious about the value of Chaucer's popular reproduction and consumption, tempted to conclude that his cultural renown perhaps prevails in spite of his popular estimation. While the register of meanings generated by his popular reception might be construed as a pastiche of simulacra, a guiding assumption of this study is that Chaucer's broad cultural renown is predicated on his continuing ability to make meaning, give pleasure, and appeal to social identities across a range of taste cultures.[35] Corrective views are not necessary because popular discrimination is selective, prizing functionality, that is, the "interconnections between a text and the immediate social situation of its readers."[36] A text is valued to the extent that it has the potential to function as a cultural resource to be plundered for pleasurable and relevant meanings at will.

And not all texts will do; popular taste, Fiske asserts, values "polysemic texts that are open to a variety of readings."[37] (One might add that professionals value Chaucer's texts for the same quality). The various adaptations, appropriations, and allusions of Chaucer's popular corpus therefore elicit a God's plenty of semiotic associations: communal inclusiveness and conviviality, confessional autobiography, educational privilege and intellectual distinction, class mobility, anti-elitism, bawdy, historical authenticity, spirituality, conservatism, etc. Social satire targeting all manner of pretension ranks high. But it is finally Chaucer's metonymic relationship with pilgrimage and tale telling that continues to resonate with a popular readership. For some, the structural frame provides a convenient literary model carrying the imprimatur of canonical capital with which to lend the illusion of generic unity to what might otherwise be perceived as a collection of short stories. But as this study demonstrates, the Chaucerian brand of pilgrimage as communal, confessional chat is repeatedly appropriated and invoked in the popular creative imagination as a narrative conceit useful for exploring competing discourses, and by extension, social divisiveness. The frame provides an imaginative space fostering the dialogue upon which the quest for collective identity (social, national, racial, intellectual) is predicated. Within a continuously fluctuating cultural semiotic, the popular Chaucerian aesthetic is presently associated with a populist myth of democratic inclusiveness and social comity. It appears to be an anodyne concept. But it is certainly a popularized ideological vision inherited from professional criticism — which constitutes an expression of high culture and is therefore presumably useful to dominant interests. The question is whether the vision can be construed as a projected ideal or as positing a reflection of social reality. That is, assuming that dominant discourses sustaining a power structure based on exclusion inevitably infiltrate popular culture, it remains debatable whether this popular version advocating Chaucer's ostensible inclusive pluralism promotes a vision of social relations that resists or simply replicates an unequal status quo.

Chapter Notes

Preface

1. Key studies in Chaucer's reception include Seth Lerer, *Chaucer and His Readers: Imagining the Author in Late Medieval England* (Princeton: Princeton University Press, 1993); Alice Miskimin, *The Renaissance Chaucer* (New Haven: Yale University Press, 1975); Theresa M. Krier, ed., *Refiguring Chaucer in the Renaissance* (Gainesville: University Press of Florida, 1998); Geoffrey W. Gust, *Constructing Chaucer: Author and Autofiction in the Critical Tradition* (New York: Palgrave Macmillan, 2009); David O. Matthews, "Speaking to Chaucer: The Poet and the Nineteenth-Century Academy," *Studies in Medievalism* 9 (1997): 5–25; and Stephanie Trigg, *Congenial Souls: Reading Chaucer from Medieval to Postmodern* (Minneapolis: University of Minnesota Press, 2002). A convenient summary of studies in Chaucer's reception is found in Kathy Cawsey, *Twentieth-Century Chaucer Criticism: Reading Audiences* (Farnham, U.K.: Ashgate, 2011), pp. 1–18.

2. Examinations of Chaucer's early popular reception include Alice Miskimin, "Illustrated Eighteenth-Century Chaucer," *Modern Philology* 77 (1979): 26–55; Betsy Bowden, ed., *Eighteenth-Century Modernizations from The Canterbury Tales*, Chaucer Studies XVI (Cambridge: D.S. Brewer, 1991); Derek Brewer, "Modernizing the Medieval: Eighteenth-Century Translations of Chaucer," in *The Middle Ages After the Middle Ages in the English-Speaking World*, ed. Marie-Françoise Alamichel and Derek Brewer (Cambridge: D. S. Brewer, 1997), pp. 103–120; John Ganim, "Mary Shelley, Godwin's *Chaucer*, and the Middle Ages," in *Chaucer and the Challenges of Medievalism*, ed. Donka Minkova and Theresa Tinkle (Frankfurt: Peter Lang, 2003), pp. 175–191; Carolyn P. Collette, "Chaucer and Victorian Medievalism: Culture and Society," *Poetica* 29–30 (1989): 115–125; Charlotte C. Morse, "Popularizing Chaucer in the Nineteenth Century," *Chaucer Review* 38 (2003): 99–125; Siân Echard, "Bedtime Chaucer: Juvenile Adaptations and the Medieval Canon," in *Printing the Middle Ages* (Philadelphia: University of Pennsylvania Press, 2008), pp. 126–161; Velma Bourgeois Richmond, *Chaucer as Children's Literature: Retellings from the Edwardian and Victorian Eras* (Jefferson, NC: McFarland, 2004); and Britton J. Harwood, "The Political Use of Chaucer in Twentieth-Century America," in *Medievalism in the Modern World: Essays in Honor of Leslie J. Workman*, ed. Richard Utz and Tom A. Shippey (Turnhout, BE: Brepols, 1998), pp. 379–392.

For overviews of Chaucer's reception, see Derek Brewer, ed., *Chaucer: The Critical Heritage*, 2 vols. (London: Routledge and Kegan Paul, 1978); Stephanie Trigg, "Chaucer's Influence and Reception," in *The Yale Companion to Chaucer*, ed. Seth Lerer (New Haven: Yale University Press, 2006), pp. 297–323; John H. Fisher, "Chaucer Since 1400," in *The Importance of Chaucer* (Carbondale: Southern Illinois University Press, 1992), pp. 141–172; and David Matthews, "Reception: Eighteenth and Nineteenth Centuries," in *Chaucer: An Oxford Guide*, ed. Steve Ellis (Oxford: Oxford University Press, 2005), pp. 512–527.

3. See, for instance, David Matthews, "What Was Medievalism?: Medieval Studies, Medievalism, and Cultural Studies," in *Medieval Cultural Studies: Essays in Honor of Stephen Knight*, ed. Ruth Evans, Helen Fulton, and David Matthews (Chicago: University of Chicago Press, 2006), pp. 9–22; David Matthews, "Chaucer's American Accent," *American Literary History* 22 (2010): 758–772; and Stephanie Trigg and Tom Prendergast, "What is Happening to the Middle Ages?" *New Medieval Literatures* 9 (2007): 215–229.

4. Steve Ellis, *Chaucer at Large: The Poet in the Modern Imagination* (Minneapolis: University of Minnesota Press, 2000); Candace Barrington, *American Chaucers* (New York: Palgrave Macmillan, 2007).

5. For surveys of Chaucer's contemporary popular reception see Stephanie Trigg, "Reception: Twentieth and Twenty-First Centuries," and Kevin J. Harty, "Chaucer in Performance," in *Chaucer: An Oxford Guide*, ed. Steve Ellis (Oxford: Oxford University Press, 2005), pp. 528–

543; 560–575; and Peter Brown, *Geoffrey Chaucer* (New York: Oxford University Press, 2011), pp. 188–212.

6. Tobin Siebers, "What Does Postmodernism Want? Utopia," in *Heterotopia: Postmodern Utopia and the Body Politic*, ed. Tobin Siebers (Ann Arbor: University of Michigan Press, 1994), p. 20.

Introduction

1. On Shakespop, see Douglas Lanier, *Shakespeare and Modern Popular Culture* (Oxford: Oxford University Press, 2002), p. 5.

2. See Hans Robert Jauss, *Toward an Aesthetic of Reception*, trans. Timothy Bahti (Minneapolis: University of Minnesota Press, 1982), p. 15: "... literature and art only obtain a history that has the character of a process when the succession of works is mediated not only through the producing subject but also through the consuming subject—through the interaction of author and public." On the idea of reception as refraction, see Christian Gutleben and Susana Onega, "Introduction," in *Refracting the Canon in Contemporary British Literature and Film*, ed. Susana Onega and Christian Gutleben (Amsterdam: Rodopi, 2004), pp. 7–15. And for the notion of literary canonization and public dialogue, see David Fishelov, *Dialogues with/and Great Books: The Dynamics of Canon Formation* (Eastbourne, U.K.: Sussex Academic Press, 2010).

3. For Ellis, *Chaucer at Large*, p. xiv, Chaucer's reception in the "modern imagination" is confined to "nonacademic discourse"; Barrington, *American Chaucers*, p. 1, defines her subject as imaginative works created by "non-academics for non-specialist, or popular" audiences.

4. Harold E. Hinds, Jr., "Popularity: The *Sine Qua Non* of Popular Culture," in *Symbiosis: Popular Culture and Other Fields*, ed. Ray B. Browne and Marshall W. Fishwick (Bowling Green, OH: Bowling Green State University Popular Press, 1988), p. 207. In order to qualify, the product must be consumed by "significant numbers of people," in more than one region or socioeconomic group (210).

5. See Raymond Williams, *Keywords: A Vocabulary of Culture and Society*, rev. ed. (London: Fontana, 1983), p. 237.

6. *A Knight's Tale*, directed by Brian Helgeland (2001; Columbia TriStar Home Entertainment, 2002), DVD.

7. John Storey, ed., *Cultural Theory and Popular Culture: An Introduction*, 4th ed. (Athens: University of Georgia Press, 2006), pp. 1, 5. Similarly, for John Street, *Politics and Popular Culture* (Philadelphia: Temple University Press, 1997), p. 9, "Popular culture is defined *against* a dominant culture."

8. Brewer, *Critical Heritage*, 2: 1–2.

9. Carolyn Collette, "Afterlife," in *A Companion to Chaucer*, ed. Peter Brown (Oxford: Blackwell, 2002), p. 16. Derek Brewer, "The Criticism of Chaucer in the Twentieth Century," in *Chaucer's Mind and Art*, ed. A. C. Cawley (Edinburgh and London: Oliver and Boyd, 1969), p. 4. Lee Patterson, "The Development of Chaucer Studies," in *Negotiating the Past: The Historical Understanding of Medieval Literature* (Madison: University of Wisconsin Press, 1987), pp. 3–39, begins his discussion of the development of Chaucer studies with the death of Frederick Furnivall (1910), the founder of the Chaucer Society (1868). On the professionalization of Chaucer studies, see also Steve Ellis, "Popular Chaucer and the Academy," *Studies in Medievalism* 9 (1997): 26–43; and Anne Middleton, "Medieval Studies," in *Redrawing the Boundaries: The Transformation of English and American Literary Studies*, ed. Stephen Greenblatt and Giles Gunn (New York: MLA, 1992), pp. 12–40.

10. See D. J. Palmer, *The Rise of English Studies* (Oxford: Oxford University Press, 1965); Gerald Graff, *Professing Literature: An Institutional History* (1987; Chicago: University of Chicago Press, 2007); Chris Baldick, *The Social Mission of English Criticism, 1848–1932*, 2nd ed. (Oxford: Oxford University Press, 1987); and Ethan Knapp, "Chaucer Criticism and Its Legacies," in *The Yale Companion to Chaucer*, ed. Seth Lerer (New Haven: Yale University Press, 2007), pp. 324–358.

11. See Patterson, *Negotiating the Past*, pp. 9–18.

12. George Lyman Kittredge, *Chaucer and His Poetry* (Cambridge: Harvard University Press, 1915). On MacKaye's popularizations, see Barrington, *American Chaucers*, pp. 43–92.

13. Barrington, *American Chaucers*, p. 2.

14. Caroline F. E. Spurgeon, *Five Hundred Years of Chaucer Criticism and Allusion, 1357–1900*, 3 vols. (Cambridge: Cambridge University Press, 1925). See also Jackson Campbell Boswell and Sylvia Wallace Holton, *Chaucer's Fame in England: STC Chauceriana, 1475–1640* (New York: Modern Language Association, 2004).

15. David Wallace, "New Chaucer Topographies," *Studies in the Age of Chaucer* 29 (2007): 17.

16. Bonnie Wheeler, "Go Litel Blog, Go Litel Thys Comedye," in Brantley L. Bryant, *Geoffrey Chaucer Hath a Blog: Medieval Studies and New Media* (New York: Palgrave Macmillan, 2010), pp. 7–14, notes the increasingly "paltry proportion of medieval sessions" at mega conferences like the MLA and AHA. The MLA Job Directory listed fewer than 15 T/T medievalist positions in 2010 and 2011.

17. David W. Marshall, "Introduction: The Medievalism of Popular Culture," in *Mass Market Medieval: Essays on the Middle Ages in Popular Culture*, ed. David W. Marshall (Jefferson, NC: McFarland, 2007), p. 8.

18. Morse, "Popularizing Chaucer in the Nineteenth Century," 117–18.

19. Richard K. Emmerson, "Medieval Studies at the Beginning of the New Millennium," in *Vital Signs: English in Medieval Studies in Twenty-First Century Higher Education*, ed. Elaine Treharne, *English Association Issues in English* 2 (2002), p. 25.

20. Ellis, *Chaucer at Large*, p. 27.

21. Barrington, *American Chaucers*, p. 156.

22. David Carlson, *Chaucer's Jobs* (New York: Palgrave Macmillan, 2008).

23. Other categorizations are available. For a convenient summary of various distinctions between popular culture and high culture, see John Storey, *Cultural Theory and Popular Culture: An Introduction*, 5th ed. (Harlow, U.K.: Pearson Education Limited, 2009), pp. 5–14; Simon During, *Cultural Studies: A Critical Introduction* (New York: Routledge, 2005), pp. 193–207; and Ray B. Browne, "Popular Culture: Notes Toward a Definition," in *Popular Culture Theory and Methodology: A Basic Introduction*, ed. Harold E. Hinds, Jr., Marilyn F. Motz, and Angela M. S. Nelson (Madison: University of Wisconsin Press, 2006), pp. 15–22.

24. Herbert J. Gans, *Popular Culture and High Culture: An Analysis and Evaluation of Taste*, rev. ed. (New York: Basic Books, 1999), p. 98. Gans differentiates "professional" taste cultures from "lay high culture," but suggests that "a good deal of technically difficult creative work which would be considered professional in other disciplines is part of lay high culture, on the assumption that the high culture public is or ought to be so well-educated that it can read technical criticism in literature" (99). Pierre Bourdieu, *The Field of Cultural Production*, ed. Randal Johnson (New York: Columbia University Press, 1993), pp. 115–120, perceives a similar market and political autonomy for the field of "restricted cultural production."

25. Gans, *Popular Culture*, p. 102: "Since the culture serves a small public that prides itself on exclusiveness, its products are not intended for distribution by the mass media ... its books are published by subsidized presses or by commercial publishers willing to take a financial loss for prestige reasons." On the current state of academic publishing see John B. Thompson, *Books in the Digital Age: The Transformation of Academic and Higher Education Publishing in Britain and the United States* (Cambridge, U.K.: Polity, 2005), pp. 81–194.

26. Street, *Politics and Popular Culture*, p. 7.

27. Gans, *Popular Culture*, p. 30.

28. Gans, *Popular Culture*, p. 76.

29. See John Fiske, "Popular Discrimination," in *Modernity and Mass Culture*, ed. James Naremore and Patrick Brantlinger (Indianapolis: Indiana University Press, 1991), pp. 103–116. See also John Fiske, *Understanding Popular Culture*, 2nd ed. (London: Routledge, 2010), pp. 102–125.

30. Louise Fradenburg, "'So That We May Speak of Them': Enjoying the Middle Ages," *New Literary History* 28 (1997): 209.

31. See Kathleen Forni, *The Chaucerian Apocrypha: A Counterfeit Canon* (Gainesville: University Press of Florida, 2001), pp. 44–105.

32. John M. Manly, *Some New Light on Chaucer* (New York: Henry Holt, 1926), p. 262, suggests that behind "Chaucer's most vital and successful sketches lay the observation of living men and women."

33. Thomas Speght, *The Workes of Our Antient and Learned English Poet, Geffrey Chaucer* (London, 1598), b3.

34. See Helen Dell, "Past, Present, and Future Perfect: Paradigms of History in Medievalism Studies," *Parergon* 25 (2008): 58–79; Louise D'Arcens, "Deconstruction and the Medieval Indefinite Article: The Undecidable Medievalism of Brian Helgeland's *A Knight's Tale*," *Parergon* 25 (2008): 80–98; David Matthews, "What the Trumpet Solo Tells Us: A Response," *Parergon* 25 (2008): 119–127; Holly A. Crocker, "Teaching Masculinities in Chaucer's Shorter Poems: Historical Myths and Brian Helgeland's *A Knight's Tale*," in *Approaches to Teaching Chaucer's Troilus and Criseyde and the Shorter Poems*, ed. Tison Pugh and Angela Jane Weisl (New York: MLA 2007), pp. 76–80; Holly A. Crocker, "Chaucer's Man Show: Anachronistic Authority in Brian Helgeland's *A Knight's Tale*," in *Race, Class, and Gender in 'Medieval' Cinema*, ed. Lynn T. Ramey and Tison Pugh (New York: Palgrave Macmillan, 2007), pp. 183–197; Barrington, *American Chaucers*, pp. 143–153; Caroline Jewers, "Hard Day's Knights: *First Knight, A Knight's Tale*, and *Black Knight*," in *The Medieval Hero on Screen: Representations from Beowulf to Buffy*, ed. Martha Driver and Sid Ray (Jefferson, NC: McFarland, 2004), pp. 192–210; Kathleen Forni, "Reinventing Chaucer: Helgeland's *A Knight's Tale*," *Chaucer Review* 37 (2003): 253–264; and Nickolas A. Haydock, "Arthurian Melodrama, Chaucerian Spectacle, and the Waywardness of Pastiche in *First Knight* and *A Knight's Tale*," *Studies in Medievalism* 12 (2002): 5–38.

35. See, for instance, "*A Knight's Tale* Slash Archive," http://aknightstale.ficology.com; "*A Knight's Tale* Fan Fiction Archive," http://www.fanfiction.net/movie/A_Knights_Tale; "Slash Asylum," http://slashasylum.livejournal.com.

36. Gans, *Popular Culture*, pp. 7, xv.

37. Fiske, *Understanding Popular Culture*, p. 103.

38. See Fiske, *Understanding Popular Culture*, pp. 102–125. Fiske's understanding of critical/aesthetic discrimination as an assertion of social distinction owes much to Pierre Bourdieu's notion of the social function of hierarchies of taste.

39. See Henry A. Giroux and Roger I. Simon, "Critical Pedagogy and the Politics of Popular Culture," *Cultural Studies* 2 (1988): 23–46; David Harris, *From Class Struggle to the Politics of Pleasure: The Effects of Gramscianism on Cultural Studies* (London: Routledge, 1992); and Graeme Turner, *British Cultural Studies: An Introduction*, 3rd ed. (London: Routledge, 2003).

40. Lawrence Grossberg, "Cultural Studies: What's in a Name? (One More Time)," in *Media/Cultural Studies: Critical Approaches*, ed. Rhonda Hammer and Douglas Kellner (New York: Peter Lang, 2009), pp. 25–48. The political assumptions embodied in contemporary cultural theory are indebted to the political analysis of Antonio Gramsci. See Tony Bennett, "Popular Culture and the 'turn to Gramsci,'" in *Cultural Theory and Popular Culture: A Reader*, 4th ed., ed. John Storey (Harlow, U.K.: Pearson Education Limited, 2009), pp. 81–87.

41. Pierre Bourdieu, *Distinction: A Social Critique of the Judgement of Taste*, trans. Richard Nice (London: Routledge and Kegan Paul, 1984), p. 254, defines the dominant as those with economic, educational, and social power. Fiske, *Understanding Popular Culture*, p. 24, refers to the "power-bloc" as "capitalism, patriarchy, racial dominance."

42. For the now classic challenge to "the bizarre claims about the absence of 'subjectivity' in 'pre-bourgeois' societies," see David Aers, "A Whisper in the Ear of Early Modernists; or, Reflections on Literary Critics Writing 'The History of the Subject,'" in *Culture and History, 1350–1600: Essays on English Communities, Identities, and Writing*, ed. David Aers (Detroit, MI: Wayne State University Press, 1992), pp. 177–203; see also Lee Patterson, "On the Margin: Postmodernism, Ironic History, and Medieval Studies," *Speculum* 65 (1990), particularly 96–100.

43. Jonathan Brody Kramnick, *Making the English Canon: Print Capitalism and the Cultural Past, 1700–1770* (Cambridge: Cambridge University Press, 1999), pp. 237, 242.

44. Matthew Arnold, *Culture and Anarchy*, ed. Samuel Lipman (New Haven: Yale University Press, 1994), p. 119.

45. Carlson, *Chaucer's Jobs*, p. 1.

46. On Chaucer's pedagogical usefulness, see Richmond, *Chaucer as Children's Literature*, pp. 15–23.

47. John Guillory, *Cultural Capital: The Problem of Literary Canon Formation* (Chicago: University of Chicago Press, 1993), p. 6. See also Bourdieu, *Distinction*, p. 7.

48. See Lee Patterson, *Chaucer and the Subject of History* (Madison: University of Wisconsin Press, 1991), pp. 32–39; and more recently, Lee Patterson, ed., *Geoffrey Chaucer's The Canterbury Tales: A Casebook* (Oxford: Oxford University Press, 2007), p. 19.

49. Alcuin Blamires, "Chaucer the Reactionary," *Review of English Studies* 51 (2000): 524.

50. On the symbiotic relationship between criticism and canonicity, see Barbara Herrnstein Smith, "Contingencies of Value," in *Canons*, ed. Robert von Hallberg (Chicago: University of Chicago Press, 1984), pp. 5–40.

51. See Stuart Hall, "Notes on Deconstructing 'The Popular,'" in *Cultural Theory and Popular Culture: A Reader*, 4th ed., ed. John Storey (Harlow, U.K.: Pearson Education, 2009), pp. 508–518. See also Fiske, *Understanding Popular Culture*, pp. 19–23.

52. Joan Acocella, "All England," *The New Yorker*, Dec. 21, 2009, pp. 140–145.

53. See Kramnick, *Making the English Canon*, pp. 237–245.

54. John Fiske, *Television Culture* (London: Methuen & Co., 1987), pp. 316–319.

55. On the opposition of productivity and pleasure peculiar to medievalists, see Fradenburg, "'So That We May Speak of Them.'"

56. Brantley L. Bryant, "Playing Chaucer," in *Geoffrey Chaucer Hath a Blog: Medieval Studies and New Media* (New York: Palgrave Macmillan, 2010), p. 17. The blog is available at houseoffame.blogspot.com.

57. Bryant, "Playing Chaucer," p. 20.

58. John Fiske, "The Cultural Economy of Fandom," in *The Adoring Audience: Fan Culture and Popular Media*, ed. Lisa A. Lewis (New York: Routledge, 1992), p. 34. Similarly, for Henry Jenkins, "'Strangers no more we sing': Filking and the Social Construction of the Science Fiction Community," in *Media Studies: A Reader*, 2nd ed., ed. Paul Marris and Sue Thornham (New York: New York University Press, 2000), p. 531, fandom "is particularly attractive to groups marginalized or subordinated in the dominant culture."

59. On some of the characteristics of neomedievalism, see Amy S. Kaufman "Medieval Unmoored," *Studies in Medievalism* 19 (2010): 1–11.

60. Jostein Gripsrud, "'High Culture' Revisited," *Cultural Studies* 3 (1989): 194–207.

61. Bryant, "Playing Chaucer," p. 22.

62. See Trigg, *Congenial Souls*, pp. 1–39; and Thomas A. Prendergast, *Chaucer's Dead Body: From Corpse to Corpus* (New York: Routledge, 2004).

63. Bryant, "Playing Chaucer," pp. 18–19.
64. Prendergast, *Chaucer's Dead Body*, p. 14.
65. See Bourdieu, *Distinction*, pp. 4–5.
66. Trigg, *Congenial Souls*, p. 4.
67. On the queering of Chaucer, see Gust, *Constructing Chaucer*, pp. 177–198; and Tison Pugh, *Sexuality and Its Queer Discontents in Middle English Literature* (New York: Palgrave Macmillan, 2008), pp. 49–100. For the quarrel with Gower, see Carolyn Dinshaw, "Rivalry, Rape, and Manhood: Gower and Chaucer," in *Chaucer and Gower: Difference, Mutuality, Exchange*, ed. Robert F. Yeager, *English Literary Studies* 51 (1991): 130–152.
68. See Joli Jensen, "Introduction: On Fandom, Celebrity, and Mediation: Posthumous Possibilities," in *Afterlife as Afterimage: Understanding Posthumous Fame*, ed. Steve Jones and Joli Jensen (New York: Peter Lang, 2005), pp. xv–xxiii.

Chapter 1

1. Ellis, *Chaucer at Large*, p. xiii.
2. Michel Foucault, *Aesthetics, Method, and Epistemology: Essential Works of Michel Foucault, 1954–1984*, ed. James D. Faubion (New York: New Press, 1998), p. 221.
3. Graham Allen, *Intertextuality* (New York: Routledge, 2000), p. 1.
4. John Frow, "Intertextuality and Ontology," in *Intertextuality: Theories and Practices*, ed. Michael Worton and Judith Still (Manchester, U.K.: Manchester University Press, 1990), p. 46.
5. Linda Hutcheon, *A Theory of Adaptation* (New York: Routledge, 2006), pp. 1–9.
6. David Cowart, *Literary Symbiosis: The Reconfigured Text in Twentieth-Century Writing* (Athens: University of Georgia Press, 1993), pp. 4–10.
7. Julie Sanders, *Adaptation and Appropriation* (London: Routledge, 2006), pp. 15–42.
8. Gérard Genette, *Palimpsests: Literature in the Second Degree*, trans. Channa Newman and Claude Doubinsky (1982; Lincoln: University of Nebraska Press, 1997), pp. 1–6.
9. Marko Juvan, *History and Poetics of Intertextuality*, trans. Timothy Pogacar (West Lafayette, IN: Purdue University Press, 2008), pp. 144–178.
10. Mary Orr, *Intertextuality: Debates and Contexts* (Cambridge, U.K.: Polity, 2003), p. 39, suggests that "prior knowledge, whether by readers or texts, remains the nub of the problem for intertextual research in general." Similarly, Michael Schudson, "The New Validation of Popular Culture: Sense and Sentimentality in Academia," in *Popular Culture Theory and Methodology: A Basic Introduction*, ed. Harold E. Hinds, Marilyn F. Motz, and Angela M. S. Nelson (Madison: University of Wisconsin Press, 2006), pp. 85–106, suggests that "the audience, in social science studies of mass media and popular culture, has been (like the weather) something that everybody talks about and nobody does anything about" (95).
11. Genette, *Palimpsests*, often pauses in his virtuoso readings to quantify the type of reader—"potential," "real," "privileged," "ordinary," "virtual"—who will be receptive to the referential resonances that Genette himself recognizes. Genette is "happily at odds" with "hypertextual hermeneutics," that is, with investing the "hermeneutic activity of the reader" with "authority and significance" that it does not warrant (9).
Michael Riffaterre, in "Compulsory Reader Response: The Intertextual Drive," in *Intertextuality: Theories and Practices*, ed. Michael Worton and Judith Still (Manchester, U.K.: Manchester University Press, 1990), pp. 56–78, emphasizes the crucial role of the reader in the generation of intertextual meaning, also presupposes a highly "competent" reader able to decode complex patterns of meaning.
12. See Schudson, "The New Validation of Popular Culture," pp. 101–102.
13. Juvan, *History and Poetics of Intertextuality*, p. 146.
14. Hutcheon, *Theory of Adaptation*, p. xiv.
15. Geoffrey Wagner, *The Novel and the Cinema* (Rutherford, NJ.: Fairleigh Dickinson University Press, 1975), p. 222.
16. Hutcheon, *Theory of Adaptation*, p. 87.
17. *I racconti di Canterbury*, directed by Pier Paolo Pasolini (1972; BFI Video, 2009), DVD.
18. Cathal Tohill and Pete Tombs, *Immoral Tales: European Sex and Horror Movies, 1956–1984* (New York: St. Martins, 1995), p. 1977: "Following the huge local success of Pasolini's *Decameron*, his 1971 film of *The Canterbury Tales* was being imitated in anticipation of its expected success even *before* it had been released. Unfortunately, somebody didn't do their homework properly, and several of the resulting films laboured under the misapprehension that Canterbury was the author of the tales in question, which lead to some strange titlings, as well as peculiar hybrids like *The Sexbury Tales* (1971), *The Lusty Wives of Canterbury* (1972), and *The Other Canterbury Tales* (1972)."
19. Sarah Cardwell, "Literature on the Small Screen: Television Adaptations," in *The Cambridge Companion to Literature on Screen*, ed. Deborah Cartmell and Imelda Whelehan (Cambridge, U.K.: Cambridge University Press, 2007), pp. 181–195.
20. *Canterbury Tales: Leaving London; Arriv-*

ing at Canterbury; The Journey Back, directed by Dave Antrobus, et al., written by Jonathan Myerson (1998–2000; Metrodome Distribution, 2005), DVD (Region 2).

21. See Paul Wells, *Animation: Genre and Authorship* (London: Wallflower, 2002), especially "Genre in Animation," pp. 41–71.

22. BBC's *Canterbury Tales*, directed by Julian Jarrold, John McKay, Marc Munden and Andy DeEmmony (2003; IMC Vision, 2004), DVD (Region 2).

Quoted from Stephen Pile, "The Scriptwriters' Tales," *The Daily Telegraph*, August 30, 2003, http://www.telegraph.co.uk/culture/tvandradio/3601561/The-scriptwriters-tales.html.

23. John Cawelti, "The Evolution of Social Melodrama," in *Imitations of Life: A Reader on Film and Television Melodrama*, ed. Marcia Landy (Detroit, MI: Wayne State University Press, 1991), p. 47, suggests that despite changes in the genre over the past one hundred years, "there are certain basic continuities of theme and structure such as the emphasis on romantic love as an ultimate value, the defense of monogamous, family-oriented relationships between men and women, and the attempt to define true and false conceptions of success and status."

24. Cowart, *Literary Symbiosis*, p. 1.

25. See Ellis, *Chaucer at Large*, pp. 121–140, for the quite numerous stage versions of *The Canterbury Tales* in the late nineteenth and twentieth centuries.

Geoffrey Chaucer and Co., a not-for-profit repertory theater based in Northern California since 1996, performs loose versions of the individual tales in Modern English, adapted by a host of different writers. See http://www.chaucertheatre.org.

26. Mike Poulton, *The Canterbury Tales* (London: Nick Hern Books, 2006). *The Canterbury Tales, 1969 Original Broadway Cast* (1969; Angel Records, 1994), Audio CD.

There are also quite a number of acting editions, suitable both for performance in smaller theatre venues and for pedagogical use. These usually focus on a handful of tales (some with musical scores), which are often updated to modern genres, and the characters provided with a modicum of realistic motivation. Martin Riley, *Geoffrey Chaucer: The Canterbury Tales* (1998; Oxford: Oxford University Press, 2003) is probably the best known. Others include John O'Connor, *The Canterbury Tales: A Play Based on the Poem by Geoffrey Chaucer* (Cheltenham, U.K.: Nelson Thornes, 2001); Susan A. Van Schuyver, *Five Tales from Chaucer: A Collection of Five Playlets Adapted from Canterbury Tales* (Droitwich, U.K.: Hanbury Plays, 1988); Derek Hyde and Kenneth Pickering, *Some Canterbury Tales: Adapted from Geoffrey Chaucer* (London: S.

French, 1988); and Thomas Eberle, *Six Canterbury Tales* (New Orleans, LA: Anchorage Press, 1993).

27. John Gardner, *The Poetry of Chaucer* (Carbondale, IL: Southern Illinois University Press, 1977), pp. 288, 297.

28. Steve Orme, Review of RSC *The Canterbury Tales*, *The British Theatre Guide* 2006, http://www.britishtheatreguide.info/reviews/RSCcanttales-rev.htm.

29. Ellis, *Chaucer at Large*, p. 164.

30. The characterization of the Squire as incompetent and self-conscious reflects a long critical tradition; see Derek Pearsall, "The Squire as Story-Teller," *University of Toronto Quarterly* 34 (1964): 82–92.

31. Steve Orme, Review of RSC *The Canterbury Tales*, praises the eclectic mix of "moralistic stories" and "lavatorial humor"; Benedict Nightingale, Review of RSC *The Canterbury Tales*, *The Times*, December 10, 2005, admires the "anal thunder galore" and "orgiastic farce" tempered with "high romance" and "picaresque adventure"; Celia Wren, "Throwing Bawdy and Soul into 'Canterbury,'" *The Washington Post*, April 16, 2006, is taken by the characters: "The irrepressible Wife of Bath; the corrupt, epicene Pardoner; the simpering Prioress with her lap dogs—these figures have a charm and vigor that befit and transcend their place in academic tomes"; and for Peter Marks, "A Canter Down Chaucer's Long and Windy Road," *The Washington Post*, April 21, 2006, "What is illuminated ... is an entire society, secular and religious, rich and poor, educated and intellectually limited.... Everyone, no matter his or her station, gets a shot."

32. Joseph Garaventa, "A Bawdy Journey to 'Canterbury,'" *The Washington Post*, April 21, 2006, http://www.washingtonpost.com/wp-dyn/content/article/2006/04/20/AR2006042000615_pf.html.

33. Alfred Hickling, Review of the Northern Broadsides' "The Canterbury Tales," *The Guardian*, March 3, 2010, p. 40.

34. Baba Brinkman, *The Rap Canterbury Tales* (Vancouver: Talon Books, 2006). An extended performance version is also available as *The Canterbury Tales Remixed* (Vancouver: Lit Fuse Records, 2012), Audio CD.

35. For an analysis of the *Miller's Tale*, see Peter G. Beidler, "It's Miller Time!: Baba Brinkman's Adaptation of the *Miller's Tale*," *LATCH* 3 (2010): 134–150.

36. Seymour Chwast, *Geoffrey Chaucer: The Canterbury Tales* (New York: Bloomsbury, 2011). For Chwast's design work, see Steven Heller and Paula Scher, ed., *Seymour: The Obsessive Images of Seymour Chwast* (San Francisco: Chronicle Books, 2009).

For the visual vocabulary of comics, see Scott McCloud, *Understanding Comics: The Invisible Art* (New York: HarperCollins, 1994); and Will Eisner, *Comics and Sequential Art: Principles and Practices from the Legendary Cartoonist* (Tamarac, FL: Poorhouse Press, 1985).

37. McCloud, *Understanding Comics*, p. 192.
38. See McCloud, *Understanding Comics*, pp. 30, 160.
39. While the incorporation of modern technology does suggest a conceptual linkage between the medieval and the modern, Chwast explained his choice of transport thus: "I'm not great at drawing horses.... And I love drawing motorcycles." Quoted from Sonia Harris, "CCI: Art of Design, AKA Comics and Design," *Comic Book Resources*, August 2, 2011. Interview available at http://www.comicbookresources.com/?page=article&id=33686.
40. Quoted from *Programme Notes* (London, 1999), p. 8. *God's Plenty* was originally performed by the Rambert Dance Company, Britain's leading modern ensemble, with financial support provided by the National Lottery through the Arts Council of England.
41. *Programme Notes*, p. 8. John Dryden, Preface to *Fables Ancient and Modern*, in *The Works of John Dryden*, Vol. VII, ed. Vinton A. Dearing (Berkeley and Los Angeles: University of California Press, 2002), 7: 37–38. Mixed reviews of *God's Plenty* include: Ismene Brown "Canterbury Fails," *The Telegraph*, September 21, 1999, http://www.telegraph.co.uk/culture/4718479-/Canterbury-fails.html; and Jenny Gilbert, "Chaucer is Jigging in His Grave," *The Independent*, September 19, 1999, http://www.independent.co.uk/arts-entertainment/dance-chaucer-is-jigging-in-his-grave-1120362.html.
42. *Programme Notes*, p. 9.
43. *Programme Notes*, p. 9.
44. *Programme Notes*, p. 8.
45. Christopher Morley, *The Trojan Horse* (Philadelphia: J. B. Lippincott, 1937); William Walton, *Troilus and Criseyde, Opera in Three Acts*, libretto by Christopher Hassell (Oxford: Oxford University Press, 1954). The legend is also invoked in the Bollywood film, *Dil Chahta Hai*, directed by Farhan Akhtar (2001; Spark Worldwide, 2001), DVD.
46. John Dryden, *Troilus and Cressida*, in *The Works of John Dryden*, Vol. XIII, ed. Maximillian E. Novak, Allan Roper, George R. Guffey, and Vinton A. Dearing (Berkeley and Los Angeles: University of California Press, 1985).
47. Alice Shields, "Criseyde: A Feminist Opera," p. 3. Available as pdf. at http://www.aliceshields.com/criseyde/about.html.
48. Information about Shields' production plans is available at http://www.aliceshields.com/criseyde/criseyde_info.pdf.

49. Robert Stam, "Introduction: The Theory and Practice of Adaptation," in *Literature and Film: A Guide to the Theory and Practice of Film Adaptation*, ed. Robert Stam and Alessandra Raengo (Oxford: Blackwell, 2005), p. 3.
50. Hutcheon, *Theory of Adaptation*, p. 175.
51. Sanders, *Adaptation*, p. 26.
52. Paul Strohm, *Social Chaucer* (Cambridge: Harvard University Press, 1994), p. 166.
53. Marilyn Nelson, *The Cachoeira Tales and Other Poems* (Baton Rouge: Louisiana State University Press, 2005), p. 11.
54. All references to Chaucer's texts are from Larry D. Benson, ed., *The Riverside Chaucer*, 3rd ed. (New York: Houghton Mifflin, 1987).
55. Jerry Ellis, *Walking to Canterbury: A Modern Journey Through Chaucer's Medieval England* (New York: Ballantine Books, 2003).
56. Dan Simmons, *Hyperion* (London: Headline Book Publishing, 1990).
57. Paul A. Freeman, *Robin Hood and Friar Tuck: Zombie Killers—A Canterbury Tale* (Winnipeg, CAN: Coscom Entertainment, 2009).
58. On zombie signification, see Stephen T. Asma, *On Monsters: An Unnatural History of Our Worst Fears* (New York: Oxford University Press, 2009), pp. 231–254; and Jeffrey Jerome Cohen, "Monster Culture (Seven Theses)," in *Monster Theory: Reading Culture*, ed. Jeffrey Jerome Cohen (Minneapolis: University of Minnesota Press, 1996), pp. 3–25.
59. Karen King-Aribisala, *Kicking Tongues* (Portsmouth, NH: Heinemann, 1998).
60. Sharyn McCrumb, *St. Dale* (New York: Kensington, 2005).
61. Ronald L. Ecker, *The Evolutionary Tales: Rhyme and Reason on Creation/ Evolution*, 3rd rev. ed. (Palatka, FL: Hodge and Braddock, 2006).
62. Chaucer is again used to pitch scientific method in Richard Dawkins's *The Ancestor's Tale: A Pilgrimage to the Dawn of Life* (New York: Houghton Mifflin, 2004), which turns to *The Canterbury Tales* in order to package evolutionary theory for a general readership. Dawkins presents his narrative as a pilgrimage backward in time, with Canterbury representing the "Concester," or "grand ancestor of all surviving life" (7). The "General Prologue" introduces the "methods and problems of reconstructing evolutionary history" which is subsequently presented as a series of digestible narratives ("The Ragworm's Tale," "The Dodo's Tale") with occasional links such as "What the Star-Nosed Mole Said to the Duckbilled Platypus." Dawkins is both narrator and host, probably not inaccurately recognizing that it would be a bit "twee" to have "let my animal and plant-tellers speak in the first person singular" (10).
63. *Broadcast* maintains an afterlife as a website: http://www.somewhere.org.uk/broadcast.

64. Jonathan Jones, "Pilgrims Like Us," *The Guardian*, September 9, 1999, http://www.guardian.co.uk/culture/1999/sep/09/artsfeatures1.
65. Gavin Douglas, *Virgil's Aeneid*, 4 vols., STS 3rd series 25, 27, 28, 30, ed. David F. C. Coldwell (Edinburgh and London: William Blackwell and Sons, 1957–1964), *Pro* 1.448. *The Insomniac Tales by Chaucer's Women* (DLSIJ Press, 2003).
66. Edmund Reiss, "The Pilgrimage Narrative and the *Canterbury Tales*," *Studies in Philology* 67 (1970): 298, 300: "It is ludicrous to imagine Chaucer's flawed journeyers being converted and saved on the pilgrimage to Canterbury."
67. Mary Devlin, *Murder on the Canterbury Pilgrimage: A Geoffrey Chaucer Murder Mystery* (Lincoln, NE: Writers Club Press, 2000). Dan Brown, *The Da Vinci Code* (New York: Doubleday, 2003).
68. Paul C. Doherty, *An Ancient Evil: The Knight's Tale...* (London: Headline, 1994); *A Tapestry of Murders: The Man of Law's Tale...* (London: Headline, 1994); *A Tournament of Murders: The Franklin's Tale...* (London: Headline, 1997); *Ghostly Murders: The Poor Priest's Tale...* (London: Headline, 1997); *The Hangman's Hymn: The Carpenter's Tale...* (London: Headline, 2002); *A Haunt of Murder* (London: Headline, 2002).
69. Doherty, *An Ancient Evil*, p. 4.
70. Doherty, *An Ancient Evil*, p. 3.
71. Doherty, *Tapestry of Murders*, p. 3.
72. See H. Marshall Leicester, "The Art of Impersonation: A General Prologue to the *Canterbury Tales*," *PMLA* 95 (1980): 213–224.
73. Devlin, *Murder on the Canterbury Pilgrimage*, p. 12.
74. Peter Ackroyd, *The Clerkenwell Tales* (New York: Anchor Books, 2005).
75. Philippa Morgan, *Chaucer and the House of Fame* (New York: Carroll and Graf, 2004); *Chaucer and the Legend of Good Women* (New York: Carroll and Graf, 2005); *Chaucer and the Doctor of Physic* (New York: Carroll and Graf, 2006).
76. Morgan, *House of Fame*, pp. 192, 27.
77. Garry O'Connor, *Chaucer's Triumph: Including the case of Cecilia Chaumpaigne, the seduction of Katherine Swynford, the murder of her husband, the interment of John of Gaunt and other offices of the flesh in the year 1399* (London: Petrak Press, 2007).
78. John Guare, *Chaucer in Rome* (New York: Dramatists Play Service, 2002).
79. Marina Lewycka, *Two Caravans* (London: Penguin Books, 2007).
80. Review of *Strawberry Fields*, *Publisher's Weekly*, May 28, 2007, http://www.publishersweekly.com/978-1-59420-137-0; Review of *Strawberry Fields*, *The New Yorker*, August 13, 2007, http://www.newyorker.com/arts/reviews/brieflynoted/2007/08/13/070813crbn_brieflynoted1.

81. See "Marina Lewycka's Dare-Devil Leap from Tractors to Caravans," *The Sunday Times*, March 18, 2007, http://women.timesonline.co.uk/tol/life_and_style/women/article1530630.ece.
82. *Mystery Train*, directed by Jim Jarmusch (1989; MGM, 2000), DVD. Quoted from Scott Cohen, "Strangers in Paradise," *Spin*, December 1989, p. 70. See also the interview in Ludvig Hertzberg, *Jim Jarmusch: Interviews* (Jackson: University Press of Mississippi, 2001), p. 127: "the form of the film is a little bit from *Canterbury Tales*, in a way. But there are a lot of streets in Memphis named after poets.... Chaucer isn't one of them, though."
83. Bennet Schaber, "Modernity and the Vernacular," *Surfaces* 1 (1991): 16.
84. Jonathan Rosenbaum, *Essential Cinema: On the Necessity of Film Canons* (Baltimore, MD: Johns Hopkins University Press, 2004), p. 216; Peter Quartermain, *Disjunctive Poetics: From Gertrude Stein and Louis Zukofsky to Susan Howe* (Cambridge: Cambridge University Press, 1992), p. 16.
85. Peter Conrad, "Arrival at Canterbury," in *To be Continued: Four Stories and Their Survival* (Oxford: Clarendon Press, 1995), pp. 7–45.
86. James Hynes, *The Lecturer's Tale* (New York: Picador, 2002).
87. David Dabydeen, *The Intended* (London: Minerva, 1992).
88. On Dabydeen's "imbrications of language, literature, and education in contemporary postcolonial societies," see Russell West-Pavlov, *Transcultural Graffiti: Diasporic Writing and the Teaching of Literary Studies* (Amsterdam: Rodopi, 2005), pp. 175–186.
89. Ted Hughes, *Birthday Letters* (New York: Farrar, Straus, and Giroux, 1999).
90. Lucas Myers, *Crow Steered Bergs Appeared: A Memoir of Ted Hughes and Sylvia Plath* (Sewanee, TN: Proctor's Hall Press, 2001), p. 48.
91. Wallace, "New Chaucer Topographies," 4: "As Chaucerians, Plath and Hughes merit places on the smartest NCS [New Chaucer Society] panels. But ... their engagement with Chaucer seems to me particularly *inward*, mystical in a Julian-like sense, tethered to the dynamics of interpersonal relationship rather than to the qualities of particular locales."
92. Caryl Churchill, *Top Girls* (1982; London: Methuen, 1991). Victoria Bazin, "[Not] Talking 'bout My Generation: Historicizing Feminisms in Carly Churchill's *Top Girls*," *Studies in the Literary Imagination* 39 (2006): 117.
93. Rebecca Cameron, "From Great Women to *Top Girls*: Pageants of Sisterhood in British Feminist Theater," *Comparative Drama* 43 (2009): 144.
94. Susan Swan, *The Wives of Bath* (New York: Knopf, 1993). The film adaptation of the

novel, *Lost and Delirious*, directed by Lea Pool (Montreal: Cite-Amerique, 2001), drops the Chaucer references.

95. Gloria Naylor, *Bailey's Café* (New York: Harcourt, Brace, Jovanovich, 1992).

96. Linda Hutcheon, "The Politics of Postmodern Parody," in *Intertextuality*, ed. Heinrich F. Plett (Berlin: Walter de Gruyter, 1991), p. 232.

97. Alex Preminger and T. V. F. Brogan, *The New Princeton Encyclopedia of Poetry and Poetics* (Princeton: Princeton University Press, 1993), p. 39, also make a distinction in their definition of allusion between the device used to create a "conceptual connection" or to "enrich a poem by incorporating further meaning" and a simple "display of knowledge" or "appeal to those sharing experience or knowledge with the poet."

98. Juvan, *History and Poetics of Intertextuality*, p. 152.

99. Ellis, *Chaucer at Large*, p. 154.

100. Nicole Galland, *The Fool's Tale* (New York: HarperCollins, 2005); Bernard Cornwall, *The Archer's Tale* (New York: HarperTorch, 2001); A. S. Byatt, *The Biographer's Tale* (New York: Alfred A. Knopf, 2000).

101. Wendy Holden, *The Wives of Bath* (New York: Plume, 2005), p. 9.

102. Thomas Augst, *The Clerk's Tale: Young Men and Moral Life in Nineteenth-Century America* (Chicago: University of Chicago Press, 2003).

103. Timothy B. Spears, Review of *The Clerk's Tale: Young Men and Moral Life in Nineteenth-Century America*, *Journal of American History* 91 (2005): 1457.

104. Wendy Cope, "The Teacher's Tale" in *If I Don't Know* (London: Faber and Faber, 2001), pp. 55–76.

105. Kate Kellaway, "Of Headless Squirrels and Men," Review of *If I Don't Know*, *The Observer*, June 3, 2001, p. 16.

106. Roger Stevens, *The Journal of Danny Chaucer (Poet)* (London: Orion Children's Books, 2002).

107. Sting, *Ten Summoner's Tales* (1993; A&M Records, 1998), Audio CD. For a fuller version of these reviews, see http://www.sting.com/discography/index/ablum/albumId/16/tag-Name/Albums.

108. *Canterbury Tales: The Best of Caravan* (1976; Universal Distribution, 1994), Audio CD.

109. An image of the original album art is available at http://picasaweb.google.com/lh/photo/8Zm6Fk__2tusM032ui_xhw.

110. See Edward Macan, *Rocking the Classics: English Progressive Rock and the Counterculture* (Oxford: Oxford University Press, 1996), pp. 129–132, 240–246. One might include here "Poison" by the American punk rock band, Rancid (*Rancid*, Los Angeles: Hellcat, 2000), which, searching for a simile to describe the kinds of toxic, materialistic relationships that might plague unexpectedly commercially successful musicians, hits upon a felicitous and quite unexpected, simile:
Like Chaucer's *Canterbury Tales*
When three men find a pot of gold
and end up killing one another in the name of greed
Some people are poison

111. Neil Gaiman, "Men of Good Fortune," *Sandman* Issue 13, "The Doll's House Part 4" (1990), reprinted in *Sandman Vol. 2: The Doll's House* (1991; New York: DC Comics, 1995). Gaiman also loosely adopts Chaucer's pilgrimage frame in *Sandman Vol. 8: Worlds' End* (1993; New York: DC Comics, 1994).

112. Juvan, *History and Poetics*, p. 182.

113. Karen Maitland, *Company of Liars: A Novel of the Plague* (London: Penguin Books, 2008).

114. Rana Dasgupta, *Tokyo Cancelled* (London: Harper Perennial, 2006). See Alev Adil, "Modern Fables Get Lost in Transit Lounge," *The Independent*, March 8, 2005, http://gala.gre.ac.uk/1684/.

115. John Fowles, *A Maggot* (Boston: Little, Brown and Co., 1985). See, for instance, Jeffrey Roessner, "Unsolved Mysteries: Agents of Historical Change in John Fowles's *A Maggot*," *Papers on Language and Literature* 36 (2000): 302–323; Peter Brigg, "Maggots, Tropes, and Metafictional Challenge: John Fowles' *A Maggot*," in *Imaginative Futures,* ed. Milton T. Wolf and Daryl F. Mallett (San Bernardino, CA: Borgo, 1995), pp. 293–305; and Frederick M. Holmes, "History, Fiction, and the Dialogic Imagination: John Fowles's *A Maggot*," *Contemporary Literature* 32 (1991): 229–243.

116. Carla Arnell, "Chaucer's Wife of Bath and John Fowles's Quaker Maid: Tale-Telling and the Trial of Personal Experience and Written Authority," *Modern Language Review* 102 (2007): 934.

117. Graham Swift, *Last Orders* (New York: Alfred A. Knopf, 1996). Quoted from Adrian Poole, Review of *Last Orders*: "Hurry up please it's time," *The Guardian*, January 12, 1996, http://www.guardian.co.uk/books/1996/jan/12/fiction.grahamswift.

118. David Malcolm, *Understanding Graham Swift* (Columbia: University of South Carolina Press, 2003), p. 173.

119. For the Frow kerfuffle, including the disappointing response of Booker committee members, see "The Sound and the Fury," *The Independent on Sunday*, March 16, 1997, http://www.independent.co.uk/news/the-sound-and-the-fury-1273239.html.

120. Graham Swift, *Ever After* (London: Picador, 1992), p. 3.
121. Juvan, *History and Poetics*, p. 153.
122. See Hutcheon, *Theory of Adaptation*, p. 31: "To think of narrative adaptation in terms of a story's fit and its process of mutation or adjustment, through adaptation, to a particular cultural environment is something I find suggestive. Stories also evolve by adaptation and are not immutable over time ... stories travel to different cultures and different media."
123. I echo Foucault, "What is an Author?" in *Aesthetics, Method, and Epistemology*, p. 221.
124. On the search for social identities and modern pilgrimage, see Peter Jan Margry, "Secular Pilgrimage: A Contradiction in Terms?" in *Shrines and Pilgrimage in the Modern World: New Itineraries into the Sacred*, ed. Peter Jan Margry (Amsterdam: Amsterdam University Press, 2008), pp. 13–46.
125. Michaela Paasche Grudin, "Discourse and the Problem of Closure in the *Canterbury Tales*," *PMLA* 107 (1992): 1163–1165.

Chapter 2

1. See Joerg O. Fichte, "Crime Fiction Set in the Middle Ages: Historical Novel and Detective Story," *Zeitschrift für Anglistik und Amerikanistik* 53 (2005): 53–70.
2. On the narrative and thematic characteristics of classical detective fiction and crime fiction, see John Scaggs, *Crime Fiction* (New York: Routledge, 2005), pp. 33–54; Stephen Knight, "The Golden Age," in *The Cambridge Companion to Crime Fiction*, ed. Martin Priestman (Cambridge: Cambridge University Press, 2003), pp. 77–94; Lee Horsley, *Twentieth-Century Crime Fiction* (New York: Oxford University Press, 2005), pp. 12–65; John G. Cawelti, *Adventure, Mystery, and Romance: Formula Stories as Art and Popular Culture* (Chicago: University of Chicago Press, 1976), pp. 80–105; Dennis Porter, *The Pursuit of Crime: Art and Ideology in Crime Fiction* (New Haven: Yale University Press, 1981), pp. 115–129; and Heta Pyrhönen, *Murder from an Academic Angle: An Introduction to the Study of the Detective Narrative* (Columbia, SC: Camden House, 1994).
3. Patricia J. Eberle, "Crime and Justice in the Middle Ages: Cases from the *Canterbury Tales* of Geoffrey Chaucer," in *Rough Justice: Essays on Crime in Literature*, ed. M. L. Friedland (Toronto: University of Toronto Press, 1991), p. 19. On some similarities between medieval literature and modern crime fiction, see Geraldine Barnes, "Medieval Murder — Modern Crime Fiction," in *Medieval Cultural Studies: Essays in Honor of Stephen Knight*, ed. Ruth Evans, Helen Fulton, and David Matthews (Chicago: University of Chicago Press, 2006), pp. 241–254.
4. See, for instance, Gerald Morgan, "Moral and Social Identity and the Idea of Pilgrimage in the *General Prologue*," *Chaucer Review* 37 (2003): 285–314.
5. Horsley, *Twentieth-Century Crime Fiction*, p. 18.
6. Gertrude Clancy and Joseph Clancy, *Death is a Pilgrim* (Aberystwyth, Wales: Northgate, 1993).
7. On the "country-house" motif within detective fiction, see Porter, *Pursuit of Crime*, pp. 189–201.
8. Porter, *Pursuit of Crime*, p. 121.
9. On the use of red herrings, see Pyrhönen, *Murder from an Academic Angle*, p. 107.
10. Trigg, *Congenial Souls*, pp. xxii, 161, 84.
11. Johannes Willem Bertens and Theo d'Haen, *Contemporary American Crime Fiction* (New York: Palgrave Macmillan, 2001), p. 146. "There is no obvious explanation for the sudden popularity of historical crime writing at the end of the twentieth century. Perhaps it is exactly the approaching end of the second millennium that has triggered the interest in history and the awareness that the past is still usable.... The past is relevant to us in historical crime fiction because it allows us to draw parallels with the contemporary world and to illuminate contemporary issues and problems" (159).
On the generic characteristics of historical crime fiction, see Scaggs, *Crime Fiction*, pp. 122–138; and Ray B. Browne and Lawrence A. Kreiser, Jr., ed., *The Detective as Historian: History and Art in Historical Crime Fiction* (Bowling Green, OH: Bowling Green State University Popular Press, 2000).
12. Duane Crowley, *Riddle Me a Murder* (London: Blue Boar Press, 1986).
13. Two of Cherith Baldry's three short whodunnits, "The Pilgrims' Tale" and "The Duke's Tale," feature a similar premise, with Chaucer's trips abroad involving him in delicate diplomatic missions. The third, "The Friar's Tale," imagines a scene similar to Ford Madox Brown's "Chaucer Reading the 'Legend of Custance' to Edward III and his Court" (1845–51) or the fifteenth-century *Troilus* frontispiece, with Chaucer an intimate and personal advisor to Richard II. All three provide on a domestic scale a reflection of disruptive national political events (an incipient Lords Appellant; the prosecution of the Hundred Years' War) which Chaucer temporarily forestalls by letting the aristocratic malefactors go free. Cherith Baldry, "The Friar's Tale," in *Royal Whodunnits: Tales of Right Royal Murder and Mystery*, ed. Mike Ashley (New York: Carroll and Graf, 1999), pp. 187–202; "The Pilgrim's Tale," in *The Mammoth Book of More Historical Whodunnits*,

ed. Mike Ashley (New York: Carroll and Graf, 2001), pp. 297–312; "The Duke's Tale," in *The Mammoth Book of New Historical Whodunnits*, ed. Mike Ashley (New York: Carroll and Graf, 2005), pp. 178–196.

14. Ian A. Bell, "Eighteenth-Century Crime Writing," in *The Cambridge Companion to Crime Fiction*, ed. Martin Priestman (Cambridge: Cambridge University Press, 2003), p. 15.

15. Similarly, in "Act Four" of the corporate-authored *House of Shadows* (in which Morgan writes as Philip Gooden), Chaucer gets "an idea for a poem" (307) after hearing of a myth concerning a giant eagle concocted by the founding brothers of Bermondsey Priory in order to perpetuate the order's fame. See Bernard Knight, Ian Morson, Michael Jecks, Philip Gooden, and Susanna Gregory, *House of Shadows: A Historical Mystery by The Medieval Murderers* (London: Pocket Books, 2007). Like Chaucer's poem, the novel is concerned with fame and the lengths gone to quell rumor and maintain reputation.

16. Charles J. Rzepka, *Detective Fiction* (Cambridge, U.K.: Polity, 2005) p. 25.

17. Mary Devlin, *The Legend of Good Women: A Geoffrey Chaucer Murder Mystery* (Lincoln, NE: Writers Club Press, 2003).

18. On the academic side of the field, Michael Foster, "On Dating the Duchess: The Personal and Social Context of *Book of the Duchess*," *Review of English Studies* 59 (2008): 185–196, argues that the relationship between Chaucer and Gaunt by way of Katherine Swynford is central to our understanding of *Book of the Duchess*. In a letter (1873), Henry Bradshaw had suggested to Frederick Furnivall a similar autobiographical conjunction between *Troilus and Criseyde* and Gaunt's liaison with Katherine. Furnivall "should like to kick Chaucer if he wrote for such a purpose." See Matthews, "Speaking to Chaucer," 18.

19. But, on Chaucer's propensity for violence, see David R. Carlson, "The Robberies of Chaucer," *English Studies in Canada* 35 (2009): 29–54.

20. Stephen Henry Rigby, *Chaucer in Context: Society, Allegory, and Gender* (Manchester: Manchester University Press, 1996), p.18.

21. John G. Cawelti, "Canonization, Modern Literature, and the Detective Story," in *Theory and Practice of Classical Detective Fiction*, ed. Jerome H. Delamater and Ruth Prigozy (Westport, CT: Greenwood Press, 1997), p. 12.

22. Cawelti, *Adventure, Mystery, and Romance*, pp. 148–149.

23. Martin Priestman, "Post-war British Crime Fiction," in *A Cambridge Companion to Crime Fiction* (Cambridge: Cambridge University Press, 2003), p. 184, suggests that the use of locations that are "half-familiar to a fair majority of readers, but chiefly identified with culture or tourism" provides "an inbuilt sense of enthralling discovery in the exposure of these places' festering underbellies."

24. Barry Lewis, *My Words Echo Thus: Possessing the Past in Peter Ackroyd* (Columbia: University of South Carolina Press, 2007), p. 130.

25. Tom Payne, "The Blood and the Beef," Review of *The Clerkenwell Tales*, *The Telegraph*, August 4, 2003, http://www.telegraph.co.uk/culture/books/3600595/The-blood-and-the-beef.html.

26. Lewis, *My Words Echo*, pp. 134–135.

27. John Maingay, "Panic on London's Streets," *Newsday*, September 18, 2004, http://www.newsday.com/entertainment/fanfare/panic-on-london-s-streets-1.697758.

28. Linda Hutcheon, *The Poetics of Postmodernism: History, Theory, Fiction* (London: Routledge, 1988), p. 20.

29. Wallace, "New Chaucer Topographies," 5.

30. Laura Marcus, "Detection and Literary Fiction," in *The Cambridge Companion to Crime Fiction*, ed. Martin Priestman (Cambridge: Cambridge University Press, 2003), p. 248.

31. Hutcheon, *Poetics of Postmodernism*, p. 16.

32. Hutcheon, *Poetics of Postmodernism*, p. 5.

33. See Ben Lowe, "Teaching in the 'Schole of Christ': Law, Learning, and Love in Early Lollard Pacificism," *The Catholic Historical Review* 90 (2004): 405–438: "Wyclif and Lollards quickly came to condemn what they considered to be the ulterior motives of popes in their promotion of war and persecution of the godly reformers. Most of these attacks were extensions of Wyclif's dominion theory.... Simply put, *dominium*—the right to hold both power and possessions, through the divine gift (*donatio*) of grace—is restricted to the predestined, since any act of a person in mortal sin leads to further sinning, and God cannot co-operate with evil" (408–409).

34. Umberto Eco, *The Limits of Interpretation* (Bloomington: Indiana University Press, 1990), p. 91.

35. For Will Hammond, "Old London Calling," *The Observer*, August 9, 2003, http://www.guardian.co.uk/books/2003/aug/10/fiction.peterackroyd, the novel lacks "a recognizable purpose"; Michael Pye, "A Mad Nun's Tale," *The New York Times*, October 31, 2004, http://www.nytimes.com/2004/10/31/books/review/31PYEL.html?8bl, finds that "for all the lovely colors in this book ... it still rings rather hollow—a gifted writer's five-finger exercise"; and for Phil Baker, "London Calling," *The Guardian*, August 15, 2003, http://www.guardian.co.uk/books/2003/aug/16/fiction.peterackroyd, the text is "almost self parodic."

36. Terry Jones, *Who Murdered Chaucer?: A Medieval Mystery* (New York: St. Martin's, 2004), p. 2.

37. Stephanie Trigg, "Medievalism and Convergence Culture: Researching the Middle Ages for Fiction and Film," *Parergon* 25 (2008): 118. There is precedent for this convergence or blurring of the popular and the professional. In Vernon Hall, Jr.'s short story, "Sherlock Holmes and the Wife of Bath," *Baker Street Journal* 3 (1948): 84–93, the detective, now retired and looking for something "to amuse me in my sedentary years," takes up "literary scholarship." He discovers that the Wife of Bath has hired Jankyn to kill her fourth husband. To Watson's rote objection that "men who devote their lives to literature" have not discovered this plot, Holmes blandly retorts that "professional scholars ... are not reasoning animals. If the murder ... has not been discovered before, it is because I never read that part of the *Canterbury Tales* until a fortnight ago" (85).

Taking up the ludic challenge, Susan Crane, "Alison of Bath Accused of Murder: Case Dismissed," *English Language Notes* 25 (1988): 10–15, exposes the strained inferences but also demonstrates that Hall's parody in fact mimics misogynistic critical trends in the 1970s. Yvonne Yaw, "Student Study Guides and the Wife of Bath," *Chaucer Review* 35 (2001): 318–332, finds that even in the wake of 40 years of feminist critical reevaluation, the cumulative effect of errors in contemporary study guides is to lead some students to believe that Alison killed not only the fourth, but indeed "all of her husbands" (318).

38. Jensen, "On Fandom," p. xxi.

39. The phantom "Book of the Lion" also features in two mid-century detective novels. Robert Robinson, *Landscape with Dead Dons* (London: Gollancz, 1956) features a medievalist who, somewhat understandably, can't bear the "slog" of sustained research and creates a sensation with his forged "Book of the Lion" (here, an allegorical prophesy of Henry Bolingbroke's usurpation). Elizabeth Daly, *The Book of the Lion* (New York: Berkley, 1948), features a lesser-known Lost Generation of writers who supplement their incomes with literary forgeries, including Chaucer's "dream vision allegory in octosyllabic couplets" (78).

40. Patterson, *Chaucer and the Subject of History*, p. 44.

41. This trait is passed on to his son Thomas in Margaret Frazer's *The Novice's Tale* (New York: Berkley, 1993), p. 9: "My place in the world would hardly change by my gaining a title. I'd simply add more duties to my life and my taxes would go up and that's an idiot's price for fancying my name." Throughout her series Frazer focuses on socioeconomic injustice and its larger effects on society as a whole.

42. Rzepka, *Detective Fiction*, p. 48.
43. Patterson, *Chaucer and the Subject of History*, p. 39.
44. Strohm, *Social Chaucer*, p. 157.
45. Carlson, *Chaucer's Jobs*, p. 61.

Chapter 3

1. *The Treasure of the Sierra Madre*, directed by John Huston (1948; Warner Home Video, 2003), DVD; *A Simple Plan*, directed by Sam Raimi (1998; Paramount, 1999), DVD.

2. *A Canterbury Tale*, directed by Michael Powell and Emeric Pressburger (1944; Criterion, 2006), DVD. In David Lazar, ed., *Michael Powell, Interviews* (Jackson: University Press of Mississippi, 2003), p. 40, Powell himself suggests that the film "doesn't have that much to do with Chaucer." But see Tison Pugh, "Perverse Pastoralism and Medieval Melancholia in Powell and Pressburger's *A Canterbury Tale*," *Arthuriana* 19 (2009): 97–113, for an engaging analysis of how Chaucer provides a "nostalgically pastoral foundation" for the film's propagandistic efforts to "posit the uniformity between past and present" (98).

3. On *I racconti di Canterbury* as an adaptation, see Martin Green, "The Dialectic of Adaptation: *The Canterbury Tales* of Pier Paolo Pasolini," *Literature/Film Quarterly* 4 (1976): 46–53; and Carol L. Robinson, "Celluloid Criticism: Pasolini's Contribution to a Chaucerian Debate," *Studies in Medievalism* 5 (1993): 115–126.

4. Quoted from Pile, "The Scriptwriters' Tales."

5. Kevin J. Harty, "Chaucer for a New Millennium: The *BBC Canterbury Tales*," in *Mass Market Medieval: Essays on the Middle Ages in Popular Culture*, ed. David W. Marshall (Jefferson, NC: McFarland, 2007), p. 25.

6. Ellis, *Chaucer at Large*, p. 139.

7. Cardwell, "Literature on the Small Screen," pp. 184, 193.

8. On the pedagogical value of fidelity, see Douglas Lanier, "William Shakespeare, Filmmaker," in *The Cambridge Companion to Literature on Screen*, ed. Deborah Cartmell and Imelda Whelehan (Cambridge: Cambridge University Press, 2007), p. 68.

9. Cardwell, "Literature on the Small Screen," p. 188: "Historically speaking, a television adaptation, unlike a film, cannot be regarded as mere entertainment. Its aim is not limited to being financially viable or even artistically successful; its accomplishments are also measured with reference to these broader conceptions of television's public role. This in part explains television adaptations' preoccupation with fidelity."

10. The BBC series inspired a similar mod-

ernizing treatment of a handful of Shakespeare's plays, and the animated version won several awards, including an Emmy, Bafta, and Academy Award nomination.

11. Robert Stam, "Beyond Fidelity: The Dialogics of Adaptation," in *Film Adaptation*, ed. James Naremore (New Brunswick, NJ: Rutgers University Press, 2000), p.58, describes a similar artistic conversation as "intertextual dialogism."

12. See Wagner, *Novel and the Cinema*, p. 223. On the various ways of evaluating and categorizing film adaptations see also Dudley Andrew, *Concepts in Film Theory* (New York: Oxford University Press, 1984), pp. 98–101; and Thomas Leitch, *Film Adaptation and Its Discontents* (Baltimore, MD: Johns Hopkins University Press, 2007), pp. 93–126.

13. *Alan Plater's Trinity Tales,* directed by Tristan de Vere Cole and Roger Tucker, written by Alan Plater (London: BBC, 1975).

14. Jane Tranter, quoted by Giles Coren, "A Kick in the Vernaculars," *The Times*, September 6, 2003 [log-in required].

15. See Harry M. Benshoff, *Dark Shadows* (Detroit, MI: Wayne State University Press, 2011), p. 38.

16. Jauss, *Toward an Aesthetic of Reception*, p. 23. Quoted from Maureen Paton, "Soap for the Wife of Bath," *The Times*, September 1, 2003, [log-in required].

17. See Fiske, *Television Culture*, pp. 21–22.

18. See Phyllis Zatlin, *Theatrical Translation and Film Adaptation: A Practitioner's View* (Clevedon, U.K.: Multilingual Matters, 2005), p. 170.

19. See "Introduction" in Marcia Landy, ed., *Imitations of Life: A Reader on Film and Television Melodrama* (Detroit, MI: Wayne State University Press, 1991), p. 15.

20. Cawelti, "The Evolution of Social Melodrama," p. 46.

21. Stam, "Introduction: The Theory and Practice of Adaptation," p. 43.

22. Sally Wainwright is quoted from "*Canterbury Tales*, Episode Guide: The Wife of Bath's Tale," BBC Online, July 9, 2006, http://www.bbc.co.uk/pressoffice/pressreleases/stories/2003/08_august/06/wifeofbath.pdf.

23. Cowart, *Literary Symbiosis*, p. 17.

24. Naomi Wolf, *The Beauty Myth: How Images of Beauty are Used Against Women* (New York: W. Morrow, 1991).

25. Robert Stretter, "Rewriting Perfect Friendship in Chaucer's *Knight's Tale* and Lydgate's *Fabula Duorum Mercatorum*," *Chaucer Review* 37 (2003): 234.

26. Quoted from Pile, "The Scriptwriters' Tales."

27. Quoted from "*Canterbury Tales*, Episode Guide: *The Knight's Tale*," BBC Online, July 9, 2006.

28. Carolyn P. Collette, *Species, Phantasms, and Images: Vision and Medieval Psychology in* The Canterbury Tales (Ann Arbor: University of Michigan Press, 2001), p. 58.

29. Avie Luthra is quoted from Jonathan Myerson, "Tales of the Unexpected," *The Guardian*, August 30, 2003, http://www.guardian.co.uk/theobserver/2003/aug/31/features.review87.

30. Janey Place, "Women in *Film Noir*," in *Women in Film Noir*, ed. E. Ann Kaplan (London: British Film Institute, 1978), p. 35.

31. Grounds is quoted from "*Canterbury Tales*: About the Show," BBC Online, July 9, 2006, http://www.bbc.co.uk/canterburytales/episodeguide/pardoners_tale/.

32. Wagner, *Novel and the Cinema*, p. 227.

33. Stam, "Introduction: The Theory and Practice of Adaptation," p. 10.

34. For a convenient summary of critical approaches to the old man, see Gudrun Richardson, "The Old Man in Chaucer's *Pardoner's Tale*: An Interpretative Study of His Identity and Meaning," *Neophilologus* 87 (2003): 323–337.

35. Olivia Hetreed is quoted from Pile, "The Scriptwriters' Tales."

36. Quoted from Pile, "The Scriptwriters' Tales." See Susan Yager, "The BBC 'Man of Law's Tale': Faithful to the Tradition," *Literature and Belief* 27 (2007): 55–68, for an insightful analysis of how the show has "key elements which connect contemporary sensibilities, emotionally and intellectually, with the medieval story" (56).

37. Mary Beth Rose, *Gender and Heroism in Early Modern English Literature* (Chicago: University of Chicago Press, 2002), pp. xi-xii.

38. A. C. Spearing, "Narrative Voice: The Case of Chaucer's *Man of Law's Tale*," *New Literary History* 32 (2001): 741.

39. According to the "unofficial overnights" provided by *The Guardian*'s "TV ratings" following the broadcast of each BBC1 episode, "The Miller's Tale" and "The Wife of Bath" garnered between 7 and 8 million viewers, or 30% of audience share. There was a decline after that with "The Knight's Tale" (watched by 5.1 million viewers) attracting a 24% audience share. "The Sea Captain's Tale" (3.6 million viewers), "The Pardoner's Tale" (4.4 million), and "The Man of Law" (4.3 million) attracted roughly 20% of audience share between 9 p.m. and 10 p.m.

40. Margaret Rogerson, "Prime-time Drama: *Canterbury Tales* for the Small Screen," *Sydney Studies in English* 32 (2006): 55.

41. Cawelti, "Evolution of Social Melodrama," p. 47.

42. "The Animator's Tale," *BBC News Online*, March 17, 1999, http://news.bbc.co.uk/2/hi/entertainment/297262.stm.

43. See Jill Nelmes, *An Introduction to Film*

Studies, 3rd ed. (New York: Routledge, 2003), p. 226.

44. The show originally aired during the Christmas holidays (1998) and subsequently on national educational television. It was also broadcast, with subtitles, in Welsh and Middle English.

45. *The Canterbury Tales*, directed by Michael Bakewell and Roderick Graham, written by Martin Starkie and Nevil Coghill (London: BBC, 1969). For further analysis, see Ellis, *Chaucer at Large*, pp. 121–124.

46. Ellis, *Chaucer at Large*, p. 139.

47. Paul Wells, "Classic Literature and Animation: All Adaptations are Equal, But Some are More Equal Than Others," in *The Cambridge Companion to Literature on Screen*, ed. Deborah Cartmell and Imelda Whelehan (Cambridge: Cambridge University Press, 2007), p. 208.

48. Barry Purves, *Basics Animation: Stop-Motion* (Lausanne: Ava Publishing, 2010), p. xvii. Some of the puppets, especially the Wife of Bath, bear a resemblance to the figures found in the Canterbury Tales Visitor Attraction in Canterbury.

49. See Carol Midgely, "Chaucer? Not many people know that," *The Times*, November 23, 1998 [log-in required].

50. Paul Wells, "'Thou art translated': Analyzing Animated Adaptations," in *Adaptations: From Text to Screen, Screen to Text*, ed. Deborah Cartmell and Imelda Whelehan (London: Routledge, 1999), p. 205.

51. Quoted from Midgely, "Chaucer? Not a lot of people know that," n.p.

52. Jean Ann Wright, *Animation Writing and Development: From Script Development to Pitch* (Burlington, MA: Focal Press, 2005), p. 182.

53. See Wells, "'Thou art translated,'" p. 208: "Animation accentuates the intended 'feeling' of the text through its very abstractness in the use of colour, form and movement ... animation simultaneously literalizes and abstracts."

54. Paul Wells, *Understanding Animation* (New York: Routledge, 1998), p. 69.

55. Wells, "'Thou Art Translated,'" p. 201.

56. Pertelote: Dreams are nothing but nonsense. It's overeating. It's vapours from the gut.
Chaunticleer: —*belches*—
Pertelote: Just listen to what Dionysius Cato has to say on the subject. "Attach no import to dreams. Too much red in you — dreams of arrows, flames, biting beasts. Too much black — bears, bulls, demons." But I won't dwell on this. What you need is a laxative. Two days of worms will stop this nonsense.
Chaunticleer: Cato, yes, Cato. He commands a certain respect. But many, many greater authorities posit quite a contrary stance. Daniel. Did he think dreams were illusions? Joseph? Pharaoh? His butler? Andromache? Croesus? St. Kenelm? Scipio Africanus? Suffice to say, this dream of mine spells adversity. No laxatives. All I need is your soft feathers nustling beside me. The perch is too narrow for anything else.

57. Wells, "'Thou Art Translated,'" p. 200.

58. Barbara Cooney, *Chanticleer and the Fox* (New York: Thomas Y. Crowell, 1958).

59. See, for instance, Saul Nathaniel Brody, "Truth and Fiction in the *Nun's Priest's Tale*," *Chaucer Review* 14 (1979): 33–47: "the tale is less about a particular moral in it than about the very existence of moral possibilities" (43).

60. Wells, "Classic Literature and Animation," p. 203.

61. On Quinn's style, see Wells, *Understanding Animation*, p. 66; and Maureen Furniss, *Art in Motion: Animation Aesthetics* (London: John Libbey, 1998), p. 33.

62. Wells, *Understanding Animation*, p. 65, suggests that "she criticizes his duplicity, promising him that she will be both — in this version chillingly illustrated by an oscillating metamorphosis between voluptuous young lover and skeletal harridan."

63. See Furniss, *Art in Motion*, p. 147.

64. On the artistic use of psychological hues, see Furniss, *Art in Motion*, p. 73.

65. See A. C. Hamilton, ed., *Spenser: The Faerie Queen*, 2nd ed. (New York: Longman, 2006), Book 4; F. J. Furnivall, ed., "John Lane's Continuation of Chaucer's *Squire's Tale*," *Chaucer Society Publications*, ser. 23 (London: K. Paul, Trench and Trubner, 1890).

66. Wells, "'Thou Art Translated,'" p. 210.

67. Kirsten Thompson, "Animation," in *Comedy: A Geographic and Historical Guide*, Vol. 1, ed. Maurice Charney (Westport, CT: Praeger, 2005), p. 141. Suzanne Buchan, "The Animated Spectator," in *Animated Worlds*, ed. Suzanne Buchan (Eastleigh, U.K.: John Libbey, 2006), pp. 15–38, suggests that 2D animation is especially effective in visualizing the sudden changes and reversals associated with comedy (26).

68. Wells, *Understanding Animation*, p. 27. On the toleration for otherwise "offensive behavior" afforded by animation, see Purves, *Animation*, p. 61. HBO nonetheless omitted the tales from its airing in the United States. See Laura Fries, "Animated Epics: The Canterbury Tales," *Variety*, May 25, 1999, http://www.variety.com/review/VE1117499827?refCatId=32.

69. Erik Hertog, *Chaucer's Fabliaux as Analogues* (Leuven, BE: Leuven University Press, 1991), p. 215: "Instead of 'moralizing' the narrative ... the fabliau does exactly the reverse and mocks the conventional, established attempt and pretensions at moralizing."

70. For an eloquent plea to deconstruct the "a priori valorization" of the literary source text, see

Stam, "Introduction: The Theory and Practice of Adaptation," pp. 1–8.
71. Dominic Strinati, *An Introduction to Studying Popular Culture* (London: Routledge, 2000), p. 156.
72. Dudley Andrew, "Adapting Cinema to History: A Revolution in the Making," in *A Companion to Literature and Film*, ed. Robert Stam and Alessandra Raengo (Oxford: Blackwell, 2004), p. 190.
73. Quoted from the media critics' roundup following the airing of "The Miller's Tale," *The Guardian*, September 12, 2003, http://www.guardian.co.uk/media/2003/sep/12/firstnight.broadcasting.
74. Nancy Banks-Smith is quoted from *The Guardian*, September 12, 2003, http://www.guardian.o.uk/media/2003/sep/12/firstnight.broadcasting.

Chapter 4

1. Wallace, "New Chaucer Topographies," 4–5.
2. Hall, "Notes on Deconstructing the Popular," p. 514.
3. See, for instance, Patricia Clare Ingham, "Contrapuntal Histories," in *Postcolonial Moves: Medieval Through Modern*, ed. Patricia Clare Ingham and Michelle R. Warren (New York: Palgrave Macmillan, 2003), pp. 47–70; Sylvia Tomasch, "Postcolonial Chaucer and the Virtual Jew," in *The Postcolonial Middle Ages*, ed. Jeffrey Jerome Cohen (New York: St. Martin's, 2000), pp. 243–260; and Kathryn R. Lynch, "Storytelling, Exchange, and Constancy: East and West in Chaucer's *Man of Law's Tale*," *Chaucer Review* 33 (1999): 409–422.
4. See John M. Bowers, "Chaucer after Smithfield: From Postcolonial Writer to Imperialist Author," in *The Postcolonial Middle Ages*, ed. Jeffrey Jerome Cohen (New York: St. Martins, 2000), pp. 53–66. For a critique of similar postcolonial critical moves, see Derek Pearsall, "Chaucer and Englishness," *Proceedings of the British Academy* 101 (1999): 77–99.
5. Henry Louis Gates, Jr., *The Signifying Monkey: A Theory of African-American Literary Criticism* (New York: Oxford University Press, 1988), p. xxvi; Linda Hutcheon, *A Theory of Parody: The Teachings of Twentieth-Century Art Forms* (1985; Champaign: University of Illinois Press, 2000), p. xii.
6. Nelson has been associated with the New Formalist movement, generally characterized by a return to traditional verse forms in preference to free verse, and narrative in preference to lyricality. See, for instance, Mark Jarman and David Mason, ed., *Rebel Angels: 25 Poets of the New Formalism* (Ashland, OR: Story Line Press, 1996).
7. Todd Edmondson, "The Ambivalence of Pilgrimage in Marilyn Nelson's *Cachoeira Tales*," *REA: A Journal of Religion, Education, and the Arts* 6 (2009): 5.
8. Wallace, "New Chaucer Topographies," 12.
9. For the full version of "The Ski Accident," see Jan Harold Brunvard, *Encyclopedia of Urban Legends* (Santa Barbara: ABC-CLIO, Inc., 2001), pp. 386–387. In a footnote Wallace, "New Chaucer Topographies," 13, relates Nelson's suggestion that the "why ol' ass can't whistle" tale is Native American (Lakota) in origin.
10. Wallace, "New Chaucer Topographies," 15.
11. I borrow the term describing a form of external intertextuality from Michael Gresset, "Of Sailboats and Kites: The 'Dying Fall' in Faulkner's *Sanctuary* and Beckett's *Murphy*," in *Intertextuality in Faulkner*, ed. Michael Gresset and Noel Polk (Jackson: University Press of Mississippi, 1985), pp. 57–72.
12. Bowers, "Chaucer after Smithfield," p. 54.
13. Evan Maina Mwangi, *Africa Writes Back to Self: Metafiction, Gender, Sexuality* (Albany: State University of New York Press, 2010), p. 140.
14. Sara Upstone, *Spatial Politics in the Postcolonial Novel* (Burlington, VT: Ashgate, 1988), p. 70.
15. On liminality and pilgrimage, see Victor Turner and Edith Turner, *Image and Pilgrimage in Christian Culture* (New York: Columbia University Press, 1978), pp. 1–39.
16. See Christopher Anyokwu, "Wordplay and Fancy: The Nigerian Question in Karen King-Aribisala's *Kicking Tongues*," *LARES: A Journal of Language and Literary Studies*, ed. V. O. Awonusi (University of Lagos, 2006): 308–19.
17. Mwangi, *Africa Writes Back*, p. 140.
18. Bowers, "Chaucer at Smithfield," pp. 54–56.
19. Upstone, *Spatial Politics*, p. 70.
20. Like Chaucer, King-Aribisala often uses array as a secondary signifier. See Eleonora Chiavetta, "The Clothing Metaphor as Signifier in the Fiction of Karen King-Aribisala," in *Bodies and Voices: The Forcefield of Representation and Discourse in Colonial and Postcolonial Studies*, ed. Merete Falck Borch, et al. (Amsterdam: Rodopi, 2008), pp. 93–102.
21. Mwangi, *Africa Writes Back*, p. 141, suggests that the narrator's "bossiness" mimics and parodies the psychology of dictatorial regimes.
22. Jennifer Wenzel, "Petro-magic-realism: Toward a Political Ecology of Nigerian Literature," *Postcolonial Studies* 9 (2006): 454.
23. Rebecca S. Wood, "'Two Warring Ideals in One Dark Body': Universalism and National-

ism in Gloria Naylor's *Bailey's Cafe*," *African American Review* 30 (1996): 385.

24. On the novel as a "blues symphony," see Sylvie Chavenelle, "Gloria Naylor's *Bailey's Café*: The Blues and Beyond," *American Studies International* 36.2 (1998): 58–73.

25. As a gendered revisioning of Scripture, see Lynn Alexander, "Signifyin(g) Sex: Gloria Naylor's *Bailey's Cafe* and Western Religious Tradition," in *He Said, She Says: An RSVP to the Male Text*, ed. Mica Howe and Sarah Appleton Aguiar (Cranbury, NJ.: Associated University Presses, 2001), pp. 91–105; Dorothy Perry Thompson, "African Womanist Revision in Gloria Naylor's *Mama Day* and *Bailey's Café*," in *Gloria Naylor's Early Novels*, ed. Margot Anne Kelley (Gainesville: University Press of Florida, 1999), pp. 89–111; Amy Benson Brown, "Writing Home: The Bible and Gloria Naylor's *Bailey's Café*," in *Homemaking: Women Writers and the Politics and Poetics of Home*, ed. Catherine Wiley and Fiona Barnes (New York: Garland, 1996), pp. 23–42; Keith Eldon Byerman, *Remembering the Past in Contemporary African American Fiction* (Chapel Hill: University of North Carolina Press, 2005), pp. 75–93; and Shirley A. Stave, "Gloria Naylor's Revisionary Theology," in *Gloria Naylor: Strategy and Technique, Myth and Magic*, ed. Shirley A. Stave (Cranbury, NJ: Associated University Presses, 2001), pp. 97–117.

Elizabeth Ann Beaulieu, *Writing African American Women* (Westport, CT: Greenwood Press, 2006), pp. 34–36, suggests that Naylor advocates a "liberation sexuality" that transcends gender roles; for Carol Bender and Roseanne Hoefel, "Toward a Literacy of Empathy: Inhabiting Gloria Naylor's *Bailey's Cafe*," in *Gloria Naylor: Strategy and Technique, Magic and Myth*, ed. Shirley A. Stave (Cranbury, NJ.: Associated University Presses, 2001), pp. 182–195, through Bailey's narrative voice, Naylor provides a "model for the reader's empathic imagination"; and Wood, "'Two Warring Ideals in One Dark Body,'" reads the novel as a synthesis of universalist and nationalist perspectives on racial identity.

26. For Naylor's use of Shakespeare, see Peter Erickson, *Rewriting Shakespeare, Rewriting Ourselves* (Berkeley and Los Angeles: University of California Press, 1991), pp. 124–145; and Julie Sanders, *Novel Shakespeares: Twentieth-Century Women Novelists and Appropriation* (Manchester, U.K.: Manchester University Press, 2001), pp. 170–90. On Naylor's practice of intertextuality more generally, see Karen Schneider, "Gloria Naylor's Poetics of Emancipation: (E)merging (Im)possibilities in *Bailey's Café*," in *Gloria Naylor's Early Novels*, ed. Margot Anne Kelley (Gainesville: University Press of Florida, 1999), pp. 1–20.

27. Donna Rifkind, Review of *Bailey's Café*, in *Gloria Naylor: Critical Perspectives Past and Present*, ed. Henry Louis Gates, Jr., and K. A. Appiah (New York: Amistad, 1993), p. 28.

28. Charles E. Wilson, Jr., "Medievalism, Race, and Social Order in Gloria Naylor's *Bailey's Café*," *Studies in Medievalism* 10 (1998): 78; Wood, "Two Warring Ideals," p. 385; Alexander, "Signifyin(g) Sex," p. 92.

29. For instance, see Charles E. Wilson, Jr., *Gloria Naylor: A Critical Companion* (Westport, CT: Greenwood Press, 2001), p. 134: "While Chaucer's characters depart from and return to the Tabard Inn, Naylor's characters find themselves in the café when they are most in need of sanctuary"; Alexander, "Signifyin(g) Sex," p. 92: "instead of a shrine, the refuge sought by the various women is Eve's boarding house/ brothel, a brownstone surrounded by a garden of wildflowers."

30. Thompson, "African Womanist Revision," p. 89. Similarly, and more forcefully, Greg Thomas, Review of *Gloria Naylor's Early Novels*, *African Literatures* 33 (2002): 223–5, decries the critical focus on literary influences as "canonical co-optation," a privileging of "high canonicity in the culture of U. S. imperialism."

31. Wilson, "Medievalism, Race, and Social Order," p. 74.

32. Wilson, *Gloria Naylor: A Critical Companion*, p. 133. In a similar approach, Schneider, "Poetics of Emancipation," p. 3, suggests that Naylor's habit is to "appropriate familiar stories from Western culture, but by modifying content and/or form she recasts them in ways that destabilize absolute ontological boundaries defined by genre, gender politics, class, and cultural/literary tradition."

33. Wood, "Two Warring Ideals," p. 385.

34. Margot Anne Kelley, ed., *Gloria Naylor's Early Novels* (Gainesville: University Press of Florida, 1999), p. xiii.

35. Compare to Chaucer: "Of wenches wolde I beren hem on honde, / Whan that for syk unnethes myghte they stonde./ Yet tikled I his herte, for that he/ Wende that I hadde of hym so greet chiertee!/ I swoor that al my walkynge out by nyghte / Was for t' espye wenches that he dighte" (III. 393-98).

36. Compare the Wife of Bath's meditation on the dubious authority of institutionalized antifeminism: "Who peynted the leon, tel me who?/ By God, if women hadde writen stories,/ As clerkes han withinne hire oratories,/ They wolde han writen of men moore wikkednesse/ Than al the mark of Adam may redresse" (III. 692–96).

37. Sanders, *Novel Shakespeares*, pp. 178, 190.

38. Benedict Anderson, *Imagined Communities: Reflections on the Origin and Spread of Nationalism* (London: Verso, 1991), pp. 53, 61, also discusses pilgrimage as a vital "organizing trope"

in the formation of imagined, national communities.
	39. Reiss, "The Pilgrimage Narrative and the *Canterbury Tales*," 303.

Chapter 5

1. See Douglas B. Holt, *How Brands Become Icons: The Principles of Cultural Branding* (Harvard Business School, 2004), pp. 8,212. See also Tilde Heding, Charlotte F. Knudtzen, and Mogens Bjerre, *Brand Management: Research, Theory, Practice* (New York: Routledge, 2009), p. 237.
2. Holt, *How Brands Become Icons*, pp. 2, 6.
3. Louise M. Bishop, "Geoffrey Chaucer," in *Icons of the Middle Ages: Rulers, Writers, Rebels, and Saints*, ed. Lister M. Matheson (Santa Barbara, CA: Greenwood Press, 2012), p. 202.
4. Andrew Moor, *Powell and Pressburger: A Cinema of Magical Spaces* (London: I. B. Taurus, 2005), p. 94.
5. Powell is quoted from Moor, *Powell and Pressburger*, pp. 102–103.
6. Moor, *Powell and Pressburger*, p. 227.
7. D. Douglas Caulkins, Vickie Schlegel, Christina Hanson, Jane Cherry, "The Politics of Authenticity and Identity in British Heritage Sites," in *Regional Development on the North Atlantic Margin*, ed. Reginald Byron, Jens Christian Hansen, and Tim Jenkins (Aldershot, U.K.: Ashgate), pp. 115–116.
8. On the concept of staged authenticity and the role of authenticity in tourism studies see Dean MacCannell, *The Tourist: A New Theory of the Leisure Class* (1973; Berkeley and Los Angeles: University of California Press, 1999), pp. 91–108.
9. Ellis, *Chaucer at Large*, p. 160.
10. See MacCannell, *The Tourist*, p. 155.
11. See Caulkins, "Politics of Authenticity," p. 113.
12. The Chaucerian finds some interesting touches. The name of the pilgrims' inn is borrowed from the *Tale of Beryn*: "They toke hir in and logged hem at mydmorowe,/ I trowe, atte Cheker of the Hope, that many a man doth knowe" (13–14). See John M. Bowers, ed., The Canterbury Tales: *Fifteenth-Century Continuations and Additions* (Kalamazoo, MI: Medieval Institute Publications, 1992). A series of carved wooden panels depicting the rioters' demise in the tavern setting of the *Pardoner's Tale* resembles the Chaucer Chest in the London Museum. See Muriel Whitaker, "The Chaucer Chest and the *Pardoner's Tale*: Didacticism and Narrative Art," *Chaucer Review* 34 (1999): 174–189.
13. G. K. Chesterton, *Chaucer* (London: Faber and Faber, 1932).
14. See especially Chesterton, *Chaucer*, pp. 186–216 ("Chaucer as an Englishman").
15. For the Chaucer Cellars collection, see http://www.bargetto.com/chaucers.shtml.
16. See Stephen M. Mullins and David C. Fastenau, *A Century of Royal Doulton Character and Toby Jugs* (Atglen, PA: Schiffer, 2008), p. 137.
17. Diana Crane, *Fashion and Its Social Agendas: Class, Gender, and Identity in Clothing* (Chicago: University of Chicago Press, 2000), pp. 178–183.
18. The portrait ultimately derives from Hoccleve's *Regiment of Princes* (see the cover of this book). Matthews, "Speaking to Chaucer," p. 6, suggests that it was "this image more than any other that readers relied upon for their ideas about Chaucer's appearance" and for "conceptions of his character" (6).
19. Thomas Speght, *The Workes of Our Ancient and Learned English Poet, Geoffrey Chaucer, newly Printed* (London, 1602).
20. Andrew Ross, *No Respect: Intellectuals and Popular Culture* (New York: Routledge, 1989), p. 231.
21. On the sartorial blurring of status, see Crane, *Fashion and Its Social Agendas*, p. 178; and Betsy Cullum-Swan and Peter K. Manning, "What is a T-shirt?" in *The Socialness of Things: Essays on the Socio-Semiotics of Objects*, ed. Stephen Harold Riggins (Berlin: Mouton de Gruyter, 1994), p. 428.
22. Dryden, *Works*, 7: 40.
23. Fiske, *Understanding Popular Culture*, p. 4.
24. See houseoffame.blogspot.com.
25. See Gripsrud, "High Culture Revisited."
26. Jenkins, "'Strangers no more, we sing,'" p. 552.
27. Henry Jenkins, *Textual Poachers: Television Fans and Participatory Culture* (New York: Routledge, 1992), p. 25.
28. Brantley L. Bryant, et al., *Geoffrey Chaucer Hath a Blog: Medieval Studies and New Media* (New York: Palgrave, 2010). On the dialectic of containment and resistance, see Hall, "Notes on Deconstructing 'The Popular,'" p. 509.
29. Fiske, "Popular Discrimination," p. 113. For Fiske, the institutionalization of academia "necessarily aligns it with the power-bloc" (114).
30. See Tony Bennett, et al., *Culture, Class, Distinction* (London: Routledge, 2009), pp. 182–190.
31. See Fradenburg, "'So that we may speak of them': Enjoying the Middle Ages," 206; Wheeler, "Introduction: Go litel blog, go litel thys comedye!" p. 7.
32. See Pierre Bourdieu, "The Intellectual Field: A World Apart," in *In Other Words: Essays Towards a Reflexive Sociology*, trans. Matthew Anderson (Palo Alto, CA: Stanford University Press, 1990), pp. 140–149.
33. See, for instance, Patterson, "On the Mar-

gin," 87: "Most literary scholars and critics consider medieval texts to be utterly extraneous to their own interests, as at best irrelevant, at worst inconsequential; and they perceive the field itself as a sight of pedantry and antiquarianism, a place to escape from the demands of modern intellectual life."

34. Riley, *Geoffrey Chaucer: The Canterbury Tales*, p. 17.
35. See Fiske, *Television Culture*, pp. 309–326.
36. Fiske, "Popular Discrimination," p. 104.
37. Fiske, "Popular Discrimination," p. 106.

Bibliography

Primary Works

Ackroyd, Peter. *The Clerkenwell Tales.* New York: Anchor Books, 2005.

Alan Plater's Trinity Tales. Directed by Tristan de Vere Cole and Roger Tucker. Written by Alan Plater. London: BBC, 1975.

Augst, Thomas. *The Clerk's Tale: Young Men and Moral Life in Nineteenth-Century America.* Chicago: University of Chicago Press, 2003.

Baldry, Cherith. "The Duke's Tale." In *The Mammoth Book of New Historical Whodunnits*, edited by Mike Ashley, 178–196. New York: Carroll and Graf, 2005.

———. "The Friar's Tale." In *Royal Whodunnits: Tales of Right Royal Murder and Mystery*, edited by Mike Ashley, 187–202. New York: Carroll and Graf, 1999.

———. "The Pilgrim's Tale." In *The Mammoth Book of More Historical Whodunnits*, edited by Mike Ashley, 297–312. New York: Carroll and Graf, 2001.

BBC's Canterbury Tales. Directed by Julian Jarrold, John McKay, Marc Munden and Andy De Emmony. 2003; IMV Vision, 2004. DVD (Region 2).

Benson, Larry D., ed. *The Riverside Chaucer.* 3rd ed. New York: Houghton Mifflin, 1987.

Brinkman, Baba. *The Rap Canterbury Tales.* Vancouver: Talon Books, 2006.

Byatt, A. S. *The Biographer's Tale.* New York: Alfred A. Knopf, 2000.

A Canterbury Tale. Directed by Michael Powell and Emeric Pressburger. 1944; Criterion, 2006. DVD.

The Canterbury Tales. Directed by Michael Bakewell and Roderick Graham. Written by Martin Starkie and Nevil Coghill. London: BBC, 1969.

Canterbury Tales: Leaving London; Arriving at Canterbury; The Journey Back. Directed by Dave Antrobus, et al. Written by Jonathan Myerson. 1998–2000; Metrodome Distribution, 2005. DVD (Region 2).

The Canterbury Tales, 1969 Original Broadway Cast. 1969; Angel Records, 1994. Audio CD. Caravan. *Canterbury Tales: The Best of Caravan.* 1976; Universal Distribution, 1994. Audio CD.

Chwast, Seymour. *Geoffrey Chaucer: The Canterbury Tales.* New York: Bloomsbury 2011.

Churchill, Caryl. *Top Girls.* 1982; London: Methuen, 1991.

Clancy, Gertrude, and Joseph Clancy. *Death is a Pilgrim.* Aberystwyth, Wales: Northgate, 1993.

Cope, Wendy. *If I Don't Know.* London: Faber and Faber, 2001.

Cornwall, Bernard. *The Archer's Tale.* New York: HarperTorch, 2001.

Crowley, Duane. *Riddle Me a Murder.* London: Blue Boar Press, 1986.

Dabydeen, David. *The Intended.* London: Minerva, 1992.

Daly, Elizabeth. *The Book of the Lion.* New York: Berkley, 1948.

Dasgupta, Rana. *Tokyo Cancelled.* London: Harper Perennial, 2006.

Dawkins, Richard. *The Ancestor's Tale: A Pilgrimage to the Dawn of Life.* New York: Houghton Mifflin, 2004.

Devlin, Mary. *Murder on the Canterbury Pilgrimage: A Geoffrey Chaucer Murder Mystery.* Lincoln, NE: Writers Club Press, 2000.

———. *The Legend of Good Women: A Geoffrey Chaucer Murder Mystery.* Lincoln, NE: Writers Club Press, 2003.

Dil Chahta Hai. Directed by Farhan Akhtar. 2001; Spark Worldwide, 2001. DVD.

Doherty, Paul C. *An Ancient Evil: The Knight's Tale...* London: Headline, 1994.

———. *Ghostly Murders: The Poor Priest's Tale...* London: Headline, 1997.

_____. *The Hangman's Hymn: The Carpenter's Tale*... London: Headline, 2002.
_____. *A Haunt of Murder*. London: Headline, 2002.
_____. *A Tapestry of Murders: The Man of Law's Tale*... London: Headline, 1994.
_____. *A Tournament of Murders: The Franklin's Tale*... London: Headline, 1997.
Eberle, Thomas. *Six Canterbury Tales*. New Orleans, LA: Anchorage Press, 1993.
Ecker, Ronald L. *The Evolutionary Tales: Rhyme and Reason on Creation/Evolution*. 3rd ed. Palatka, FL: Hodge and Braddock, 2006.
Ellis, Jerry. *Walking to Canterbury: A Modern Journey Through Chaucer's Medieval England*. New York: Ballantine Books, 2003.
Fowles, John. *A Maggot*. New York: Little, Brown, 1985.
Frazer, Margaret. *The Novice's Tale*. New York: Berkley, 1993.
Freeman, Paul A. *Robin Hood and Friar Tuck: Zombie Killers — A Canterbury Tale*. Winnipeg, CAN: Coscom Entertainment, 2009.
Gaiman, Neil. "Men of Good Fortune." *Sandman* Issue 13, "The Doll's House Part 4" (1990). Reprinted in *Sandman Vol. 2: The Doll's House*. 1991; New York: DC Comics, 1995.
_____. *Sandman Vol. 8: Worlds' End*. 1993; New York: DC Comics, 1994.
Galland, Nicole. *The Fool's Tale*. New York: HarperCollins, 2005.
Guare, John. *Chaucer in Rome*. New York: Dramatists Play Service, 2002.
Hall, Vernon, Jr. "Sherlock Holmes and the Wife of Bath." *Baker Street Journal* 3 (1948): 84–93.
Holden, Wendy. *The Wives of Bath*. New York: Plume, 2005.
Hughes, Ted. *Birthday Letters*. New York: Farrar, Straus, and Giroux, 1999.
Hyde, Derek, and Kenneth Pickering. *Some Canterbury Tales: Adapted from Geoffrey Chaucer*. London: S. French, 1988.
Hynes, James. *The Lecturer's Tale*. New York: Picador, 2002.
I racconti di Canterbury. Directed by Pier Paolo Pasolini. 1972; BFI Video, 2009. DVD.
The Insomniac Tales by Chaucer's Women. DLSJ Press, 2003.
Jones, Terry. *Who Murdered Chaucer?: A Medieval Mystery*. New York: St. Martin's, 2004.

King-Aribisala, Karen. *Kicking Tongues*. Portsmouth, NH: Heinemann, 1998.
Knight, Bernard, Ian Morson, Michael Jecks, Philip Gooden, and Susanna Gregory. *House of Shadows: A Historical Mystery by The Medieval Murderers*. London: Pocket Books, 2007.
A Knight's Tale. Directed by Brian Helgeland. 2001; Columbia TriStar Home Entertainment, 2002. DVD.
Lewycka, Marina. *Two Caravans*. London: Penguin, 2007.
Maitland, Karen. *Company of Liars: A Novel of the Plague*. London: Penguin, 2008.
McCrumb, Sharyn. *St. Dale*. New York: Kensington, 2005.
Morgan, Philippa. *Chaucer and the Doctor of Physic*. New York: Carroll and Graf, 2006.
_____. *Chaucer and the House of Fame*. New York: Carroll and Graf, 2004.
_____. *Chaucer and the Legend of Good Women*. New York: Carroll and Graf, 2005.
Morley, Christopher. *The Trojan Horse*. Philadelphia: J. B. Lippincott, 1937.
Mystery Train. Directed by Jim Jarmusch. 1989; MGM, 2000. DVD.
Naylor, Gloria. *Bailey's Café*. New York: Harcourt Brace Jovanovich, 1992.
Nelson, Marilyn. *The Cachoeira Tales and Other Poems*. Baton Rouge: Louisiana State University Press, 2005.
O'Connor, Garry. *Chaucer's Triumph: Including the Case of Cecilia Chaumpaigne, the Seduction of Katherine Swynford, the Murder of her Husband, the Interment of John of Gaunt and Other Offices of the Flesh in the Year 1399*. London: Petrak Press, 2007.
O'Connor, John. *The Canterbury Tales: A Play Based on the Poem by Geoffrey Chaucer*. Cheltenham: Nelson Thornes, 2001.
Poulton, Mike. *The Canterbury Tales*. London: Nick Hern Books, 2006.
Rancid. "Poison." *Rancid*. Los Angeles: Hellcat, 2000. Audio CD.
Riley, Martin. *Geoffrey Chaucer: The Canterbury Tales*. 1998; Oxford: Oxford University Press, 2003.
Robinson, Robert. *Landscape with Dead Dons*. London: Gollancz, 1956.
Simmons, Dan. *Hyperion*. London: Headline Book Publishing, 1990.
A Simple Plan. Directed by Sam Raimi. 1998; Paramount, 1999. DVD.
Stevens, Roger. *The Journal of Danny Chaucer (Poet)*. London: Orion Children's Books, 2002.

Sting. *Ten Summoner's Tales*. 1993; A&M Records, 1998. Audio CD.
Swan, Susan. *The Wives of Bath*. New York: Alfred A. Knopf, 1993.
Swift, Graham. *Ever After*. London: Picador, 1992.
_____. *Last Orders*. New York: Alfred A. Knopf, 1996.
The Treasure of the Sierra Madre. Directed by John Huston. 1948; Warner Home Video, 2003. DVD.
Van Schuyver, Susan A. *Five Tales from Chaucer: A Collection of Five Playlets Adapted from Canterbury Tales*. Droitwich, U.K.: Hanbury Plays, 1988.
Walton, William. *Troilus and Criseyde, Opera in Three Acts*. Libretto by Christopher Hassell. Oxford: Oxford University Press, 1954.

Secondary Works

Acocella, Joan. "All England." *The New Yorker*, Dec. 21, 2009, 140–145.
Adill, Alev. "Modern Fables Get Lost in Transit Lounge." *The Independent*, March 8, 2005.
Aers, David. "A Whisper in the Ear of Early Modernists; or, Reflections on Literary Critics Writing 'The History of the Subject.'" In *Culture and History, 1350–1600: Essays on English Communities, Identities, and Writing*, edited by David Aers, 177–203. Detroit, MI: Wayne State University Press, 1992.
Alexander, Lynn. "Signifyin(g) Sex: Gloria Naylor's *Bailey's Cafe* and Western Religious Tradition." In *He Said, She Says: An RSVP to the Male Text*, edited by Mica Howe and Sarah Appleton Aguiar, 91–105. Cranbury, NJ: Associated University Presses, 2001.
Allen, Graham. *Intertextuality*. New York: Routledge, 2000.
Anderson, Benedict. *Imagined Communities: Reflections on the Origin and Spread of Nationalism*. London: Verso, 1991.
Andrew, Dudley. "Adapting Cinema to History: A Revolution in the Making." In *A Companion to Literature and Film*, edited by Robert Stam and Alessandra Raengo, 189–204. Oxford: Blackwell, 2004.
_____. *Concepts in Film Theory*. New York: Oxford University Press, 1984.
"The Animator's Tale." *BBC News Online*, March 17, 1999.*http://news.bbc.co.uk/2/hi/entertainment/297262.stm*.
Anyokwu, Christopher. "Wordplay and Fancy: The Nigerian Question in Karen King-Aribisala's *Kicking Tongues*." *LARES: A Journal of Language and Literary Studies*. Ed. V. O. Awonusi. Lagos: University of Lagos, 2006. 308–319.
Arnell, Carla. "Chaucer's Wife of Bath and John Fowles's Quaker Maid: Tale-Telling and the Trial of Personal Experience and Written Authority." *Modern Language Review* 102 (2007): 933–946.
Arnold, Matthew. *Culture and Anarchy*. Ed. Samuel Lipman. New Haven: Yale University Press, 1994.
Asma, Stephen T. *On Monsters: An Unnatural History of Our Worst Fears*. New York: Oxford University Press, 2009.
Baker, Phil. "London Calling." *The Guardian*, August 15, 2003. http://www.guardian.co.uk/books/2003/aug/16/fiction.peterackroyd.
Baldick, Chris. *The Social Mission of English Criticism, 1848–1932*, 2nd ed. Oxford: Oxford University Press, 1987.
Barnes, Geraldine. "Medieval Murder — Modern Crime Fiction." In *Medieval Cultural Studies: Essays in Honor of Stephen Knight*, edited by Ruth Evans, Helen Fulton, and David Matthews, 241–254. Chicago: University of Chicago Press, 2006.
Barrington, Candace. *American Chaucers*. New York: Palgrave Macmillan, 2007.
Bazin, Victoria. "[Not] Talking 'bout My Generation: Historicizing Feminisms in Carly Churchill's *Top Girls*." *Studies in the Literary Imagination* 39 (2006): 115–134.
Beaulieu, Elizabeth Ann. *Writing African American Women*. Westport, CT: Greenwood Press, 2006.
Beidler, Peter G. "It's Miller Time!: Baba Brinkman's Adaptation of the *Miller's Tale*." *LATCH* 3 (2010): 134–150.
Bell, Ian A. "Eighteenth-Century Crime Writing." In *The Cambridge Companion to Crime Fiction*, edited by Martin Priestman. Cambridge: Cambridge University Press, 2003.
Bender, Carol, and Roseanne Hoefel. "Toward a Literacy of Empathy: Inhabiting Gloria Naylor's *Bailey's Café*." In *Gloria Naylor: Strategy and Technique, Magic and Myth*, edited by Shirley A. Stave, 182–195. Cranbury, NJ: Associated University Presses, 2001.
Bennett, Tony. "Popular Culture and the 'turn to Gramsci.'" In *Cultural Theory and*

Popular Culture: A Reader, 4th ed., edited by John Storey, 81–87. Harlow, U.K.: Pearson Education Limited, 2009.
_____, et al. *Culture, Class, Distinction*. London: Routledge, 2009.
Benshoff, Harry M. *Dark Shadows*. Detroit, MI: Wayne State University Press, 2011.
Bertens, Johannes Willem, and Theo d'Haen. *Contemporary American Crime Fiction*. New York: Palgrave Macmillan, 2001.
Bishop, Louise M. "Geoffrey Chaucer." In *Icons of the Middle Ages: Rulers, Writers, Rebels, and Saints,* edited by Lister M. Matheson, 174–204. Santa Barbara, CA: Greenwood Press, 2012.
Blamires, Alcuin. "Chaucer the Reactionary." *Review of English Studies* 51 (2000): 523–539.
Boswell, Jackson Campbell and Sylvia Wallace Holton. *Chaucer's Fame in England: STC Chauceriana, 1475–1640*. New York: Modern Language Association, 2004.
Bourdieu, Pierre. *Distinction: A Social Critique of the Judgement of Taste*. Trans. Richard Nice. London: Routledge and Kegan Paul, 1984.
_____. *The Field of Cultural Production*. Ed. Randal Johnson. New York: Columbia University Press, 1993.
_____. "The Intellectual Field: A World Apart." In *In Other Words: Essays Towards a Reflexive Sociology,* translated by Matthew Anderson, 140–49. Palo Alto, CA: Stanford University Press, 1990.
Bowden, Betsy, ed. *Eighteenth-Century Modernizations from* The Canterbury Tales. Chaucer Studies XVI. Cambridge: D.S. Brewer, 1991.
Bowen, Christopher. "The Choreographer's Tale." *Scotland on Sunday*, Oct. 17, 1999.
Bowers, John M., ed. The Canterbury Tales: *Fifteenth-Century Continuations and Additions*. Kalamazoo, MI: Medieval Institute Publications, 1992.
_____."Chaucer after Smithfield: From Postcolonial Writer to Imperialist Author." In *The Postcolonial Middle Ages,* edited by Jeffrey Jerome Cohen, 53–66. New York: St. Martins, 2000.
Brewer, Derek, ed. *Chaucer: The Critical Heritage*, 2 vols. London: Routledge and Kegan Paul, 1978.
_____. "The Criticism of Chaucer in the Twentieth Century." In *Chaucer's Mind and Art,* edited by A. C. Cawley, 3–28. Edinburgh and London: Oliver and Boyd, 1969.

_____. "Modernizing the Medieval: Eighteenth-Century Translations of Chaucer." In *The Middle Ages After the Middle Ages in the English-Speaking World,* edited by Marie-Françoise Alamichel and Derek Brewer, 103–120, Cambridge: D. S. Brewer, 1997.
Brigg, Peter. "Maggots, Tropes, and Metafictional Challenge: John Fowles' *A Maggot*." In *Imaginative Futures,* edited by Milton T. Wolf and Daryl F. Mallett, 293–305. San Bernardino, CA: Borgo, 1995.
Brody, Saul Nathaniel. "Truth and Fiction in the *Nun's Priest's Tale*." *Chaucer Review* 14 (1979): 33–47
Brown, Amy Benson. "Writing Home: The Bible and Gloria Naylor's *Bailey's Café*." In *Homemaking: Women Writers and the Politics and Poetics of Home,* edited by Catherine Wiley and Fiona Barnes, 23–42.New York: Garland, 1996.
Brown, Ismene. "Canterbury Fails." *The Telegraph,* September 21, 1999. http://www.telegraph.co.uk/culture/4718479-/Canterbury-fails.html.
Brown, Peter. *Geoffrey Chaucer*. New York: Oxford University Press, 2011.
Browne, Ray B. "Popular Culture: Notes Toward a Definition." In *Popular Culture Theory and Methodology: A Basic Introduction,* edited by Harold E. Hinds, Jr., Marilyn F. Motz, and Angela M. S. Nelson, 15–22. Madison: University of Wisconsin Press, 2006.
_____, and Lawrence A. Kreiser, Jr., eds. *The Detective as Historian: History and Art in Historical Crime Fiction*. Bowling Green, OH: Bowling Green State University Popular Press, 2000.
Brunvard, Jan Harold. *Encyclopedia of Urban Legends*. Santa Barbara: ABC-CLIO, Inc., 2001.
Bryant, Brantley L. "Playing Chaucer." In *Geoffrey Chaucer Hath a Blog: Medieval Studies and New Media,* edited by Brantley L. Bryant, 15–28. New York: Palgrave Macmillan, 2010.
Buchan, Suzanne. "The Animated Spectator." In *Animated Worlds,* edited by Suzanne Buchan, 15–38. Eastleigh, U.K.: John Libbey, 2006.
Byerman, Keith Eldon. *Remembering the Past in Contemporary African American Fiction*. Chapel Hill: University of North Carolina Press, 2005, 75–93.
Cameron, Rebecca. "From Great Women to

Top Girls: Pageants of Sisterhood in British Feminist Theater." *Comparative Drama* 43 (2009): 143–166.

"*Canterbury Tales*: About the Show." *BBC Online*, July 9, 2006. http://www.bbc.co.uk/canterburytales/episodeguide/pardoners_tale/.

"*Canterbury Tales*, Episode Guide: The Knight's Tale." *BBC Online*, July 9, 2006.

"*Canterbury Tales*, Episode Guide: The Wife of Bath's Tale." *BBC Online*, July 9, 2006. http://www.bbc.co.uk/pressoffice/pressreleases/stories/2003/08_august/06/wifeofbath.pdf.

Cardwell, Sarah. "Literature on the Small Screen: Television Adaptations." In *The Cambridge Companion to Literature on Screen*, edited by Deborah Cartmell and Imelda Whelehan, 181–195. Cambridge: Cambridge University Press, 2007.

Carlson, David R. *Chaucer's Jobs*. New York: Palgrave Macmillan, 2008.

_____. "The Robberies of Chaucer." *English Studies in Canada* 35 (2009): 29–54.

Caulkins, D. Douglas, Vickie Schlegel, Christina Hanson, and Jane Cherry. "The Politics of Authenticity and Identity in British Heritage Sites." In *Regional Development on the North Atlantic Margin*, edited by Reginald Byron, Jens Christian Hansen, and Tim Jenkins, 103–121. Aldershot, U.K.: Ashgate.

Cawelti, John G. *Adventure, Mystery, and Romance: Formula Stories as Art and Popular Culture*. Chicago: University of Chicago Press, 1976.

_____. "Canonization, Modern Literature, and the Detective Story." In *Theory and Practice of Classical Detective Fiction*, edited by Jerome H. Delamater and Ruth Prigozy. Westport, CT: Greenwood Press, 1997.

_____. "The Evolution of Melodrama." In *Imitations of Life: A Reader on Film and Television Melodrama*, edited by Marcia Landy, 33–49. Detroit, MI: Wayne State University Press, 1991.

Cawsey, Kathy. *Twentieth-Century Chaucer Criticism: Reading Audiences*. Farnham, U.K.: Ashgate, 2011.

Chavenelle, Sylvie. "Gloria Naylor's *Bailey's Café*: The Blues and Beyond." *American Studies International* 36.2 (1998): 58–73.

Chesterton, G. K. *Chaucer*. London: Faber and Faber, 1932.

Chiavetta, Eleonora. "The Clothing Metaphor as Signifier in the Fiction of Karen King-Aribisala." In *Bodies and Voices: The Forcefield of Representation and Discourse in Colonial and Postcolonial Studies*, edited by Merete Falck Borch, Eva Rask Knudsen, Martin Leer, and Bruce Clunies Ross, 93–102. Amsterdam: Rodopi, 2008.

Cohen, Jeffrey Jerome. "Monster Culture (Seven Theses)." In *Monster Theory: Reading Culture*, edited by Jeffrey Jerome Cohen, 3–25. Minneapolis: University of Minnesota Press, 1996.

Cohen, Scott. "Strangers in Paradise." *Spin*, December 1989, 70.

Collette, Carolyn. "Afterlife." In *A Companion to Chaucer*, edited by Peter Brown, 8–22. Oxford: Blackwell, 2002.

_____. "Chaucer and Victorian Medievalism: Culture and Society." *Poetica* 29–30 (1989): 115–125.

_____. *Species, Phantasms, and Images: Vision and Medieval Psychology in* The Canterbury Tales. Ann Arbor: University of Michigan Press, 2001.

Conrad, Peter. *To be Continued: Four Stories and Their Survival*. Oxford: Clarendon Press, 1995.

Cooney, Barbara. *Chanticleer and the Fox*. New York: Thomas Y. Crowell, 1958.

Coren, Giles. "A Kick in the Vernaculars." *The Times*, September 6, 2003.

Cowart, David. *Literary Symbiosis: The Reconfigured Text in Twentieth-Century Writing*. Athens: University of Georgia Press, 1993.

Crane, Diana. *Fashion and Its Social Agendas: Class, Gender, and Identity in Clothing*. Chicago: University of Chicago Press, 2000.

Crane, Susan. "Alison of Bath Accused of Murder: Case Dismissed." *English Language Notes* 25 (1988): 10–15.

Crocker, Holly A. "Chaucer's Man Show: Anachronistic Authority in Brian Helgeland's *A Knight's Tale*." In *Race, Class, and Gender in 'Medieval' Cinema*, edited by Lynn T. Ramey and Tison Pugh, 183–197. New York: Palgrave Macmillan, 2007.

_____. "Teaching Masculinities in Chaucer's Shorter Poems: Historical Myths and Brian Helgeland's *A Knight's Tale*." In *Approaches to Teaching Chaucer's Troilus and Criseyde and the Shorter Poems*, edited by Tison Pugh and Angela Jane Weisl, 76–80. New York: MLA 2007.

Cullum-Swan, Betsy, and Peter K. Manning. "What is a T-shirt?" In *The Socialness of*

Things: Essays on the Socio-Semiotics of Objects, edited by Stephen Harold Riggins, 415–434. Berlin: Mouton de Gruyter, 1994.

D'Arcens, Louise. "Deconstruction and the Medieval Indefinite Article: The Undecidable Medievalism of Brian Helgeland's *A Knight's Tale.*" *Parergon* 25 (2008): 80–98.

Dell, Helen. "Past, Present, and Future Perfect: Paradigms of History in Medievalism Studies." *Parergon* 25 (2008): 58–79.

Dinshaw, Carolyn. "Rivalry, Rape, and Manhood: Gower and Chaucer." In *Chaucer and Gower: Difference, Mutuality, Exchange,* edited by Robert F. Yeager, *English Literary Studies* 51 (1991): 130–152.

Douglas, Gavin. *Virgil's Aeneid.* Ed. David F. C. Coldwell. Edinburgh and London: William Blackwell and Sons, 1957–1964.

Dryden, John. Preface to *Fables Ancient and Modern. The Works of John Dryden.* 20 vols. Ed. Vinton A. Dearing. Berkeley and Los Angeles: University of California Press, 2000.

During, Simon. *Cultural Studies: A Critical Introduction.* New York: Routledge, 2005.

Eberle, Patricia J. "Crime and Justice in the Middle Ages: Cases from the *Canterbury Tales* of Geoffrey Chaucer." In *Rough Justice: Essays on Crime in Literature,* edited by M. L. Friedland, 19–51. Toronto: University of Toronto Press, 1991.

Echard, Siân. *Printing the Middle Ages.* Philadelphia: University of Pennsylvania Press, 2008.

Eco, Umberto. *The Limits of Interpretation.* Bloomington: Indiana University Press, 1990.

Edmondson, Todd. "The Ambivalence of Pilgrimage in Marilyn Nelson's *Cachoeira Tales.*" *REA: A Journal of Religion, Education, and the Arts* 6 (2009): 1–18.

Eisner, Will. *Comics and Sequential Art: Principles and Practices from the Legendary Cartoonist.* Tamarac, FL: Poorhouse Press, 1985.

Ellis, Steve. *Chaucer at Large: The Poet in the Modern Imagination.* Minneapolis: University of Minnesota Press, 2000.

_____. "Popular Chaucer and the Academy." *Studies in Medievalism* 9 (1997): 26–43.

Emmerson, Richard K. "Medieval Studies at the Beginning of the New Millennium." In *Vital Signs: English in Medieval Studies in Twenty-First Century Higher Education,* edited by Elaine Treharne (English Association Issues in English, 2, 2002): 17–27.

Erickson, Peter. *Rewriting Shakespeare, Rewriting Ourselves.* Berkeley and Los Angeles: University of California Press, 1991.

Fichte, Joerg O. "Crime Fiction Set in the Middle Ages: Historical Novel and Detective Story." *Zeitschrift für Anglistik und Amerikanistik* 53 (2005): 53–70.

Fishelov, David. *Dialogues with/and Great Books: The Dynamics of Canon Formation.* Eastbourne, U.K.: Sussex Academic Press, 2010.

Fisher, John H. *The Importance of Chaucer.* Carbondale: Southern Illinois University Press, 1992.

Fiske, John. "The Cultural Economy of Fandom." In *The Adoring Audience: Fan Culture and Popular Media,* edited by Lisa A. Lewis. New York: Routledge 1992.

_____. "Popular Discrimination." In *Modernity and Mass Culture,* edited by James Naremore and Patrick Brantlinger, 103–116. Indianapolis: Indiana University Press, 1991.

_____. *Television Culture.* London: Methuen & Co., 1987.

_____. *Understanding Popular Culture.* 2nd ed. London: Routledge, 2010.

Forni, Kathleen. *The Chaucerian Apocrypha: A Counterfeit Canon.* Gainesville: University Press of Florida, 2001.

_____. "Reinventing Chaucer: Helgeland's *A Knight's Tale.*" *Chaucer Review* 37 (2003): 253–264.

Foster, Michael. "On Dating the Duchess: The Personal and Social Context of *Book of the Duchess.*" *Review of English Studies* 59 (2008): 185–196.

Foucault, Michel. *Aesthetics, Method, and Epistemology: Essential Works of Michel Foucault, 1954–1984,* edited by James D. Faubion. New York: New Press, 1998.

Fradenburg, Louise. "'So That We May Speak of Them': Enjoying the Middle Ages." *New Literary History* 28 (1997): 205–230.

Fries, Laura. "Animated Epics: *The Canterbury Tales.*" *Variety,* May 25, 1999. http://www.variety.com/review/VE1117499827?refCatId=32.

Frow, John. "Intertextuality and Ontology." In *Intertextuality: Theories and Practices,* edited by Michael Worton and Judith Still, 45–55. Manchester, U.K.: Manchester University Press, 1990.

Furniss, Maureen. *Art in Motion: Animation Aesthetics.* London: John Libbey, 1998.

Furnivall, F. J., ed. "John Lane's Continuation

of Chaucer's Squire's Tale." *Chaucer Society Publications*, 2nd ser. 23. London: K. Paul, Trench and Trubner, 1890.

Ganim, John. "Mary Shelley, Godwin's *Chaucer*, and the Middle Ages." In *Chaucer and the Challenges of Medievalism*, edited by Donka Minkova and Theresa Tinkle, 175–191. Frankfurt: Peter Lang, 2003.

Gans, Herbert J. *Popular Culture and High Culture: An Analysis and Evaluation of Taste*. Rev. ed. New York: Basic Books, 1999.

Garaventa, Joseph. "A Bawdy Journey to 'Canterbury.'" *The Washington Post*, April 21, 2006.

Gardner, John. *The Life and Times of Chaucer*. Carbondale: Southern Illinois University Press, 1977.

Gates, Henry Louis, Jr. *The Signifying Monkey: A Theory of African-American Literary Criticism*. New York: Oxford University Press, 1988.

Genette, Gérard. *Palimpsests: Literature in the Second Degree*. Trans. Channa Newman and Claude Doubinsky. 1982; Lincoln: University of Nebraska Press, 1997.

Gilbert, Jenny. "Chaucer is Jigging in His Grave." *The Independent*, Sept. 19, 1999. http://www.independent.co.uk/arts-entertainment/dance-chaucer-jigging-in-his-grave-1120362.html.

Giroux, Henry A., and Roger I. Simon. "Critical Pedagogy and the Politics of Popular Culture." *Cultural Studies* 2 (1988): 23–46.

Graff, Gerald. *Professing Literature: An Institutional History*. 1987; Chicago: University of Chicago Press, 2007.

Grant, Kevin, ed. *The Art of David Dabydeen*. Leeds, U.K.: Peepal Tree Press, 1997.

Green, Martin. "The Dialectic of Adaptation: *The Canterbury Tales* of Pier Paolo Pasolini." *Literature/Film Quarterly* 4 (1976): 46–53.

Gresset, Michael. "Of Sailboats and Kites: The 'Dying Fall' in Faulkner's *Sanctuary* and Beckett's *Murphy*." In *Intertextuality in Faulkner*, edited by Michael Gresset and Noel Polk, 57–72. Jackson: University Press of Mississippi, 1985.

Gripsrud, Jostein. "'High Culture' Revisited." *Cultural Studies* 3 (1989): 194–207.

Grossberg, Lawrence. "Cultural Studies: What's in a Name? (One More Time)." In *Media/Cultural Studies: Critical Approaches*, edited by Rhonda Hammer and Douglas Kellner, 25–48. New York: Peter Lang, 2009.

Grudin, Michaela Paasche. "Discourse and the Problem of Closure in the *Canterbury Tales*," *PMLA* 107 (1992): 1157–1167.

Guillory, John. *Cultural Capital: The Problem of Literary Canon Formation*. Chicago: University of Chicago Press, 1993.

Gust, Geoffrey W. *Constructing Chaucer: Author and Autofiction in the Critical Tradition*. New York: Palgrave Macmillan, 2009.

Gutleben, Christian and Susana Onega. "Introduction." In *Refracting the Canon in Contemporary British Literature and Film*, edited by Susana Onega and Christian Gutleben. Amsterdam: Rodopi, 2004.

Hall, Stuart. "Notes on Deconstructing 'The Popular.'" In *Cultural Theory and Popular Culture: A Reader*, 4th ed., edited by John Storey, 508–518. Harlow, U.K.: Pearson Education, 2009.

Hammond, Will. "Old London Calling." *The Observer*, August 9, 2003. http://www.guardian.co.uk/books/2003/aug/10/fiction.peterackroyd.

Harris, David. *From Class Struggle to the Politics of Pleasure: The Effects of Gramscianism on Cultural Studies*. London: Routledge, 1992.

Harris, Sonia. "CCI: Art of Design, AKA Comics and Design." *Comic Book Resources*, August 2, 2011. http://www.comicbookresources.com/?page=article&id=33686.

Harty, Kevin J. "Chaucer for a New Millennium: The BBC *Canterbury Tales*." In *Mass Market Medieval: Essays on the Middle Ages in Popular Culture*, edited by David W. Marshall, 13–27. Jefferson, NC: McFarland, 2007.

———. "Chaucer in Performance." In *Chaucer: An Oxford Guide*, edited by Steve Ellis, 560–575. Oxford: Oxford University Press, 2005.

Harwood, Britton J. "The Political Use of Chaucer in Twentieth-Century America." In *Medievalism in the Modern World: Essays in Honor of Leslie J. Workman*, edited by Richard Utz and Tom A. Shippey, 379–392. Turnhout, BE: Brepols, 1998.

Haydock, Nickolas A. "Arthurian Melodrama, Chaucerian Spectacle, and the Waywardness of Pastiche in *First Knight* and *A Knight's Tale*." *Studies in Medievalism* 12 (2002): 5–38.

Heding, Tilde, Charlotte F. Knudtzen, and Mogens Bjerre. *Brand Management: Research, Theory, Practice*. New York: Routledge, 2009.

Heller, Steven, and Paula Scher, eds. *Seymour: The Obsessive Images of Seymour Chwast*. San Francisco: Chronicle Books, 2009.

Herrnstein Smith, Barbara. "Contingencies of Value." In *Canons*, edited by Robert von Hallberg, 5–40. Chicago: University of Chicago Press, 1984.

Hertog, Erik. *Chaucer's Fabliaux as Analogues*. Leuven, BE: Leuven University Press, 1991.

Hertzberg, Ludvig. *Jim Jarmusch: Interviews*. Jackson: University Press of Mississippi, 2001.

Hickling, Alfred. Review of the Northern Broadsides "The Canterbury Tales." *The Guardian*, March 3, 2010.

Hinds, Harold E., Jr. "Popularity: The *Sine Qua Non* of Popular Culture." In *Symbiosis: Popular Culture and Other Fields*, edited by Ray B. Browne and Marshall W. Fishwick, 207–216. Bowling Green, OH: Bowling Green State University Popular Press, 1988.

Holmes, Frederick M. "History, Fiction, and the Dialogic Imagination: John Fowles's *A Maggot*." *Contemporary Literature* 32 (1991): 229–243.

Holt, Douglas B. *How Brands Become Icons: The Principles of Cultural Branding*. Harvard Business School, 2004.

Horsley, Lee. *Twentieth-Century Crime Fiction*. New York: Oxford University Press, 2005.

Hutcheon, Linda. *The Poetics of Postmodernism: History, Theory, Fiction*. London: Routledge, 1988

_____. "The Politics of Postmodern Parody." In *Intertextuality*. Ed. Heinrich F. Plett. Berlin: Walter de Gruyter, 1991. 225–236.

_____. *A Theory of Adaptation*. New York: Routledge, 2006.

_____. *A Theory of Parody: The Teachings of Twentieth-Century Art Forms*. 1985; Champaign: University of Illinois Press, 2000.

Ingham, Patricia Clare. "Contrapuntal Histories." In *Postcolonial Moves: Medieval Through Modern*, edited by Patricia Clare Ingham and Michelle R. Warren, 47–70. New York: Palgrave Macmillan, 2003.

Jarman, Mark, and David Mason, eds. *Rebel Angels: 25 Poets of the New Formalism*. Ashland, OR: Story Line Press, 1996.

Jauss, Hans Robert. *Toward an Aesthetic of Reception*. Trans. Timothy Bahti. Minneapolis: University of Minnesota Press, 1982.

Jenkins, Henry. "'Strangers no more we sing': Filking and the Social Construction of the Science Fiction Community." In *Media Studies: A Reader*, 2nd ed., edited by Paul Marris and Sue Thornham, 547–556. New York: New York University Press, 2000.

_____. *Textual Poachers: Television Fans and Participatory Culture*. New York: Routledge, 1992.

Jensen, Joli. "Introduction: On Fandom, Celebrity, and Mediation: Posthumous Possibilities." In *Afterlife as Afterimage: Understanding Posthumous Fame*, edited by Steve Jones and Joli Jensen, xv–xxiii. New York: Peter Lang, 2005.

Jewers, Caroline. "Hard Days Knights: *First Knight*, *A Knight's Tale*, and *Black Knight*." In *The Medieval Hero on Screen: Representations from Beowulf to Buffy*, edited by Martha Driver and Sid Ray, 192–210. Jefferson, NC: McFarland, 2004.

Jones, Jonathon. "Pilgrims Like Us." *The Guardian*, September 9, 1999. http://www.guardian.co.uk/culture/1999/sep/09/arts-features1.

Juvan, Marko. *History and Poetics of Intertextuality*. Trans. Timothy Poga_ar. West Lafayette, IN: Purdue University Press, 2008.

Kaufman, Amy S. "Medieval Unmoored." *Studies in Medievalism* 19 (2010): 1–11.

Kellaway, Kate. "Of Headless Squirrels and Men." *The Observer*, June 3, 2001, p. 16.

Kelley, Margot Anne, ed. *Gloria Naylor's Early Novels*. Gainesville: University Press of Florida, 1999.

Kittredge, George Lyman. *Chaucer and his Poetry*. Cambridge: Harvard University Press, 1915.

Knapp, Ethan. "Chaucer Criticism and Its Legacies." In *The Yale Companion to Chaucer*, edited by Seth Lerer, 324–358. New Haven: Yale University Press, 2007.

Knight, Stephen. "The Golden Age." In *The Cambridge Companion to Crime Fiction*, edited by Martin Priestman, 77–94. Cambridge: Cambridge University Press, 2003.

Kramnick, Jonathan Brody. *Making the English Canon: Print Capitalism and the Cultural Past, 1700–1770*. Cambridge: Cambridge University Press, 1999.

Krier, Theresa M., ed. *Refiguring Chaucer in the Renaissance*. Gainesville: University Press of Florida, 1998.

Landy, Marcia, ed. *Imitations of Life: A Reader on Film and Television Melodrama*.

Detroit, MI: Wayne State University Press, 1991.

Lanier, Douglas. *Shakespeare and Modern Popular Culture.* Oxford: Oxford University Press, 2002.

———. "William Shakespeare, Filmmaker." In *The Cambridge Companion to Literature on Screen,* edited by Deborah Cartmell and Imelda Whelehan, 61–74. Cambridge: Cambridge University Press, 2007.

Lazar, David, ed. *Michael Powell, Interviews.* Jackson: University Press of Mississippi, 2003.

Leicester, H. Marshall. "The Art of Impersonation: A General Prologue to the *Canterbury Tales.*" *PMLA* 95 (1980): 213–224.

Leitch, Thomas. "Adaptation Studies at a Crossroads." *Adaptation* 1 (2008): 63–77.

———. *Film Adaptation and Its Discontents.* Baltimore, MD: Johns Hopkins University Press, 2007.

Lerer, Seth. *Chaucer and His Readers: Imagining the Author in Late Medieval England.* Princeton: Princeton University Press, 1993.

Lewis, Barry. *My Words Echo Thus: Possessing the Past in Peter Ackroyd.* Columbia: University of South Carolina Press, 2007.

Lowe, Ben. "Teaching in the 'Schole of Christ': Law, Learning, and Love in Early Lollard Pacificism." *The Catholic Historical Review* 90 (2004): 405–438.

Lynch, Kathryn R. "Storytelling, Exchange, and Constancy: East and West in Chaucer's *Man of Law's Tale.*" *Chaucer Review* 33 (1999): 409–422.

Macan, Edward. *Rocking the Classics: English Progressive Rock and the Counterculture.* Oxford: Oxford University Press, 1996.

MacCannell, Dean. *The Tourist: A New Theory of the Leisure Class.* 1973; Berkeley and Los Angeles: University of California Press, 1999.

Maingay, John. "Panic on London's Streets." *Newsday,* September 18, 2004. http://www.newsday.com/entertainment/fanfare-/panic-on-london-s-streets-1.697758.

Malcolm, David. *Understanding Graham Swift.* Columbia: University of South Carolina, 2003.

Malkin, Arthur Thomas. *The Gallery of Portraits: With Memoirs.* 3 vols. London: C. Knight, 1834.

Manly, John M. *Some New Light on Chaucer.* New York: Henry Holt, 1926.

Marcus, Laura. "Detection and Literary Fiction." In *The Cambridge Companion to Crime Fiction,* edited by Martin Priestman, 245–268. Cambridge: Cambridge University Press, 2003.

Margry, Peter Jan. "Secular Pilgrimage: A Contradiction in Terms?" In *Shrines and Pilgrimage in the Modern World: New Itineraries into the Sacred,* edited by Peter Jan Margry, 13–46. Amsterdam: Amsterdam University Press, 2008.

"Marina Lewycka's Dare-Devil Leap from Tractors to Caravans." *The Sunday Times,* March 18, 2007. http://women.timesonline.co.uk/tol/life_and_style/women/article1530630.ece.

Marks, Peter. "A Canter Down Chaucer's Long and Windy Road." *The Washington Post,* April 21, 2006.

Marshall, David W. "Introduction: The Medievalism of Popular Culture." In *Mass Market Medieval: Essays on the Middle Ages in Popular Culture,* edited by David W. Marshall, 1–12. Jefferson, NC: McFarland, 2007.

Matthews, David. "Chaucer's American Accent." *American Literary History* 22 (2010): 758–772.

———. "Reception: Eighteenth and Nineteenth Centuries." In *Chaucer: An Oxford Guide,* edited by Steve Ellis, 512–527. Oxford: Oxford University Press, 2005.

———. "Speaking to Chaucer: The Poet and the Nineteenth-Century Academy." *Studies in Medievalism* 9 (1997): 5–25.

———. "What the Trumpet Solo Tells Us: A Response." *Parergon* 25 (2008): 119–127.

———. "What Was Medievalism?: Medieval Studies, Medievalism, and Cultural Studies." In *Medieval Cultural Studies: Essays in Honor of Stephen Knight,* edited by Ruth Evans, Helen Fulton, and David Matthews, 9–22. Chicago: University of Chicago Press, 2006.

McCloud, Scott. *Understanding Comics: The Invisible Art.* New York: HarperCollins, 1994.

Middleton, Anne. "Medieval Studies." In *Redrawing the Boundaries: The Transformation of English and American Literary Studies,* edited by Stephen Greenblatt and Giles Gunn, 12–40. New York: MLA, 1992.

Midgely, Carol. "Chaucer? Not a lot of people know that." *The Times,* November 23, 1998.

Miskimin, Alice. "Illustrated Eighteenth-Century Chaucer." *Modern Philology* 77 (1979): 26–55.

_____-. *The Renaissance Chaucer.* New Haven: Yale University Press, 1975.

Moor, Andrew. *Powell and Pressburger: A Cinema of Magical Spaces.* London: I. B. Taurus, 2005.

Morgan, Gerald. "Moral and Social Identity and the Idea of Pilgrimage in the *General Prologue.*" *Chaucer Review* 37 (2003): 285–314.

Morse, Charlotte C. "Popularizing Chaucer in the Nineteenth Century." *Chaucer Review* 38 (2003): 99–125.

Mullins, Stephen M., and David C. Fastenau. *A Century of Royal Doulton Character and Toby Jugs.* Atglen, PA: Schiffer, 2008.

Mwangi, Evan Maina. *Africa Writes Back to Self: Metafiction, Gender, Sexuality.* New York: State University of New York Press, 2010.

Myers, Lucas. *Crow Steered Bergs Appeared: A Memoir of Ted Hughes and Sylvia Plath.* Sewanee, TN: Proctor's Hall Press, 2001.

Myerson, Jonathan. "Tales of the Unexpected." *The Guardian,* August 31, 2003.

Nelmes, Jill. *An Introduction to Film Studies,* 3rd ed. New York: Routledge, 2003.

Nightingale, Benedict. Review of RSC *The Canterbury Tales. The Times,* December 10, 2005.

Orme, Steve. Steve Orme, Review of RSC *The Canterbury Tales.* The British Theatre Guide, 2006. http://www.britishtheatreguide.info/reviews/RSCcanttales-rev.htm.

Orr, Mary. *Intertextuality: Debates and Contexts.* Oxford: Blackwell, 2003.

Palmer, D. J. *The Rise of English Studies.* Oxford: Oxford University Press, 1965.

Paton, Maureen. "Soap for the Wife of Bath." *The Times,* September, 1, 2003.

Patterson, Lee. *Chaucer and the Subject of History.* Madison: University of Wisconsin Press, 1991.

_____, ed. *Geoffrey Chaucer's The Canterbury Tales: A Casebook.* Oxford: Oxford University Press, 2007.

_____. *Negotiating the Past: The Historical Understanding of Medieval Literature.* Madison: University of Wisconsin Press, 1987.

_____. "On the Margin: Postmodernism, Ironic History, and Medieval Studies." *Speculum* 65 (1990): 87–108.

Payne, Tom. "The Blood and the Beef." *The Telegraph,* August 4, 2003. http://www.telegraph.co.uk/culture/books/3600595-/The-blood-and-the-beef.html.

Pearsall, Derek. "Chaucer and Englishness." *Proceedings of the British Academy* 101 (1999): 77–99.

_____. "The Squire as Story-Teller." *University of Toronto Quarterly* 34 (1964): 82–92.

Pile, Stephen. "The Scriptwriters' Tales." *The Daily Telegraph,* August 30, 2003. http://www.telegraph.co.uk/culture/tvandradio/3601561/The-scriptwriters-tales.html.

Place, Janey. "Women in *Film Noir.*" In *Women in Film Noir,* edited by E. Ann Kaplan, 35–55. London: British Film Institute, 1978.

Poole, Adrian. Review of *Last Orders:* "Hurry up please it's time." *The Guardian,* January 12, 1996.

Porter, Dennis. *The Pursuit of Crime: Art and Ideology in Crime Fiction.* New Haven: Yale University Press, 1981.

Preminger, Alex, and T. V. F. Brogan. *The New Princeton Encyclopedia of Poetry and Poetics.* Princeton: Princeton University Press, 1993.

Prendergast, Thomas A. *Chaucer's Dead Body: From Corpse to Corpus.* New York: Routledge, 2004.

Priestman, Martin. "Post-war British Crime Fiction." In *A Cambridge Companion to Crime Fiction,* 173–190. Cambridge: Cambridge University Press, 2003.

Pugh, Tison. "Perverse Pastoralism and Medieval Melancholia in Powell and Pressburger's *A Canterbury Tale.*" *Arthuriana* 19 (2009): 97–113

_____. *Sexuality and Its Queer Discontents in Middle English Literature,* 48–100. New York: Palgrave Macmillan, 2008.

Purves, Barry. *Basics Animation: Stop-Motion.* Lausanne: Ava Publishing, 2010.

Pye, Michael. "A Mad Nun's Tale." *The New York Times,* October 31, 2004. http://www.nytimes.com/2004/10/31/books/review/31PYEL.html?8bl.

Pyrhönen, Heta. *Murder from an Academic Angle: An Introduction to the Study of the Detective Narrative.* Columbia, SC: Camden House, 1994.

Quartermain, Peter. *Disjunctive Poetics: From Gertrude Stein and Louis Zukofsky to Susan Howe.* Cambridge: Cambridge University Press, 1992.

Reiss, Edmund. "The Pilgrimage Narrative and the *Canterbury Tales.*" *Studies in Philology* 67 (1970): 295–305.

Review of *Strawberry Fields. Publisher's Weekly,* May 28, 2007. http://www.publishersweekly.com/978-1-59420-137-0.

Review of *Strawberry Fields*. *The New Yorker*, August 13, 2007. http://www.newyorker.com/arts/reviews/brieflynoted/2007/08/13/070813crbn_brieflynoted1.

Richardson, Gudrun. "The Old Man in Chaucer's Pardoner's Tale: An Interpretative Study of His Identity and Meaning." *Neophilologus* 87 (2003): 323–337.

Richmond, Velma Bourgeois. *Chaucer as Children's Literature: Retellings from the Edwardian and Victorian Eras.* Jefferson, NC: McFarland, 2004.

Riffaterre, Michael. "Compulsory Reader Response: The Intertextual Drive." In *Intertextuality: Theories and Practices*, edited by Michael Worton and Judith Still, 56–78. Manchester, U.K.: Manchester University Press, 1990.

Rifkind, Donna. Rev. of *Bailey's Café*. In *Gloria Naylor: Critical Perspectives Past and Present*, edited by Henry Louis Gates, Jr., and K. A. Appiah, 28–30. New York: Amistad, 1993.

Rigby, Stephen Henry. *Chaucer in Context: Society, Allegory, and Gender.* Manchester: Manchester University Press, 1996.

Robinson, Carol L. "Celluloid Criticism: Pasolini's Contribution to a Chaucerian Debate." *Studies in Medievalism* 5 (1993): 115–126.

Roessner, Jeffrey. "Unsolved Mysteries: Agents of Historical Change in John Fowles's *A Maggot*." *Papers on Language and Literature* 36 (2000): 302–323.

Rogerson, Margaret. "Prime-Time Drama: *Canterbury Tales* for the Small Screen." *Sydney Studies in English* 32 (2006): 45–63.

Rose, Mary Beth. *Gender and Heroism in Early Modern English Literature.* Chicago: University of Chicago Press, 2002.

Rosenbaum, Jonathan. *Essential Cinema: On the Necessity of Film Canon.* Baltimore, MD: Johns Hopkins University Press, 2004.

Ross, Andrew. *No Respect: Intellectuals and Popular Culture.* New York: Routledge, 1989.

Rzepka, Charles J. *Detective Fiction.* Cambridge, U.K.: Polity, 2005.

Sanders, Julie. *Adaptation and Appropriation.* London: Routledge, 2006.

_____. *Novel Shakespeares: Twentieth-Century Women Novelists and Appropriation.* Manchester, U.K.: Manchester University Press, 2001.

Scaggs, John. *Crime Fiction.* New York: Routledge, 2005.

Schaber, Bennet. "Modernity and the Vernacular." *Surfaces* 1 (1991): 6–38.

Schneider, Karen. "Gloria Naylor's Poetics of Emancipation: (E)merging (Im)possibilities in *Bailey's Café*." In *Gloria Naylor's Early Novels*, edited by Margot Anne Kelley, 1–20. Gainesville: University Press of Florida, 1999.

Schudson, Michael. "The New Validation of Popular Culture: Sense and Sentimentality in Academia." In *Popular Culture Theory and Methodology: A Basic Introduction*, edited by Harold E. Hinds, Marilyn F. Motz, and Angela M. S. Nelson, 85–106. Madison: University of Wisconsin Press, 2006.

Shields, Alice. "Criseyde: A Feminist Opera." http://www.aliceshields.com/criseyde/about.html.

Siebers, Tobin. "What Does Postmodernism Want? Utopia." In *Heterotopia: Postmodern Utopia and the Body Politic*, edited by Tobin Siebers, 1–39. Ann Arbor: University of Michigan Press, 1994.

"The Sound and the Fury." *The Independent on Sunday*, March 16, 1997.

Spearing, A. C. "Narrative Voice: The Case of Chaucer's *Man of Law's Tale*." *New Literary History* 32 (2001): 715–746.

Spears, Timothy B. Review of *The Clerk's Tale: Young Men and Moral Life in Nineteenth-Century America*, *Journal of American History* 91 (2005): 1457.

Speght, Thomas. *The Workes of Our Antient and Learned English Poet, Geffrey Chaucer, newly printed.* London, 1598.

_____. *The Workes of Our Ancient and Learned English Poet, Geoffrey Chaucer, newly Printed.* London, 1602.

_____. *The Workes of Our Ancient and Learned English Poet, Geffrey Chaucer.* London, 1602.

"Spinning the Tales." *The Age*, August 11, 2005. http://www.theage.com.au/news/tv—radio/spinning-the-tales/2005/08/09/1123353323615.html.

Spurgeon, Caroline F. E. *Five Hundred Years of Chaucer Criticism and Allusion, 1357–1900.* 3 vols. Cambridge: Cambridge University Press, 1925.

Stam, Robert. "Beyond Fidelity: The Dialogics of Adaptation." In *Film Adaptation*, edited by James Naremore, 54–76. New Brunswick, NJ: Rutgers University Press, 2000.

_____. "Introduction: The Theory and Practice of Adaptation." In *Literature and Film: A Guide to the Theory and Practice of Film Adaptation*, edited by Robert Stam and Alessandra Raengo. Oxford: Blackwell, 2005.

Stave, Shirley A. "Gloria Naylor's Revisionary Theology." In *Gloria Naylor: Strategy and Technique, Myth and Magic*, edited by Shirley A. Stave, 97–117. Cranbury, NJ: Associated University Presses, 2001.

Storey, John, ed. *Cultural Theory and Popular Culture: An Introduction*. 5th ed. Harlow, U.K.: Pearson Education Limited, 2009.

_____. ed. *Cultural Theory and Popular Culture: An Introduction*. 4th ed. Athens: University of Georgia Press, 2006.

Street, John. *Politics and Popular Culture*. Philadelphia: Temple University Press, 1997.

Stretter, Robert. "Rewriting Perfect Friendship in Chaucer's *Knight's Tale* and Lydgate's *Fabula Duorum Mercatorum*." *Chaucer Review* 37 (2003): 234–252.

Strinati, Dominic. *An Introduction to Studying Popular Culture*. London: Routledge, 2000.

Strohm, Paul. *Social Chaucer*. Cambridge: Harvard University Press, 1994.

Thomas, Greg. Review of *Gloria Naylor's Early Novels*. *Research in African Literatures* 33 (2002): 223–25.

Thompson, Dorothy Perry. "African Womanist Revision in Gloria Naylor's *Mama Day* and *Bailey's Café*." In *Gloria Naylor's Early Novels*, edited by Margot Anne Kelley, 89–111. Gainesville: University Press of Florida, 1999.

Thompson, John B. *Books in the Digital Age: The Transformation of Academic and Higher Education Publishing in Britain and the United States*. Cambridge, U.K.: Polity, 2005.

Thompson, Kirsten. "Animation." In *Comedy: A Geographic and Historical Guide*, Vol. 1, edited by Maurice Charney, 135–152. Westport, CT: Praeger, 2005.

Tohill, Cathal, and Pete Tombs. *Immoral Tales: European Sex and Horror Movies, 1956–1984*. New York: St. Martins, 1995.

Tomasch, Sylvia. "Postcolonial Chaucer and the Virtual Jew." In *The Postcolonial Middle Ages*, edited by Jeffrey Jerome Cohen, 243–260. New York: St. Martin's, 2000.

Trigg, Stephanie. "Chaucer's Influence and Reception." In *The Yale Companion to Chaucer*, edited by Seth Lerer, 297–323. New Haven: Yale University Press, 2006.

_____. *Congenial Souls: Reading Chaucer from Medieval to Postmodern*. Minneapolis: University of Minnesota Press, 2002.

_____. "Medievalism and Convergence Culture: Researching the Middle Ages for Fiction and Film." *Parergon* 25 (2008): 99–118.

_____. "Reception: Twentieth and Twenty-First Centuries." In *Chaucer: An Oxford Guide*, edited by Steve Ellis, 528–543. Oxford: Oxford University Press, 2005.

_____. and Tom Prendergast. "What is Happening to the Middle Ages?" *New Medieval Literatures* 9 (2007): 215–229.

Turner, Graeme. *British Cultural Studies: An Introduction*. 3rd ed. London: Routledge, 2003.

Turner, Victor, and Edith Turner. *Image and Pilgrimage in Christian Culture*. New York: Columbia University Press, 1978.

Upstone, Sara. *Spatial Politics in the Postcolonial Novel*. Burlington, VT: Ashgate, 1988.

Wagner, Geoffrey. *The Novel and the Cinema*. Rutherford, N J: Fairleigh Dickinson University Press, 1975.

Wallace, David. "New Chaucer Topographies." *Studies in the Age of Chaucer* 29 (2007): 3–19.

Wells, Paul. *Animation: Genre and Authorship*. London: Wallflower, 2002.

_____. "Classic Literature and Animation: All Adaptations are Equal, But Some are More Equal Than Others." In *The Cambridge Companion to Literature on Screen*, edited by Deborah Cartmell and Imelda Whelahan, 199–211. Cambridge: Cambridge University Press, 2007.

_____. "'Thou art translated': Analyzing Animated Adaptations." *Adaptations: From Text to Screen, Screen to Text*, edited by Deborah Cartmell and Imelda Whelahan, 199–213. London: Routledge, 1999.

_____. *Understanding Animation*. New York: Routledge, 1998.

Wenzel, Jennifer. "Petro-magic-realism: Toward a Political Ecology of Nigerian Literature." *Postcolonial Studies* 9 (2006): 449–464.

West-Pavlov, Russell. *Transcultural Graffiti: Diasporic Writing and the Teaching of Literary Studies*. Amsterdam: Rodopi, 2005.

Wheeler, Bonnie. "Go Litel Blog, Go Litel Thys Comedye." In *Geoffrey Chaucer Hath a Blog: Medieval Studies and New Media*, edited by Brantley L. Bryant, 7–14. New York: Palgrave Macmillan, 2010.

Whitaker, Muriel. "The Chaucer Chest and the *Pardoner's Tale*: Didacticism and Narrative Art." *Chaucer Review* 34 (1999): 174–189.

Williams, Raymond. *Keywords: A Vocabulary of Culture and Society*. Rev. ed. London: Fontana, 1983.

Wilson, Charles E., Jr. *Gloria Naylor: A Critical Companion*. Westport, CT: Greenwood Press, 2001.

———. "Medievalism, Race, and Social Order in Gloria Naylor's *Bailey's Café*." *Studies in Medievalism* 10 (1998): 74–91.

Wolf, Naomi. *The Beauty Myth: How Images of Beauty Are Used Against Women*. New York: W. Morrow, 1991.

Wood, Rebecca S. "Two Warring Ideals in One Dark Body: Universalism and Nationalism in Gloria Naylor's *Bailey's Cafe*." *African American Review* 30 (1996): 381–395.

Wren, Celia. "Throwing Bawdy and Soul into 'Canterbury.'" *The Washington Post*, April 16, 2006. http://www.washingtonpost.com

Wright, Jean Ann. *Animation Writing and Development: From Script Development to Pitch*. Burlington, MA: Focal Press, 2005.

Yager, Susan. "The BBC 'Man of Law's Tale': Faithful to the Tradition." *Literature and Belief* 27 (2007): 55–68.

Yaw, Yvonne. "Student Study Guides and the Wife of Bath." *Chaucer Review* 35 (2001): 318–332.

Zatlin, Phyllis. *Theatrical Translation and Film Adaptation: A Practitioner's View*. Clevedon, U.K.: Multilingual Matters, 2005.

Index

Ackroyd, Peter 16, 45, 77–80
Acocella, Joan 16
adaptation 21–23, 35
Aers, David 136n42
Alan Plater's Trinity Tales 86
Alexander, Lynn 117
Allen, Graham 21
The Ancestor's Tale 139n62
An Ancient Evil 64–66
Anderson, Benedict 149n38
Andrew, Dudley 145n12, 147n72
Anyokwu, Christopher 147n16
appropriation 35–36, 43
Arnell, Carla 57–58
Arnold, Matthew 6, 15
Asma, Stephen T. 139n58
Augst, Thomas 54

Bailey's Café 53, 106–107, 116–120
Baldick, Chris 134n10
Baldry, Cherith 142n13
Barnes, Geraldine 142n3
Barrington, Candace 2, 9, 11, 134n3
Bazin, Victoria 140n92
BBC Canterbury Tales (2003, tv) 4, 24–25, 84–96
BCC The Canterbury Tales (1969, tv) 4, 25–26, 84–96
Beaulieu, Elizabeth Ann 148n25
Beidler, Peter G. 138n35
Bell, Ian A. 143n14
Bennett, Tony 136n40, 149n30
Birthday Letters 50–51
Blamires, Alcuin 16
The Book of the Lion 144n39
Bourdieu, Pierre 18, 129, 143n14, 135n24, 136n38, 136n41
Bowden, Betsy 133n2
Bowers, John M. 114, 147n4, 149n12
branding 5, 56, 122–126
Brewer, Derek 8, 9, 133n2, 134n9
Brinkman, Baba 29–31
British cultural studies 14–15
Broadcast 41–42
Brody, Saul Nathaniel 146n59
Brown, Amy Benson 148n25

Brown, Peter 134n5
Browne, Ray B. 135n23
Bryant, Brantley L. 17–19
Buchan, Suzanne 146n67
Byerman, Keith Eldon 148n25

The Cachoeira Tales 5, 36, 106–111
Cameron, Rebecca 140n93
A Canterbury Tale (1944, film) 84, 123, 144n2
The Canterbury Tales (1969, stage) 26
The Canterbury Tales (1969, tv) 97
Canterbury Tales (1998–2000, animated) 5, 24–25, 84–85, 96–105
The Canterbury Tales (2006, stage) 26–29
Canterbury Tales: The Best of Caravan 55
Canterbury Tales Visitor Attraction 123–125
Cardwell, Sarah 24, 85
Carlson, David R. 12, 13, 15, 143n19
Cawelti, John G. 75, 96, 138n23, 142n2
Cawsey, Kathy 133n1
Chaucer, Philippa 69, 70, 72, 73, 74, 75
Chaucer and the Doctor of Physic 46–47, 70–72
Chaucer and the House of Fame 46–47, 70–72
Chaucer and the Legend of Good Women 46–47, 70–72
Chaucer in Rome 47–48
Chaucer's Triumph 46, 73–75
Chavenelle, Sylvie 148n24
Chesterton, G.K. 125
Chiavetta, Eleonora 147n20
Churchill, Caryl 52
Chwast, Seymour 31–32
citation 47, 54
Clancy, Gertrude 62–64
Clancy, Joseph 62–64
Clerkenwell Tales 45, 77–80
Cohen, Jeffrey Jerome 139n58
Collette, Carolyn 91, 133n2, 134n9
Company of Liars 56
Conrad, Peter 49
Cooney, Barbara 101
Cope, Wendy 54–55
Cowart, David 22, 25, 85, 89
Crane, Diana 126
Crane, Susan 144n37

165

Criseyde (2009, opera) 34–35
Crocker, Holly A. 135*n*34
Crowley, Duane 68–69

Dabydeen, David 50
Daly, Elizabeth 144*n*39
D'Arcens, Louise 135*n*34
Dasgupta, Rana 56–57
Dawkins, Richard 139*n*62
Death Is a Pilgrim 62–64
Dell, Helen 135n34
Devlin, Mary 44, 66–68, 72–73
Dil Chahta Hai 139*n*45
Doherty, Paul C. 64–66
double access 18
Dryden, John 33, 34, 127
During, Simon 135*n*23

Eberle, Patricia J. 62
Eberle, Thomas 138*n*26
Echard, Siân 133*n*2
Ecker, Ronald L. 40–41
Eco, Umberto 68, 79
Edmondson, Todd 147*n*7
Eisner, Will 139*n*36
Ellis, Jerry 36–37
Ellis, Steve 2, 10–11, 21, 27, 54, 98, 124
Emmerson, Richard K. 10
Erickson, Peter 148*n*26
Ever After 58
The Evolutionary Tales 40–41

fan culture 19, 128–129
Fichte, Joerg O. 142*n*1
Fishelov, David 134*n*2
Fisher, John H. 133*n*2
Fiske, John 13, 14, 16–17, 87, 122, 128, 129, 130, 136*n*38, 136*n*41
Forni, Kathleen 135n31, 135*n*34
Foster, Michael 143*n*18
Foucault, Michel 21, 142*n*123
Fowles, John 57–58
Fradenburg, Louise 13, 129
Frazer, Margaret 144*n*41
Freeman, Paul A. 38–39
Frow, John 22, 58, 141*n*119
Furniss, Maureen 146*n*61, 146*n*64

Gaiman, Neil 55–56, 141*n*111
Ganim, John 133*n*2
Gans, Herbert J. 12–13
Gardner, John 26
Gates, Henry Louis, Jr. 107, 112
Gaunt, John of 46, 67, 69, 72, 73–74
Genette, Gérard 22, 137*n*11
Geoffrey Chaucer Hath a Blog 17–19, 128–129
Ghostly Murders 64
Graff, Gerald 134*n*10
Green, Martin 144*n*3
Gresset, Michael 147*n*11

Gripsrud, Jostein 18
Grossberg, Lawrence 14–15
Grudin, Michaela Paasche 60
Guare, John 47–48
Guillory, John 136*n*47
Gust, Geoffrey W. 133n1, 137*n*67
Guthrie, Karen 41
Gutleben, Christian 134*n*2

Hall, Stuart 106, 136*n*51
Hall, Vernon, Jr. 144n37
The Hangman's Hymn 64, 66
Harris, David 136*n*39
Harty, Kevin J. 144*n*5, 133*n*5
Harwood, Britton J. 133*n*2
A Haunt of Murder 64
Haydock, Nickolas A. 135*n*34
Heding, Tilde 149*n*1
Herrnstein Smith, Barbara 136*n*50
Hertog, Erik 146*n*69
Hertzberg, Ludvig 140*n*82
Hinds, Harold E., Jr. 134*n*4
Hines, James 49–50
Holden, Wendy 54
Holmes, Frederick M. 141*n*115
Holt, Douglas B. 149*n*1
Horsley, Lee 62, 142*n*2
House of Shadows 143*n*15
Hughes, Ted 50–51
Hutcheon, Linda 22, 29, 35, 53, 78–79, 107
Hyperion 37–38

Ingham, Patricia Clare 147*n*3
The Insomniac Tales by Chaucer's Women 42–43
The Intended 50
intertextuality 4, 21–23, 147n11
invocation 47

Jarmusch, Jim 49
Jauss, Hans Robert 86, 134*n*2
Jenkins, Henry 129, 136*n*58
Jensen, Joli 80, 137*n*68
Jewers, Caroline 135*n*34
Jones, Terry 80–82
The Journal of Danny Chaucer (poet) 55
Juvan, Marko 22, 23, 53, 56, 59

Kaufman, Amy S. 136*n*59
Kelley, Margot Anne 118
King-Aribisala, Karen (*Kicking Tongues*) 5, 39, 106–107, 112–116
Kittredge, George Lyman 9, 93
Knapp, Ethan 134*n*10
Knight, Stephen 142*n*2
A Knight's Tale 8, 12–14, 24, 84
Kramnick, Jonathon Brody 15, 136*n*53
Krier, Theresa M. 133*n*1

Landscape with Dead Dons 144*n*39

Index

Landy, Marcia 145*n*19
Lanier, Douglas 134*n*1, 144*n*8
Last Orders 58
The Lecturer's Tale 49–50
The Legend of Good Women: A Geoffrey Chaucer Murder Mystery 72–73
Leicester, H. Marshall 140*n*72
Leitch, Thomas 145*n*12
Lerer, Seth 133*n*1
Lewis, Barry 77
Lewycka, Marina 48–49
Lowe, Ben 143*n*33
Lynch, Kathryn R. 147*n*3

Macan, Edward 141*n*110
MacCannell, Dean 149*n*8
A Maggot 57–58
Maitland, Karen 56
Malcolm, David 58
Manly, John M. 13
Marcus, Laura 79
Margry, Peter Jan 142*n*124
Marshall, David W. 10
Matthews, David 133*n*1, 133*n*2, 133*n*3, 135*n*34, 149*n*18
McCloud, Scott 31, 139n36
McCrumb, Sharyn 40
melodrama 5, 25, 84
Middleton, Anne 134*n*9
Miskimin, Alice 133*n*1,*n*2
Moor, Andrew 123, 149*n*5
Morgan, Gerald 142*n*4
Morgan, Philippa 45–46, 70–72
Morley, Christopher 34
Morse, Charlotte C. 10, 133*n*2
Murder on the Canterbury Pilgrimage 44, 66–68
Mwangi, Evan Maina 113
Myers, Lucas 51
Myerson, Jonathan 24–25, 96–104
Mystery Train 49

Naylor, Gloria 53, 106–107, 116–120
Nelmes, Jill 146*n*43
Nelson, Marilyn 5, 36, 106–111

O'Connor, Garry 46, 73–75
O'Connor, John 138*n*26
Onega, Susan 134*n*2
Orr, Mary 137*n*10

Palmer, D.J. 134*n*10
Pasolini, Pier Paolo 24, 84
Patterson, Lee 9, 81–82, 134*n*9, 134*n*11, 136*n*42, 136*n*48, 150*n*33
Pearsall, Derek 138*n*30, 147*n*4
Place, Janey 145*n*30
Plath, Sylvia 50–51
Pope, Nina 41
popular (definition) 8–9

popular discrimination 13
Porter, Dennis 142*n*2
Poulton, Mike 26–29
Prendergast, Thomas A. 18, 133*n*3, 136*n*62
Priestman, Martin 143*n*23
Pugh, Tison 135*n*34, 137*n*67, 144*n*2
Purves, Barry 98
Pyrhönen, Heta 142*n*2

I racconti di Canterbury 24, 84
Rancid 141*n*110
The Rap Canterbury Tales 29–31
Reiss, Edmund 43, 121
Richardson, Gudrun 145*n*34
Richmond, Velma Bourgeois 133*n*2, 136*n*46
Riddle Me a Murder 68–69
Riffaterre, Michael 137*n*11
Rigby, Stephen Henry 75
Riley, Martin 130, 138*n*26
Robin Hood and Friar Tuck: Zombie Killers 38–39
Robinson, Carol L. 144*n*3
Robinson, Robert 144*n*39
Roessner, Jeffrey 141*n*115
Rogerson, Margaret 96
Rose, Mary Beth 95
Rosenbaum, Jonathon 49
Ross, Andrew 127
Rzepka, Charles J. 143*n*16

St. Dale 40
Sanders, Julie 22, 35, 120, 148*n*26
Sandman 55–56
Scaggs, John 142n2, 142*n*11
Schneider, Karen 148*n*26, 148*n*32
Schudson, Michael 137*n*10, 137*n*12
"Sherlock Holmes and the Wife of Bath" 144n37
Shields, Alice 34–35
Siebers, Tobin 6
Simmons, Dan 37–38
A Simple Plan 84
Spearing, A.C. 145*n*38
Spears, Timothy B. 141*n*103
Speght, Thomas 14, 69, 127
Spurgeon, Caroline F.E. 9
Stam, Robert 89, 139*n*49, 145*n*11, 147*n*70
Stave, Shirley A. 148*n*25
Stevens, Roger 55
Sting 55
Storey, John 8, 135*n*23
Street, John 12, 134*n*7
Stretter, Robert 90
Strinati, Dominic 147*n*71
Strohm, Paul 36, 82
Swan, Susan 52–53
Swift, Graham 58

A Tapestry of Murders 64, 66, 76
"The Teachers Tale" 54–55

Ten Summoner's Tales 55
textual poaching 129
Thomas, Greg 148*n*30
Thompson, Dorothy Perry 118, 148*n*25
Thompson, John B. 135*n*25
Thompson, Kirsten 146*n*67
Tokyo Cancelled 56–57
Tomasch, Sylvia 147*n*3
Top Girls 52
A Tournament of Murders 64, 65, 76
The Treasure of the Sierra Madre 84, 93
Trigg, Stephanie 18, 68, 80, 133*n*1,*n*2,*n*3,*n*5, 144*n*37
Troilus and Criseyde, Opera in Three Acts 34
The Trojan Horse 34
Turner, Edith 147*n*15
Turner, Graeme 136*n*39
Turner, Victor 147*n*15
Two Caravans 48–49

Upstone, Sara 112

Van Schuyver, Susan A. 138*n*26

Wagner, Geoffrey 23, 93, 145*n*12
Walking to Canterbury 36–37
Wallace, David 10, 51, 79, 106, 108, 111
Walton, William 34
Wells, Paul 25, 100, 101, 103
Wenzel, Jennifer 115
West-Pavlov, Russell 144*n*88
Wheeler, Bonnie 134*n*16, 149*n*51
Whitaker, Muriel 149*n*12
Who Murdered Chaucer? 80–82
Williams, Raymond 146*n*52
Wilson, Charles E., Jr. 117, 118, 148*n*29
The Wives of Bath 52–53
Wolf, Naomi 90
Wood, Rebecca S. 118, 148*n*23, 148*n*25
Wren, Celia 138*n*31
Wright, Jean Ann 146*n*52

Yager, Susan 145*n*36
Yaw, Yvonne 144*n*37

Zatlin, Phyllis 145*n*18

www.ingramcontent.com/pod-product-compliance
Ingram Content Group UK Ltd.
Pitfield, Milton Keynes, MK11 3LW, UK
UKHW042016140426
5217IPUK00015B/1204